MW00681769

RE-INVENTING

HR

CHANGING ROLES
TO CREATE THE
HIGH-PERFORMANCE
ORGANIZATION

Editor and Contributor
Margaret Butteriss

JOHN WILEY & SONS

Toronto • New York • Chichester • Weinheim • Brisbane • Singapore

John Wiley & Sons Canada Limited
22 Worcester Road
Etobicoke, Ontario
M9W 1L1

Canadian Cataloguing in Publication Data

Main entry under title:

Re-inventing HR : changing roles to create the high-performance organization

ISBN 0-471-64247-9

1. Personnel management. 2. Organizational change. I. Butteriss, Margaret.

HF5549.R443 1998   658.3   C98-930673-9

Production Credits
Cover & text design, JAQ, RGD
Printer: Tri-Graphic Printing

Printed in Canada

10 9 8 7 6 5 4 3 2 1

To members of the Harris and Butteriss families,
past and present

CONTENTS

ACKNOWLEDGEMENTS

MﾊNY PEOPLE HELPED me create this book, and I wish to thank them all. First, there are the contributors, who graciously offered to write the chapters, in spite of being incredibly busy with internal and external clients.

I specifically want to thank all those senior executives who were interviewed and provided material for the chapters that I wrote. Again, these were busy people who spared the time to talk about business effectiveness and HR management in their respective organizations.

Vic Ackerman, President, Roche Canada; Bernard Cormier, Vice-President, Corporate Human Resources, Bell Canada; Brian Harrison, Chairman, A.T. Kearney, Canada; John Ellsworth, Vice-Chairman of Human Resources, KPMG Canada; Jane Graydon, Senior Manager, Change Management, Information Services, Nortel; Bruce Hamilton, Director of Labour Relations, Noranda Metallurgy Inc.; Steve Heddle, President, Noranda Aluminum Inc.; Ian Hendry, Vice-President Human Resources, Royal Dominion Securities, the investment arm of the Royal Bank of Canada; Bernt Hoegberg, former President, Ericsson, Canada, and now President of Ericsson Radio Access, Sweden; Allan Kupcis, former President and CEO of Ontario Hydro; Geri Markvoort, Director of Human Resources GTA, KPMG Canada; Yves Meunier, President of the Steelworkers Local at CCR, Noranda; Larry Morden, former Senior Vice-President, Ault Foods; Chris Nelson, General Manager, Searle, Canada, a division of Monsanto; Dee Parkinson-Marcoux, former President, CS Resources, and now President of Gulf Heavy Oil; Courtney Pratt, President, and now Chairman of Noranda, Inc; Carrie Shea, Principal, Strategic Services, A.T. Kearney.

I would like to thank Jackie Robertson for transcribing the interview material, and Judie Stewart and Dave Woods for doing literature searches and reviews for me.

I owe an enormous debt to Penny Hozy who provided writing services and edited the drafts of the chapters. This allowed me to continue my consulting work while I wrote the book. She also provided great support and encouragement to this whole project.

Lastly, I would like to thank my family—my husband Brian and my sons, Robin and Jeremy. They all encouraged me to write this book, and to share the experience I have gained over the years in Europe and North America in aligning the HR function with business strategies. Robin provided me access to his friends who could help me with the early research, and Jeremy helped with some of the initial editing of the book.

Finally, my thanks go to Karen Milner, Editor at John Wiley & Sons Canada Ltd, for agreeing to publish the book and for offering very constructive advice on its structure and form, and to Elizabeth McCurdy, Assistant Editor at John Wiley Sons Canada Ltd.

Ｈ OW MANY TIMES have we heard it said by major corporations that people are their most important asset, that their strength is their people?
These phrases are bandied about by many organizations in their vision
and mission statements, and their annual reports. We read them in
advertisements and even see them framed and hanging on the walls of
corporate headquarters. Senior management repeat these statements
in their communications to external stakeholders and employees. But
many of us are skeptical. We've heard it all so often, we no longer
believe it. How can senior management continue to say these things
while organizations continue to downsize, lay off people, and seeming-
ly ignore the value of the people side of the business?

It's easy for organizations to say people are their most important
asset when the economy is good, and they can pay more, give all kinds
of benefits, and engage in training and development. But when the
economy turns down, what's the first thing to go? In many cases, it's HR
benefits and processes, such as training and development.

As well, many of us are told we're responsible for our own employability: we are given no guarantee of job security. This new employment
contract creates little loyalty, either on the part of the individual or the
organization. As markets grow and the demand for workers, particularly knowledge workers, increases, companies may have trouble attracting and keeping the best people.

The rapidly changing nature of business in today's economy
requires a fundamental rethinking of many HR processes. For example,
many organizations are finding that customer satisfaction is linked to
employee satisfaction. In order to provide customer value and improve
profitability, businesses must pay attention to the people in the organization.

Thus, HR is increasingly becoming an important part of executive
planning and actions and far more of an integral part of management
than ever before. We see such things as performance management,

creating a high-performance organization, improving organizational and individual competence, creating flexible work teams, and satisfying customers' needs becoming a major part of the strategic planning of senior management. All of this creates a strong dependence on people to build high-performance organizations.

External pressures such as globalization, competition, deregulation and free trade, rationalization and consolidation, and technology have created internal pressures on organizations to alter business. These internal changes include re-engineering, cost reduction, flexibility of attitudes and work practices, and the need to be agile and speedy in meeting and exceeding customer needs. Other changes, such as building workforces from various types of employees other than full-time, including part-timers, temporary contractors, and consultants, are designed to make operations more flexible and, in many cases, to reduce costs.

This new type of workforce can create additional concerns, such as high employee turnover, especially as the market demand for specialists gets stronger. We've all become free agents of one kind or another, whether we work as freelancers, on contract, or as permanent staff.

The HR function itself is increasingly being asked to take on new roles, and not all of its practitioners are equally equipped and ready to do this. We are in a time when the competencies of individual HR practitioners must be developed to better support the business organization. If the HR function does not meet the challenges of today's global business environment, it is in danger of being outsourced or cut out completely.

The ever increasing use of technology means that changes are taking place in virtually every aspect of the business environment, often in previously unimagined areas. These changes create a demand for more knowledge workers, highly trained and, in some cases, extremely specialized individuals who are able to use this technology to allow companies to be more flexible and adaptive.

In more traditional organizations where technology is increasingly being introduced and incorporated, it is important that the existing workforce be equipped, willing, and able to learn how to use that technology. The changing environment of ever increasing customer demands, competition in a global environment and the need for cost effectiveness, demands that employees be on top of what's going on in the world and know what it takes to differentiate an organization from its competitors. In some cases, this is a matter of basic survival. In most organizations, it is necessary to sustain and increase growth. A flexible, well-trained workforce is required to compete in this new environment. And so it all comes back to people. Indeed, people are and will continue to be our most important asset if this kind of expansion is to succeed.

Against this backdrop is the changing role of the Human Resources function itself. Some organizations are cutting costs in Human Resources and outsourcing HR because they still see it largely as a transactional and reactive function that can effectively be done by outside organizations. Others are building more strategic partnerships between line, management, and HR experts and are creating a consultative role for HR to cope with the rapidly changing business realities. They recognize that HR can no longer be simply transactional and administrative, but must be far more proactive in assisting senior management plan for the future.

This book was written with both senior executives and HR practitioners in mind. I wanted to share my experience, as both an internal and external Human Resources and organization development practitioner. I also wanted to share some of the valuable tools and techniques I've acquired along the way. I asked a number of seasoned practitioners, some from the highest levels of management, to contribute to this book and it is full of practical how-to's and case studies that provide advice on creating a high-performance organization through the Human Resources function and Human Resources practices.

Many pointed to the need for more partnership between corporations and individuals to demonstrate an alignment of vision, goals, and outcomes. Such a partnership requires improving performance, communications, and management. It means that HR practices have to be better linked to business goals and not conceived of as stand-alone programs that have very little to do with the realities of business.

The book is divided into four parts. The first part covers the views of senior executives, including both CEOs and HR practitioners, and the pressures they are experiencing in terms of external and internal changes facing their organizations. They also look at the implications of these changes for HR in today's world and particularly for the role of the HR function itself.

The second part focuses on the changing role of the Human Resources function. In order to support organizations and assist them in dealing with the numerous changes brought on by globalization, the

Human Resources role is changing fundamentally. This part looks at those changes and the reasons for them. It looks at moving HR from being solely a transactional, administrative, and reactive function, to being proactive and consultative, working with senior executives to create the high-performance organization. This part includes two case studies of organizations that are currently reinventing their Human Resources role. It also looks at measuring the effectiveness of both the Human Resources function itself and Human Resources processes, from a total business perspective, as HR supports the organization's goals.

The third part looks at managing change. Change is viewed from a series of perspectives. First, there is change that affects the total organization. Secondly, there is the change affecting business units and teams. And thirdly, we look at managing change at the individual level. This part includes case studies of two organizations undergoing fundamental change. Part Three also concentrates on the human resources role in assisting organizations to effectively manage change.

The final part looks at HR processes and systems that create and support a high-performance organization and contains a series of practical how-to's in terms of systems that are required to support business direction. These include executive development, performance management, developing competencies and their related use in organizations, developing a compensation strategy, and specifically, at competency-based compensation.

CONTRIBUTORS

Sherrill Burns is the President of Transform*Action Inc.*, a management consulting firm based in Toronto, Canada, which is focused on supporting the people side of large scale change in organizations. She has worked with both large and small organizations transitioning their structures, systems, and people toward new strategic directions and operating models. Her organization has recently been involved in supporting enterprise-wide system implementations, shifts in business models and value disciplines, and mergers and acquisitions. Her work points to the need to support people through major changes and the related personal transitions which must occur by building personal and group commitment, confidence, credibility, and capability.

Margaret Butteriss is a management consultant with over twenty years experience in organization effectiveness and human resource management. She manages her own consulting business which assists senior management teams to align their organizations and processes with business goals and strategy. Her clients include Fidelity Investments Canada Limited, Loblaw Companies Limited, and Nortel. Prior to setting up her own business, Margaret held senior human resource and organization effectiveness positions with Shell International in the UK, Shell Canada, and Ontario Hydro.

She has a B.Sc. (Econ) and a M.Sc. (Econ) from the UK and has authored two books entitled *Job Enrichment and Employee Participation*, Institute of Personnel Management U.K. and *New Management Tools*, Prentice-Hall Inc., 1978.

Nancie Evans, M.A., is the President of Mount Albert, Ontario-based Impact Associates. She is an acknowledged expert in enhancing the effectiveness of organizations through the application of organizational learning principles to strategy development, major organizational change initiatives and leadership and executive development. Prior to embarking on a consulting career in January 1994, Nancie spent ten years in general management with high-tech organizations, including management roles in operations, finance, information technology, customer service, sales, and marketing. This was followed by seven years experience in senior management roles, focusing on leadership, executive, and organization development. She holds a Master's degree in Organization Development from the University of Toronto, and is pursuing her doctoral studies in Management Learning at Lancaster University in the United Kingdom.

Mark Jackson, M.A., Director, Human Resources Planning and Development, Hay Management Consultants. Mark Jackson is the National Director of Hay/McBer's Human Resources Planning and Development Practice in Canada. His areas of expertise include design and implementation of integrated competency-based Human Resources management systems. Over the past sixteen years, he has designed, managed, and implemented projects involving job competency model development, selection system design, individual assessments for selection and staffing, multi-rater performance management systems, and leadership development and succession planning processes. He has developed and managed integrated human resources management projects for both public and private sector clients. His clients include national and multi-national organizations. Mark obtained his Bachelor's and Master's degree in psychology from the University of British Columbia. He is a frequent speaker at national and international Human Resources conferences on issues relevant to Human Resources planning and development.

Rick Lash, Ph.D., C.Psych., is a Senior Consultant with Hay/McBer's Human Resources Planning and Development Practice. He brings over ten years of experience in the design implementations of Human Resources applications to accelerate and maximize the learning process and performance management systems, as well as executive assessment. Rick holds a doctorate in psychology from the University of Toronto with specialization in cognitive science and instructional technology. He is also recognized as an expert in the technologies of organizational change, including the use of simulations and games. He has spoken widely on the topic of creating and sustaining superior performing cultures and linking competency assessment to individual development.

John Lewis has more than twenty years experience in Human Resources management in Canada and abroad. He has worked in medium and large industrial organizations, including the European and Caribbean operations of an international metals firm, and as a consultant. He has a degree in mathematics from Oxford University. He is currently the manager of Compensation and Benefits in a large professional services firm.

Ellie Maggio is a senior consultant and Principal with William M. Mercer Limited's Human Resource & Compensation Management Practice. Ellie has been with the company since 1989 and provides consulting assistance to private and public sector organizations, in a variety of industry sectors. Prior to joining Mercer, Ms. Maggio worked as a consultant at a strategic management consulting firm in the financial services industry. In addition, she has worked in a research capacity on several public sector contracts with the Ontario Legislative Assembly and Revenue Canada. Ms. Maggio is the Regional Vice-President, Ontario West, of the Canadian Compensation Association (CCA), a planning committee member of the Canadian Human Resource Planners (CHRP) and is an advisor to *HR Reporter*. She is published and speaks regularly at Human Resources and compensation management conferences. She has an honours B.A. in public policy and administration from York University.

Larry Morden has held progressive senior management, director and executive positions with responsibility for Human Resources management, corporate affairs and strategy functions throughout his career. Industries served include financial, retail, mining, pulp and paper, steel, manufacturing, and packaged goods. Most recently he was Senior Vice-President Human Resources and Corporate Affairs of Ault Foods Ltd. Currently he consults to private and public organizations undergoing significant change and development in the areas of Human Resources management and corporate strategy.

Robert Paterson is President of the Renewal Consulting Group, which specializes in designing organization and processes that use the principles building on intellectual capital. Prior to being in private practice, he worked for a major international financial services organization in the investment banking, brokerage, and banking functions, becoming

Senior Vice-President in both the marketing and Human Resources functions. He has also worked as a line investment banker for fourteen years and covered many markets throughout the world. He has an M.A. Honours from Oxford University.

Tony Roithmayr is an HR professional who has over twenty years experience helping organizations align their performance with the results required by their business, particularly through leadership practices. His experience includes customized performance management systems, competency-based capability and career development systems, as well as improvement projects to respond to a variety of business problems and opportunities that require change in employee and leader performance. A particular focus in recent years has been the orchestration of changes to organizations and cultures. Tony has held internal consulting and Human Resources management positions in financial services, consumer packaged goods, and the energy sectors. As an external consultant he also worked in the high-tech industry.

Anne Stephen has specialized in Human Resources and organizational development since 1980. The primary focus of her work has been the design, development, and implementation of planned change efforts which support of corporate strategy and improve management practices. Anne has a broad base of consulting experience working with U.S. and Canadian clients in a variety of industries including computers, financial services, pharmaceuticals, food manufacturing/retail, and transportation. Her experience working as both an internal and external consultant has focused her efforts on translating organizational effectiveness concepts into practical business solutions.

Part One

Senior Executives on the Role of HR in Today's Organizations

CHAPTER 1, *Human Resources in the Changing World*, is based on data from interviews I had with senior executives and Vice-Presidents of Human Resources representing a broad spread of predominantly global organizations.

They discussed the challenges facing their organizations due to changes in both the workplace and the marketplace. They then examined the organization capabilities required to meet these challenges, as well as the people implications of change. Finally, they talked about the role of Human Resources in their organizations and the initiatives needed to meet current and future business requirements.

The changes they considered most important included: operating in a global environment; greater competition from all parts of the world; deregulation and free trade as governments privatize and relax regulations; rationalization and consolidation of companies leading to a tremendous number of mergers, acquisitions and, in some cases, outsourcing of different businesses; and the increasing impact of technology in the workplace.

The executives identified seven initiatives Human Resources should undertake in order to help organizations cope with change. They are:

1. Creating a common company-wide value system,

2. Developing a "competency-based" personnel framework,

3. Providing leadership assessment and development,

4. Moving people within the company for best advantage,

5. Guaranteeing the workplace diversity that allows success in a company's varied national and global markets,

6. Handling the question of compensation, and

7. Re-engineering the corporate Human Resources function as a consulting centre to company management on hiring, training, managing, paying, retaining, and developing an organization's human assets.

CHAPTER ONE

Human Resources
in the
Changing World

Margaret Butteriss

W HEN BUSINESS LOOKS ahead to the 21st century, it sees challenges that
have already changed dramatically the expectations about the role of
people within organizations and the role of Human Resources. In fact,
perhaps nowhere has the pervasive atmosphere of change been so
deeply felt as in the corporate HR function.

The equation of Human Resources with the processing of personnel forms—payroll, benefits, evaluation, etc.—no longer makes sense
to companies driven by global markets, global competition, and new
technology. While management still expects Human Resources to perform its transactional role—at reduced cost, HR is also being called on
for new contributions in its traditional area of expertise, dealing with
people.

Never before has the people dimension been so crucial to organizational success. As businesses move into new markets and face new
competitors, they need competent people in all operations, people who
can respond quickly to change, people who understand and can satisfy
the changing needs of their customers.

To learn firsthand about how changes in our society and within
individual organizations are causing HR to reinvent itself, I spoke to ten
executives in large Canadian companies and Canadian divisions of

multinational corporations representing a broad spectrum of industries, including manufacturing, utilities, and financial services. They were unanimous about the need for business to rethink all operations: customer relations, business style, employee culture, core values, people management, etc. They also could offer many concrete examples from their own organizations of ways the HR function has already begun to change as a result of this re-examination.

HR's role in change is by no means a passive one; on the contrary, it is one of the key catalysts of its own reinvention. HR experts in business and the academy have developed a broad range of new tools allowing companies to find, hire, train, motivate, retain, and "travel" the right people for the right jobs. Even more important, they have developed proven models for ways in which HR can contribute materially to corporate re-engineering for significant competitive improvement. Later chapters in this book will provide details of these theories and case studies of their application, many of which will be mentioned here also.

HOW CHANGE IS AFFECTING ORGANIZATIONS AND THE HR FUNCTION

In this chapter, we will be guided through changing Canadian companies with the expert help of senior executives and HR Vice-Presidents. We will examine three major factors causing widespread change in organizations:

- globalization, particularly expansion into global markets;
- competition, not only increased competition in established markets but also competition with new rivals for control of new markets; and
- changes in the tools of business, particularly in information technology, with the resulting new demand for constant worker re-education and flexibility in job functions.

We will treat each of these three factors under three headings:

- the pressures each factor brings to bear on organizations,
- the changes organizations need to make in response, and
- the new role of the HR function in these organizational changes.

The Executive Participants and their Companies

Vic Ackermann, President, Roche Canada, at the time of the interview. He now holds a senior position in the European operations of Roche Pharmaceuticals, which is the world's sixth largest pharmaceutical company. It has four main divisions: pharmaceuticals, which accounts for 60% of its sales; bulk vitamins and fine chemicals; diagnostics; and flavours and fragrances.

Bernard Cormier, Vice-President, Corporate Human Resources, Bell Canada. Bell Canada, Canada's largest supplier of telecommunications services with 42,000 employees, provides advanced voice data and image communications to more than seven million business and residential customers in Ontario and Quebec. At the end of 1996 it had 69% of the long-distance market and 100% of the local-access market; its 1997 earnings were $852 million. Bell Canada is currently in the middle of a three-year program to transform the company into a more customer-focused, competitive organization.

Brian Harrison, Chairman, A.T. Kearney, Canada. A.T. Kearney Inc., the management consulting subsidiary of EDS, is a global management consulting and executive search firm with worldwide headquarters in Chicago. It has offices in thirty countries throughout the Americas, Asia Pacific, and Europe.

Ian Hendry, Vice-President and Director of Human Resources, RBC Dominion Securities, an investment dealer within the Royal Bank Financial Group. RBC DS, the most profitable full-service investment dealer in Canada, specializes in offering non-discretionary and discretionary investment service and advice to high net worth Canadian investors. It also manages the fixed income, foreign exchange, money market and capital markets businesses of the Royal Bank Financial Group.

Bernt Hoegberg, President, Ericsson, Canada, at the time of the interview. He is now President of Ericsson Audio Access in Sweden. Ericsson is a Swedish-based telecommunications company which employs 90,000 people worldwide.

Allan Kupcis, President and CEO of Ontario Hydro at the time of the interview. Ontario Hydro is a provincial utility that generates and distributes electricity throughout Ontario, and is increasing its sales of electricity to other provinces in Canada and to the U.S. It has 21,000 employees and revenues of $9 billion. Kupcis resigned after a report issued to Ontario Hydro's Management Board cited a lack of authoritative and accountable management leadership as a fundamental problem in the utility's nuclear organization. Kupcis, who had commissioned a group of U.S. nuclear experts to conduct to study, resigned to demonstrate that he took full accountability for the problem.

Larry Morden, Senior Vice-President, Ault Foods, at the time of the interview. Ault Foods was originally the dairy foods division of Labatts. After becoming an independent company in 1993, it has gradually sold off non-core business units, such as the ice cream division. Its core operations are cheese, tablespreads, and licensing dairy technologies. It now employs 1,500 people and estimates its revenues will be $992 million in 1998. In July 1997, Ault Foods was purchased by Parmalat Finanziaria SpA of Italy, who are merging it with Beatrice Foods Inc. to create a single Canadian operation.

Chris Nelson, General Manager, Searle Canada, a Division of Monsanto. Searle is an international pharmaceutical company with 8,500 people worldwide, and revenues of US $3 billion. In Canada, it currently employs about 180 people in the pharmaceutical sector, having recently moved its manufacturing sector to the U.K. and Puerto Rico. Monsanto was recently split into two entirely separate companies—the chemicals company, which is called Solutia; and the life sciences company, which will still be called Monsanto. Searle is part of the life sciences company.

Dee Parkinson-Marcoux, President, CS Resources at the time of the interview. CS Resources was purchased by Pan-Canadian and merged into 80% of their heavy oil division. She is now President of **Gulf Heavy Oil.**

Courtney Pratt, President, and now Chairman, Noranda. Noranda Inc. is a diversified natural resources company that operates in three sectors—mining and metals, forest products, and oil and gas. It employs 33,000 people and had total assets of $15 billion in 1996. Eighty per cent of its products are sold in markets outside Canada.

Interestingly, the executives interviewed provide several examples of the rapid change that is taking place in today's business world. Vic Ackermann and Bernt Hoeghberg moved on to different assignments within the global operations of their respective companies. Allan Kupcis resigned from Ontario Hydro, and Larry Morden and Dee Parkinson-Marcoux were subject to takeovers as part of the continuing rationalization and consolidation of their respective industries.

Key HR Initiatives in Response to Change

From my research, I identified seven key ways in which HR can contribute to dealing with changes in the marketplace and workplace. The first six concern services which HR can provide to the organization at large. They are:

1. Creating a common company-wide vision and value system,

2. Developing a "competency-based" personnel framework,

3. Providing leadership assessment and development,

4. Moving people within the company for best advantage,

5. Guaranteeing the workplace diversity that allows success in a company's varied national and global markets, and

6. Handling the question of change.
   Specific company initiatives reflecting all six of these points were described by the executives I interviewed and will be mentioned below under the change factor to which they are most closely related, although all of them have relevance to all aspects of company improvement. The seventh key way is:

7. Re-engineering the corporate Human Resources function as a consulting centre to company management on hiring, training, managing, paying, retaining, and developing an organization's human assets.
   This final way is implicit in all the other initiatives, because they all rely on a new company-wide attitude toward HR.

How Executives See the New HR

According to Vic Ackermann of Roche, the HR function is one of the most challenged in the organization. HR staff have moved from being primarily concerned with transactional activities to assisting the business in the management of change and organization development. They now provide the framework to create a learning organization and to enhance knowledge capital. They function as an equal partner in the business. At Roche, each line manager is responsible for his or her staff, with the HR function acting in an advisory capacity.

Bernard Cormier of Bell Canada tells a similar story of HR in transition. "Success in terms of people effectiveness is a system of checks and balances, and HR has a key role to play there. It's kind of a two-pronged challenge," he continues. "On the one hand, [change] is very challenging and presents tons of opportunities, but on the other hand, it's not easy because HR now has to play a much more proactive role. In the telecommunications industry in general, HR has traditionally been more reactive and administrative, but all the changes that are happening are related to people and their effectiveness. HR has a front-line role to play in terms of making sure the right people are deployed in the right way and are effective. This means challenging people while at the same time working with senior leaders in the company and taking more of an operating role."

Bell Canada has had to bring in people from outside the company to perform these new HR roles, but their biggest change has been in trying to set up a more generalist structure, similar to an account management or product management structure, where each function or business within Bell has an HR manager or director who provides a whole host of different support services, whether it's organization effectiveness, design initiatives, compensation, benefits, or training.

In the past, Bell was organized on a more classical type of structure in which each function, including HR, would provide expertise more on a content/area basis than on the basis of broad general knowledge. For example, in the past, the HR consultant would not be involved in the area of industrial relations. "What we've done," says Bernard Cormier, "is slowly shift to an organization that retains a core competency at the executive/corporate level for some of the major industrial relations initiatives, but more and more, the day-to-day Industrial Relations and Human Resources issues are being handled by the HR generalist."

These HR managers need to be able to network within Bell, at the corporate level, to pull in the right resources, or go outside the company for these resources depending on the issue or the case. "The HR person now needs to be more of a business person," says Cormier, "able to look at opportunities to improve employee or team organization effectiveness and come up with the tools to either get it done personally or bring in some help from outside the company."

Line management has to develop a clear sense of how they want to address HR issues, say Courtney Pratt of Noranda. "The trend of HR has always been to look at programs rather than strategy, and this is where the challenge is. It is incumbent on HR to understand all the business issues and give their input from a strategic perspective. Line management is expecting something from HR that in a lot of cases HR has trouble delivering. I think that many HR people really do not understand what a business strategy is. However," he continues, "businesses are now recognizing that their people really are the key to their success. You have heard people talking about this for years, but they didn't mean it. Now they do."

RBC Dominions Securities' Ian Hendry says, "HR strategies need to be aligned with the changing business realities and corporate goals and objectives. As they change, HR's policy, practices and programs, all of which must be integrated, must be reviewed in sync. For example, a recruitment strategy may need to be developed to staff a new business line. Compensation design may need to follow. Perhaps there is a compelling justification to differentiate pay levels for this group because of unique market pressures. What is the impact on benefits—do they continue to meet the needs? How do the new initiatives affect the mandate or change direction for the Training and Development Group? In short, HR strategy, like cogs in a wheel, should be turning as the company wheel moves."

He continues, "At the bottom of all of this, of course, is the underlying assumption that HR understands the business. This becomes the prerequisite if HR plans to enhance its visibility as a proactive, value-added member of senior management. In some organizations, HR is also endeavouring to change the corporate mind-set of itself, against a backdrop of being the destructive Grim Reaper at the forefront of industry downsizings. No mean feat."

Searle sees HR as the champions of change, helping people work through the challenges brought on by changes in the workplace and the world. "HR has been pivotal in our central planning," says Chris Nelson, "and as drivers of the processes for our strategic people planning."

Larry Morden at Ault says HR has to be more concerned with operation effectiveness and efficiency. They must be the agents of change and help with vision-based planning. He believes that when HR people are hired from the outside, they should be put through an operational exposure so they can effectively participate on the management team. Just adding HR programs to the business does not work.

"We need better measures of HR investment," says Morden. "We need to treat investment in HR programs the same way we do capital investments and need to work out the return on investment. We have moved away from the traditional measures of HR such as turnover or the number of arbitrations We are working to find linkage between HR decisions and operational effectiveness. For example," he says, "we look at the discounted cash flow of investments in training programs. We want to see impacts in terms of units produced per hour, lower labour costs, reduction in absenteeism, and better efficiency. We measure return on investment against these impacts over a given time period. The HR expectation is to have a rate of return and to have a positive impact on the operational side of the business."

GLOBALIZATION: CHANGING ORGANIZATIONS, CHANGING HR

For many North American companies, emerging markets around the world represent a crucial new hope for growth. At the same time this requires building an effective presence in an unfamiliar business climate fast enough to establish a customer base ahead of rival firms. Global expansion is often attempted through the formation of partnerships and alliances with firms already operating in the new markets, which means a new type of organizing strategy is needed for the parent business. Many of the six HR initiatives listed above are closely linked to solving the problem of globalization; the two which will be discussed in detail here are creating a company-wide value system and providing leadership assessment and development.

The Extent of the Change

Conducting business in the global marketplace is the key to growth for many organizations. Companies facing saturated markets must increasingly operate where there is growth demand for products if they are to grow and sustain their business.

"Globalizing the Corporation," a study published in 1996 by A.T. Kearney, examined 778 European and North American companies and found that more than half of these companies expected to increase the international scope of their activities within three to five years. Many had already expanded into new markets. The study also suggests that by 2020 nine of today's developing economies will be among the fifteen largest economies in the world, due to factors such as a surge in world population, increased living standards, an increase in trade and financial flow, and a liberal economic model on which to base economic activity. The developing economies that are predicted to grow significantly include China, India, Indonesia, Brazil and Mexico.

Dee Parkinson-Marcoux of Gulf Heavy Oil says, "The impetus to globalization is being driven by increased demand in different parts of the world. Companies must now go where the resources exist in order to expand their business. This is particularly true for resource-based businesses such as oil and gas, mining and forest products This move to globalization is also being driven by the need to increase shareholder value."

According to Brian Harrison, Chairman of A.T Kearney, Canada, "We are seeing more and more emphasis on growth. Companies are seeking top-line growth and are expanding their operations."

Another impetus to global expansion comes from the many countries freeing up governmental regulations and privatizing many state-run industries. World trade is becoming easier in areas such as utilities, for example, which can provide growth opportunities for Canadian firms like telecommunications giant Nortel.

What an Organization Needs

Some very exciting changes and business opportunities are emerging in the new marketplace, says Allan Kupcis. "We can now take advantage of the integration and convergence of information technology, telecommunications and electrical supplies. For instance," he says, "the same cables and electricity power line can be used to deliver Internet, telecommunications advance and electricity supply to customers at the same time, which provides real added value to them. Of course, this will require a different executive competence to integrate what is out there in the market."

At Noranda, "we have to be good at finding natural resource assets, such as oil and gas and the minerals we deal in," says Courtney Pratt. "We also have to be good at operating and getting the maximum out of our plants. This requires focus on both the technical and people dimensions. We are good at the technical dimension and have been able to integrate operating technology and information technology," he continues. "Now we have to focus on upgrading the competencies of people to operate and optimally use this technology and also be responsive to constant change."

As of August, 1997, Monsanto was split into two independently traded companies, Chemical and Life Sciences. Searle was merged into the new Life Sciences company which consists of three major sectors: agriculture, food and nutrition, and pharmaceuticals. The new company will operate on a matrix system, with such functions as Finance, HR, and Information Systems being provided centrally and across all sectors. There will be major integration of the sectors and transfer of knowledge as well as combining of research and development ideas across them, allowing for the creation of new product and service offerings. Each sector will focus on manufacturing and selling rather than corporate functions.Coupled with this major organizational change at the worldwide and Canadian levels, is the move to new premises, introducing new layouts and office furniture to facilitate teamwork and decision making.

One of the biggest challenges facing Searle is how to continue to meet the demands of the shareholder and the customer while meeting the financial challenge of launching new products. "We've traditionally been an opportunistic company, built up through licensing various products in different parts of the world," says Chris Nelson. "We've never done a global launch before and that requires a new way of thinking. We've got to learn how to do launches at that level of capability and we've got about two years to get ourselves ready for it."

Many organizations are taking advantage of the increased potential for global business by entering into strategic alliances and joint ventures with companies that are situated where the opportunities exist. This gives them access to knowledge of the local and regional markets and to existing operating, sales, and distribution networks.

Allan Kupcis says that Ontario Hydro must move to alliances and joint ventures both within the North American markets and those in other parts of the world if it is to market its electrical supply, technology services, and knowledge in all parts of the globe.

Ericsson, a Swedish-based telecommunications company, came to Canada thirty years ago and now has a major foothold in the North American market with its cellular technology. The first major equipment vendor to focus on wireless technology, it had a head start that enabled it to expand into markets that might not otherwise have been available to it. Through partnering with a major supplier (Cantel), it has enhanced its presence and visibility in both the global and Canadian markets. Capitalizing on the technology and business strength it has developed over the last thirty years, it is now moving into more joint ventures and gaining a greater slice of the world business in its market.

How HR Can Help

There are two things companies need most from Human Resources in order to meet the challenges of global expansion:

1. creating a common company-wide value system, which holds together the many business units and gives them direction; and

2. providing leadership development and assessment, which ensures the communication of the company value system and company continuity through providing for executive succession.

Creating a Common Company-Wide Vision and Value System

As organizations become larger and more diverse and are spreading throughout many parts of the world, they recognize the need to have common values to hold them together.

HR plays a major part in helping Roche create a common culture by extracting values from acquired organizations and communicating them across the organization. This is achieved through training, formation of teams whose focus is evolving and meeting future demands on the organization.

Ericsson, too, finds itself focusing more effort on culture change. The company's markets are spread all over the world, with its largest market, the United States, representing only 12% of its sales. Now that the marketplace for telecommunications is becoming more global, they must find ways to take advantage of investment and ownership opportunities. "Thirty years ago," says Bernt Hoegberg, "we had really different products for each different market. Now we've moved towards having a few global products and are gaining more global customers. As a result, we need to be competent and consistent partners around the world with our global customers."

Therefore, Hoeberg says, it has become essential to develop a common culture in the company throughout the world to act as a bond between activities that are scattered around the globe. "We have to develop the company as one unit, irrespective of where we operate. To do this we have developed a common mission and a set of values that incorporate professionalism, respect and perseverance. We are working hard to find practical ways to implement these values. In a recent scenario planning session we concluded that we need to put more focus on management development if we are to meet this future requirement."

Globalization means building teams in different parts of the world with people who may only communicate by video-conferencing, telephone or e-mail. More joint ventures and strategic alliances will demand a new kind of cultural competency.

Dee Parkinson-Marcoux of Gulf Heavy Oil noted that it is important to create a vision together with long-term plans and make sure that the vision is distinctive and clearly articulated to all key stakeholders. As she said, "The vision has to be compelling and understood. It needs to pass the 'Xerox' test. If your company's vision statement is left on the copy machine, would employees recognize it as their own."

"At Hydro," says Allan Kupcis, "we have an entitlement culture, but now we have to focus on the customers and their needs. We have to establish a performance-based organization that is results-oriented. This means that we have to change the mind-set of our employees," he says. "That mind-set has been that we are a monopoly and as such we do not care about prices. This has to change now as we enter a competitive market."

"We have three prime stakeholders," he continues, "shareholders, customers and employees. We have to give all three, and especially the employees, a clear sense of where we are going and why. Employees need to know this, and become committed to that vision and direction. This means we have to put a great deal of effort into communication, and then we have to give the employees the training and development so that they have the skills and capabilities to reach the required visions."

Ault Foods initially had a culture of taking care of people, but it is being modified to remove some inefficient operational aspects. "We need to develop people's competencies and make sure we are business-oriented," says Larry Morden. "We cannot shy away from those decisions that reinforce the right core competencies for the business. How we treat people in terms of their development, and even their termination, is critical." Ault believes strongly in frequent face-to-face communication, whether one-on-one or in small groups, to explain what is being done and why.

Creating a vision of the future also involves planning to meet potentially different scenarios. This is a new skill for many senior executives, since many of them have been used to responding to situations, rather than creating their own future in an aggressive manner.

Courtney Pratt said that Noranda recently undertook a 12-month scenario planning exercise in which a team looked at the openness of geopolitical systems and considered the impact of open borders, free flow of trade and information, and the evolution of technology on Noranda's operations.

They mapped out ten-, fifteen- and twenty-year horizons to determine which businesses should receive major capital investments. The planning process enabled them to test their plans in a new way and choose the scenario with the most promising outcome.

According to Larry Morden, Ault has worked hard over the last ten years to develop an effective planning process. It has moved from a financial planning process to a more facilitated process designed around vision-based planning. This involves various groups within the organization defining what business they want to be in and then looking at the assets and liabilities within the company. The material is then gathered for a managerial review. This vision now drives financial planning, rather than the other way around.

Although senior management bears ultimate responsibility for creating and communicating this common value system and vision, HR is an important partner in the process. HR should be recognized for its expertise in articulating an organization's goals and on ways to keep this message current for all employees.

Company expansion, as we have seen, involves both a strong central presence plus the ability to decentralize operations and form strategic alliances. This principle can be applied to HR itself, as traditional transactional roles—benefits, training, development and payroll, are outsourced, but other HR roles are centralized to cope with globalization. A.T. Kearney, for example, has centralized most HR processes such as performance management, career development and promotion, and left compensation, benefits, and recruitment to local offices. A.T. Kearney's philosophy of creating consistent excellence around the world makes it critical to have common HR systems.

Providing Leadership Assessment and Development

Leadership is seen as one of the key factors that enable organizations to be successful and sustain long-term competitive advantage.

A.T. Kearney's 1997 white paper on *"Global Best Practices in Human Resource Management"* found that "an organization's long-term growth and prosperity are directly related to its leaders. Companies with strong leaders excel in workforce performance, growth and quality of their products. The best leaders are highly mobile and have global mindsets. They are adept at leading reorganization efforts while instilling a corporate culture that is comfortable with change and ambiguity and generates employee enthusiasm."

Ian Hendry of RBC Dominion Securities sees a need for people to have problem-solving and creativity skills to solve customer issues and problems. Organizations can no longer go by the rule book, or generate solutions where one size fits all. Different thinking skills and an empowered structure are required. "At RBC Dominion Securities, we recognize the need for strong leadership throughout our organization, if we are going to compete in the global markets and do well," says Hendry. "Leaders will constantly need to inspire people, get them committed, get them wanting to do a good job, and get them interested in making improvements."

Dee Parkinson-Marcoux of Gulf Heavy Oil believes in using exception management, a technique in which management only gets involved in situations that have not been encountered before. This allows the organization to get on with what it does very well without a lot of interference. "Co-opt people who are good," says Parkinson-Marcoux. "I would say that 95% of people who do good are underutilized rather than pushed. People stretch themselves; you don't have to stretch them. In fact," she says, "only about 5% don't live up to expectations."

Global performance, then, depends on the effective identification of and development of executive skills.

The A.T. Kearney study "Globalizing the Corporation" suggests that global performance depends on the effective development of the capacity to execute plans. This includes critical capabilities transfer, human resources management processes and corporate culture. Critical capability transfer refers to the identification of critical people skills and knowledge in the organization and ensuring smooth and ready access to those capabilities on a global basis. Execution capability appears to be the engine for global success. The most powerful element in execution capacity is the effective transfer of critical capabilities, which is defined as the processes used to develop, leverage and renew the product or service that is being offered to the marketplace. Examples of these processes include a company's business and organizational competencies, various forms of intellectual property such as patents, trademarks and software technology, and non-patented but exclusive technological products and processes.

Companies must first agree on which critical capabilities to transfer and then install permanent mechanisms for the transfer. They see critical capabilities as the means and mechanisms used to deliver value to customers that uniquely position and reward the firm. Capabilities are not the company's product or service itself, but the processes used to develop, leverage and renew the product or services.

The A.T. Kearney study found that companies with a 20% greater capacity to transfer critical capabilities were rewarded with a 7% improvement in global performance. But they must be explicit and rigorous in communicating and practising critical capabilities. They must also develop and use effective global management and Human Resources processes to improve their capacity to develop and transfer these capabilities. This means nurturing global management talent and focusing on leadership development to create forward thinking and culturally adept leaders.

As an example, Brian Harrison noted that small organizations that have merged with ABB, the Swedish global conglomerate, can capitalize on the organization's strength and knowledge by learning about the products, technology, and way of doing business in other parts of the conglomerate.

At Ericsson, says Bernt Hoegberg, "We identify those with management potential and take them through a systematic leadership process. As a management group in Canada, we have put special emphasis on developing ourselves in terms of leadership. In our regular offsite meetings, we spend time on developing and enhancing our competencies."

Ontario Hydro has undertaken a real assessment of leadership skills as well as thorough management assessments. They have consulted outside the corporation, using the Hay Organization, who have identified eight key attributes and competencies deemed necessary for senior positions. Hydro management have used this material as a way to develop competencies. "We have undertaken a strata-by-strata assessment of management and leadership potential," says Al Kupcis, "and are using this data to identify our talent pool for the coming years and as a basis for leadership development."

At Bell Canada, annual programs and processes has been put in place to assess every individual on achievement, leadership skills, and technical capabilities, as they relate to Bell values. This assessment also helps people get an inventory of their own skills, says Bernard Cormier, and helps them evaluate how they're doing and where they have to improve. For the most part, this assessment process is for managerial and professional employees.

It is noteworthy that Dee Parkinson-Marcoux of Gulf Heavy Oil believes that the need to develop skills in executing strategy is not only required in the leaders of an organization, but in all its employees.

COMPETITION: CHANGING ORGANIZATIONS, CHANGING HR

Perhaps the greatest single challenge of the global marketplace is increased competition, not only in new markets but in familiar ones as well. Many of the executives interviewed spoke of ways in which their companies were being forced to change in large measure due to increased competition from imports. They identified four key ways in which companies need to address pressure from competition: satisfying customers, cutting costs, rationalizing operations, and knowing the marketplace well, especially the competition. As in our discussion of globalization, many of the six HR initiatives listed above are closely linked to solving the problem of competition; the two which will be discussed in detail here are moving people within the company for best advantage and handling the question of compensation.

The Extent of the Change

According to Bernt Hoegberg, President of Ericsson, the competitive forces facing suppliers of telecommunications equipment are changing completely and will only intensify in the coming years. Ericsson has been forced into a new style of doing business as new technologies come onto the market. It has to work increasingly with strategic business partners, and operate on a global basis, rather than on an individual country or region basis. This has in turn enhanced its presence and visibility in the global market.

A major impact of the spread of the global marketplace is that more organizations from other countries are moving into Canada creating increased competition on a national basis. According to Brian Harrison, as the competition becomes more fierce, companies must provide more value-added products and services with ever increasing quality, speed and focus on cost containment.

Bell Canada, according to Human Resources V.P. Bernard Cormier, has had to determine what is in the core business for Bell in terms of both local and long distance service. It's a much tougher business, says Cormier, because it is evolving so quickly into a commodity. This provides outstanding opportunities, but the core business is facing much more competition as the industry faces deregulation.

Ian Hendry of RBC Dominion Securities suggests that over the past decade, the financial services industry has undergone fundamental change. With more and more international banks and finance companies doing business in Canada, local firms must ask themselves if they can compete across the board. Without additional capital investment, they may choose to spin off parts of their business and concentrate on specialty segments. "The market is moving towards larger companies," he says, "and niche players who are able to provide very specific services for their clients. Niche players are mainly people who have left mainline firms to start their own investment houses and some of them are doing surprisingly well. They have specialized skills and good relationships with their clients. But the mid-sized firms are having a difficult time," claims Hendry, "because the capital expenditure required to do business on a global basis is enormous, with no guarantee of return on that investment."

Deregulation of the traditional four pillars has meant that the banks have become an even more dominant force. Like other industries, financial services organizations are facing the challenge of increased competition and shrinking margins. Investment dealers, trust companies and more recently, insurance companies, are all being forced to evaluate the cost of staying in business. Capital outlays to stay on the leading edge of technology, coupled with the cost of competing in international markets has precipitated many of the mergers and acquisitions that have occurred, with the result that it is the mid-sized firms that are being squeezed out of the marketplace. The chasm between the big, dominant organizations, leveraging their ability to provide an all-encompassing range of products and services to clients, and the smaller niche players is widening.

Courtney Pratt of Noranda says, "It's not good enough to be the best in Canada or North America. You have to be among the best in the world. These pressures have forced a tremendous competitive focus that was never there before. In the last five years it has got increasingly stronger and it is not going to go away."

However, there is evidence to suggest that Canadian companies are picking up the challenge to become globally competitive. For example, the number of Canadian company stock listings appearing on US exchanges has increased. The mining industry, albeit pre Bre-X, was being touted as the centre of the global mining universe, forcing international brokerage houses to assign analysts to cover the Canadian market. The possibility exists that as the profile of Canadian companies is raised, more and more global firms will want to establish representation in Canada, hence an increase in competition.

The pharmaceutical industry in Canada, too, faces substantial challenges: a small domestic market and a very high price tag for developing new products. Less than 10% of the total cost of healthcare is spent on drugs, and less than 3% on prescription drugs. Drug companies have sales of $7 billion in Canada, compared to General Motors, for example, which has $35 billion in sales in Canada. They also face severe price controls due to government pressure and spending cutbacks.

One of the major things that's happened at Searle is that Monsanto talent injected into R & D over the past five or six years is now showing results. "We have at least half a dozen compounds, each with a billion dollar potential globally, that will be coming through in the next few years," says Nelson. "One product can do amazing things for your ranking," he continues, "as Prozac did for Lilly, or Zantac for Glaxo."

At the same time, up-front costs, including research and development, are extremely high. There is skepticism in the pharmaceutical industry, says Chris Nelson of Searle Canada, regarding the notion of increased size creating increased revenues. According to Nelson, Bristol-Myers Squibb is the only company which has shown increased revenues with a new, bigger company. All the other, are actually underperforming on the revenue line, but Nelson says, the efficiencies they are capturing through economies of scale are really paying off and they've been able to reduce costs.

The [global] costs of bringing a new product to market are huge. "If you believe the latest numbers," says Nelson, "we're talking about US$500 or US$600 million to take a product that you've already identified and prepare it for market. There's a very high risk. Marginal improvements to a product are no longer successful in the marketplace."

What an Organization Needs

The executives interviewed emphasized four areas in which companies need to improve in order to meet new competition:

- satisfying customers,
- cutting costs,
- rationalizing operations, and
- knowing the marketplace.

Satisfying Customers

The current competitive marketplace requires an increased awareness of customers' needs and demands. This calls for a very different orientation for organizations, particularly if they have enjoyed a monopolistic advantage in the past. As Dee Parkinson-Marcoux of Gulf Heavy Oil says, "Everyone has to work harder to protect their market niche. We can't take those for granted anymore. If you don't take into account the needs of the market, you can easily be bumped out of that market."

"We have to look at how we do our work and the processes we use, and we have to remove things that add no value to customers," says Allan Kupcis of Ontario Hydro. Over time we have developed ways of working that resulted from being a monopoly, and these are not valid today. We are now benchmarking ourselves against other companies and seeing where we can remove non-value-added processes.

Bell Canada has also had to become much more customer-focused, with regard to how they're organized, how they reward people and the structures they have in place. Their biggest challenge has been marrying technology and business so that the customer benefits. "Translating customer demand and betting on certain technologies from a customer pull point of view," says Bernard Cormier, "means making real decisions, which is not easy because there are so many choices."

"At Ericsson we have to make sure that our products are kept up-to-date, both on a local and global basis," says Bernt Hoegberg. Ericsson invests 20% of their sales revenue in research and development in order to keep up-to-date and to keep ahead of their competition in a fiercely competitive market.

According to Hoegberg, of the 90,000 or so people in the worldwide Ericsson organization, 20,000 are working on technical development. It is essential to keep up with the needs of their customers, especially adding new features to cell phones and PCs. The company's main concern is how many new services are actually required to provide customers and systems suppliers with a competitive advantage. In Canada, Ericsson has tripled sales in two years by supplying different services to main telephone suppliers. As Hoegberg says, "We can only be successful if we manage to make our customers successful. That puts demands on us as a supplier. We need to understand our customers and what is important to them."

"Because of the competition, we are running faster and margins are getting tighter. Our business is becoming more and more competitive," says Ian Hendry, of RBC Dominion Securities. "As our business becomes more and more complex, our ability to provide value-added services with unique, creative solutions is ultimately where the game is going to be played. We increasingly need to draw on the skills and capabilities of our people and challenge them, individually or collectively, to solve customer issues on a case-by-case basis. This is where we have to maximize our intellectual capital. The solution we provide has to be skillfully tailored to meet the unique needs of each client."

Cutting Costs

Companies are having to get their costs down in order to remain competitive in the global marketplace. They are also coming under greater pressure to increase shareholder value. Many companies have been insulated from this pressure, but it is no longer possible to avoid it. Without barriers to prevent a company from shifting its business from one country to another, business is often being done where there is the lowest level of both labour and energy costs.

According to Brian Harrison, organizations frequently resort to downsizing, re-engineering and restructuring as cost-cutting measures. "There is a continuing emphasis on reducing cost through re-engineering." The major impact on employees is that more and more jobs are lost to contractors and contingent staff. The loyalty of the remaining employees may be eroded, which in turn could have a negative effect on productivity. Managing the change resulting from such cost reductions is critical if productivity is to be sustained.

Allan Kupcis says he has had to establish a sense of urgency with Ontario Hydro management to deal with cost structures. "We are concerned about getting the costs of electricity down. Electricity is now viewed as a commodity product and is priced on the worldwide commodity markets. Currently there are huge differences in prices across North America, with Ontario Hydro tending to be in the middle."

"We have to be sensitive to the global nature of our customers," he continues, "and ensure that we do not increase their costs. We have to help them maintain their competitive pricing in the world markets. Customers now benchmark prices and go where they can get the best prices."

Bernard Cormier notes that Bell Canada is adding value by trying to "bundle" some of the core services and products while at the same time simplifying customer interface. "Much as we want to hang on to market and maintain margins," says Cormier, "the competitive situation makes it very difficult, so we have to organize cost-wise for a marketplace that's much more commodity-oriented in our core business."

The prices of many of the commodities Noranda deals in, such as oil and metals, are set on the world market. Noranda's challenge is to reduce operating costs and differentiate itself from its competitors in other ways, such as customer service and product delivery.

Rationalizing Operations

Increasing competition in the global marketplace has led to the need for rationalization and consolidation in many industries. Companies must grow in order to take advantage of economies of scale; rationalization is also being driven by a move to greater efficiency and less duplication, which in turn will lead to reduced costs.

A study by the federal government and the National Dairy Council suggests that within the dairy industry there will be more imports from global companies. Since Canada does not, at this time, participate aggressively in the export sector in dairy products, the industry is at risk, because it is not able to offset income lost to these imports by income from exports. The consequences to the industry, particularly at the processor level, will be significant unless this issue is addressed in the very near future. The study suggested that there will have to be significant rationalization, partly because of a slight decline in the industry; partly because of the number of imports; and partly because of the change in consumer demand, for low-fat products, for example.

In the past, the Canadian dairy industry was primarily a domestic outlet for milk from dairy farms. Ault Foods has recently changed its thinking, according to Larry Morden, and made the decision to look to the market and design products specifically for it, rather than just to get them off the farm. With global firms like Nestle and Unilever entering the Canadian market and generating competition, Ault has had to consider the question of rationalization. "When Beatrice didn't bump out of the fluid milk industry," says Morden, "we decided we would be the ones to sell because there had to be a rationalization in the industry."

"And a similar thing happened in the frozen division," he continues. "We were the predominant ice cream maker in Canada, but unless we were prepared to put a lot of money into the frozen business, we would remain a regional player with the big global players like Unilever and Nestle stepping into our marketplace. It became very obvious that we would either have to reinvest back into the business at a local level or sell to a global player. Nestle was knocking at our door and we made the decision to sell to them."

At the same time, Ault is actively pursuing export business in remaining divisions, with a target of expanding them to 30%–40% of its business. Over the past five years they have set up an international division which has contributed significantly to their profits. Currently, only one other Canadian company has shown up in the top twenty export companies in the world dairy industry. There is huge potential for Canadian companies to expand in this export market, and Ault has even partnered with its unions and employees to go with them to Ottawa to argue the case for deregulation.

Rationalization is also coming in the pharmaceutical industry. According to Vic Ackermann, President of Roche Canada, of ninety new drugs produced, only three are likely to be approved, and only one is likely to repay the development costs. Currently there are fifty major and 200 smaller companies fighting for market share in a highly fragmented industry. It is expected that by 2005 there will be no more than three major companies defined by a 10% market share—surviving from the current fifty.

Knowing the Marketplace

As Dee Parkinson Marcoux of Gulf Heavy Oil says, "You have to find out if your competitors are providing products and services in a better way.

It is important to really understand what is going on in the competitive environment. This is new for many organizations."

How HR Can Help

There are two things companies need most from Human Resources in order to meet the challenge of increased competition:

1. moving people within the company for best advantage, which requires hiring, training, and motivating workers with the skills needed for the new marketplace; and

2. handling the change which requires competitive pay and benefit packages to attract skilled workers, while remaining in line with the need for cost efficiencies.

Moving People within the Company

Competition requires organizations to do business in different ways from the ones they are traditionally used to, and to understand different and diverse cultures. Since organizations must compete, both in their own countries and in the global market with new rivals, they need more employees who are able to perform in an entirely different culture with different ways of doing business.

According to Brian Harrison, a company's ability to compete globally is dependent on its ability to "travel their people," that is, move them to different markets and locations and adapt the company knowledge to the local markets and the specifics of the marketplace. This means they can use the existing knowledge and practices to set up new locations and offices and use the infrastructure that already exists.

However, says Harrison, people may be reluctant to move for a variety of reasons. At A.T. Kearney, one of the criteria for promotion is a willingness to relocate. The firm uses financial incentives and develops career and promotion paths to ensure that movement creates a challenge for employees, but it also provides a safety net for returning to the base country.

At Ericsson, cross-country exchanges are used for development purposes. "We have sent a large number of our people around the world," says Bernt Hoegberg, "especially at levels below senior management. The top positions in the company are filled by the head office in Sweden.

People who demonstrate potential are sent on leadership programs around the world. The idea is that this contributes to the exchange of ideas and develops skills and knowledge of the worldwide market."

"We may need to work in collaborative teams to meet the needs of customers," says RBC Dominion Securities' Ian Hendry. "Not everyone can know everything. We also have to allow people to have autonomy in teams when solving customer problems, since they are closest to the customer. This does not mean abdication of leadership, however, but a commitment to giving the workforce the tools, resources and support to get the job done."

Handling Change

Constant change and how to deal with it on both an organizational and human resources level is a major challenge to today's corporate leaders and managers. They recognize the need to be bold and innovative at the organizational level, but know they must tread carefully in the area of employee relations, particularly in unionized organizations.

"Many of our employees are anxious and uneasy," says Hydro's Allan Kupcis, "and are trying to understand the major changes that are taking place around them. They do not understand the environment they are working in. Many feel that the social contract with them has been broken. Hydro traditionally attracted people straight from schools and colleges who liked the idea of stability and long term-security. The real entrepreneurs did not join the company. Today we need those entrepreneurs."

Ontario Hydro also has to fundamentally change the way it manages its employee relations with union staff. "Our culture has traditionally been one of avoiding conflict with unions," says Allan Kupcis, "and this has led us to make special deals in the past. We now need far more management accountability for our labour relations. For many people, their jobs will not change, he says, but the performance standards and expectations of them will change. "We are trying to move to a reward system based on performance standards such as bonuses, which our senior people already have, but this is being resisted by the union."

Courtney Pratt of Noranda agrees that change is hard in a unionized environment. "There is tremendous pressure to be flexible and that's hard in a company that is heavily unionized and used to a paternalistic environment. We need to be much more flexible and adaptive to meet the global market demands. Dealing with unions is becoming a core competence for us."

An additional challenge is that many mining and forest companies have often been the main employer in a town, which makes employee transfers to other locations difficult. The impact of change has already been seen with many jobs being cut, but an increase in global markets has seen the number of jobs growing again.

"We need people who are flexible and adaptive," says Courtney Pratt. "They have to be able to operate in different environments, work fast and be customer-focused. They must learn to work with advanced technology and give up fixed ways of working in silos and only concentrating on their own area. We have to hire and develop those people with a commitment to change."

According to Vic Ackermann, the ability to manage change in a proactive fashion is paramount to Roche and other drug companies. They must continually absorb new companies with different cultures if they are to bring new products to the market. They are constantly reducing jobs in some areas as they strive to streamline the business, and creating jobs in others as they grow. In Canada, for example, the number of manufacturing jobs at Roche has declined and been replaced by technically skilled sales and research positions.

At Ault Foods, they are using a mutual gains bargaining approach which identifies common interests for both unions and management. "Our attempt is to bring unions into the business of expanding the pie, and then sharing the wealth," says Larry Morden. "We are trying such things as unions and management going together to lobby the government regarding free trade issues. These are issues that have to be resolved for both long-term business and job security."

Bell Canada is heavily unionized, says Bernard Cormier and Bell is looking at old work rules and ways of doing things and trying to modify them working hand in hand with the unions. "The difficult part for the unions," says Cormier, "is that total Bell employment numbers are coming down, along with the number of unionized employees. Looking at productivity and workplace reorganization will ultimately affect a lot of employees and it's not easy to make changes, but we're still working together." Change often requires a change in the way people are compensated.

Hydro, on the other hand, has introduced a base pay scheme and broad banding, and developed an incentive scheme for non-unionized staff. The professional union has also recently received an incentive pay program.

Bell Canada's compensation structure has made bigger chunks of total employee compensation variable right across the organization, mainly based on overall company financial measurements. A CEO Award program is in place so that people get rewarded if they contribute in a really substantial way to the company's bottom line.

Roche has moved away from incentive bonuses to salary schemes only. The employees were given a choice of what system they would like and preferred the salary system that gave them a higher base, and hence, higher levels of pension and benefits.

Compensation and benefits is often a very misunderstood area, says Dee Parkinson-Marcoux, Gulf Heavy Oil. It is an area in which a Human Resources professional is required, who knows that lack of fairness and perceived lack of fairness corrodes people's confidence and loyalty.

"I personally don't believe that money provides an incentive to people," says Parkinson-Marcoux. "But, on the other hand, how do you stay competitive with organizations who do use money as an incentive? Even though money doesn't necessarily provide an incentive to individuals," she says, "it sure can discourage them if it isn't handled properly at the compensation level."

THE TECHNOLOGY AND SKILLS OF BUSINESS: CHANGING ORGANIZATONS, CHANGING HR

Computer skills are perhaps the most important new job expertise being demanded in the workplace today, and the way that companies should address this need provides insight into how all required skills should be treated. A commitment to Information Technology seems indispensable, especially for companies building a global operation, but matching computer systems and workforce depends on identifying the core competencies needed to support a company's business strategy and committing to hiring and training workers on the basis of those core competencies. Thus, in this section, we will discuss the HR initiative of developing a "competency-based" personnel framework. In addition, we will explore the final HR initiative, that is, guaranteeing workplace diversity.

The Extent of the Change

Technology has always been a driver of change for organizations; however, breakthroughs are now more rapid than ever before. Technology is having a major impact on the way business is done. It is increasing the nature and scope of communications and learning around the world, and increasing both operating and process efficiencies. It is changing the way business is being done in many industries—especially in the financial services sector. It is also opening up new lines of business and opportunities in areas such as the telecommunications and pharmaceutical industries.

Technology is definitely impacting on the way business is being conducted, according to Brian Harrison. The biggest changes have come about through the introduction of the Internet and the Worldwide Web. As a tool to market services around the world and introduce channels of distribution, it allows organizations to reach more customers and provides opportunities for growth. Greater interaction with customers provides more data with which to better assess buying habits and preferences. Communication is enhanced through direct dialogue, which will become even easier as the Internet increasingly uses voice interactions. Employees are increasingly required to be extremely computer literate and to constantly develop and train themselves to be proficient with the ever changing technology.

Technology is exploding in the telecommunications industry, says Bernard Cormier of Bell Canada. Different fields, i.e., telephone, computer, cable, and media, are coming together, and information systems are integrating very quickly. Bell is faced with meshing these changes with business opportunities.

"The translation into people and how they're affected and effective is very important," says Cormier, "and our ability to learn new skills, and to hire and retain new people with those skills becomes very critical to the business. It is not a static situation."

For professional services consulting firms, knowledge has traditionally been their only competitive edge. In a world where knowledge is power, the Internet has made the hoarding of knowledge impossible. A consultant with a firm that was not part of the interview sample, commented in a private conversation with me that, "We have to create a culture where sharing information becomes the norm in order to make the whole organization stronger. This requires a lot of trust. It means using the technology to understand information, create new products and get a competitive edge. It also means we have the ability to communicate globally in real time. Telecommunications aids such as video-conferencing and e-mail eliminate menial tasks, make global coordination of businesses easier, and allow us to set up networks to store common files and proposals, access them, and change them instantly."

Ian Hendry claims that technology is changing the nature of the way things are done in the banking world. He points to The Bank of Montreal's electronic Mbanx, which is based solely on electronic banking, as one example of the way things are changing to suit customers' needs. On the securities front, smaller niche players are utilizing the Internet to buy and sell stocks, as a way to compete against the major full-service brokerage houses.

Courtney Pratt of Noranda says, "Technology is having an enormous impact on our operation in terms of production and process technologies. It is dramatically altering the way our operations work, and is creating greater efficiency and substantially increasing our quality. It is also allowing us to do things we have not been able to do before. For instance, the introduction of horizontal drilling has allowed us to obtain greater economies from oil and gas reserves."

In their diagnostic division, Roche Canada is faced with continual change and technological innovation in order to lower the price of testing and testing equipment. In the vitamin and chemical manufacturing end of the business, they face huge competition from companies in China and India who can make products much more cheaply due to their lower labour costs. Roche must survive by continually finding ways to decrease their manufacturing costs.

"Although there has been more money available to throw at R & D," says Chris Nelson of Searle, "it hasn't necessarily been productive in the technology end of the business. However, we've recently made a considerable investment in technology and are now pretty reliant on it."

What an Organization Needs

Many organizations believe that they need to better utilize technology and information systems. This means being able to store and access information across worldwide organizations. It also means using various technologies in order to communicate in real time. Brian Harrison of A.T.

Kearney indicates that the use of information technology must follow two roads: capturing knowledge and passing on knowledge. Information technology makes knowledge available to people, but it is important to ensure that people are able to use the technology. Studies are finding that those born before 1960 are not very comfortable with technology. The use of technology has become a core competency, and a strong Information Technology infrastructure can provide a competitive edge.

Harrison comments "Not all people are good at passing on acquired knowledge and information. Just knowing your stuff is not enough in a world where intellectual capital has become a key component in performance management and compensation systems. In our firm, more funds are being directed to projects that capture information, access it and link it around the world."

There is now a need to allow small or newly acquired business units of large corporations to share their functional expertise with their counterparts in other countries. The intellectual capital that they bring can be a selling point to customers and can help expand a company's markets. This information can be shared through the Internet, training programs, distance learning centres, networking, conferences, virtual teaming and previously undreamed of modes of communication.

Courtney Pratt of Noranda agrees. "Jobs will keep changing with technological advances. This is going to be hard in an industry where a lot of people have spent their whole careers doing the same things." Some will not be able to adapt, he says, and that is a challenge in a world where jobs are becoming more and more reliant on technology and computers and where it is necessary to be able to read and follow complex instructions and commands.

The skills of employees have to be upgraded in both technological and other areas. "We have to convince people to accept responsibility for their own careers," says Pratt. "They will no longer be able to say that the company is responsible for me and will look after me. This idea of individual responsibility goes to the heart of a turnaround in core values and employee development."

Noranda is putting a great deal of effort into becoming an employer of choice. Every company wants to attract the brightest and the best in their field. "In many of our operations," he says, "we are putting a concerted effort into upgrading the quality of our people because the demands are getting greater. We need people who can relate to corporate strategy, plant strategy and the culture of the plant. We have deliberately tried to upgrade the quality of people at the plant level. It is also critical that we have people who are skilled at working with unions in the new partnership style."

"We need people who not only do things that can be done by ATMs, but those who bring added value to customers. We need people who are conversant with a variety of products and services and have knowledge and skills over a variety of areas. They need to be able to think creatively, not just give stock answers."

The ability to learn quickly is critical to Bell Canada. "We have to have processes in place, from a people point-of-view," say Bernard Cormier, "that move people around the organization and develop them quickly. Technical training has to be deployed in a rapid way to keep our people up-to-date." Cormier believes the key is an organizational structure that empowers people, is flexible, and puts a premium on decision-making.

"We need people who are comfortable with change and can deal with ambiguity," says Chris Nelson of Searle. "They need to be flexible and also have a lot of analytical capability. Traditionally, we have run on intuition and experience rather than modeling," he continues. "Now we have to become much better at the modeling process."

Brian Harrison sees more emphasis on decentralization, with decision making closer to business units and customers. With technology, better data and a better educated workforce, employees can be empowered to make decisions related to customers rather than going to higher management for resolution.

"We've got to learn to do more with less," says Chris Nelson of Searle Canada. "This means learning how to work in a different way at the same time you're doing the work. We need people who can learn fast and be pretty self-reliant because there isn't time to coddle people. They have to be self-starters and learners, able to see opportunities and go to them. We are in what I call the 'New Deal,'" says Nelson. "The 'New Deal' is not employment for life anymore. The deal is, if you're here, you're going to learn an awful lot and you are going to be very employable in the future. It's not employment anymore, it's employability."

Says Dee Parkinson-Marcoux, "We have to recognize that we're in a constant learning environment and that we must invest in training.

However," she continues, "most organizations are reluctant to spend money on training. I think one of the reasons for this is that if you invest in training and become a really good trainer, other companies just filch your people. So you don't recover your investment."

She believes that development within an organization should very much be on a partnership basis. "People must continually communicate what they like about their job and what they feel they should be learning, she says, "and your obligation is to listen to that. This kind of openness goes hand in hand with communication and training."

According to Brian Harrison, there is a huge pent-up demand for training and development in most companies. It is critical in today's market to keep up-to-the-minute in technological developments, product knowledge, diversity, language training and personal safety and security within parent and acquired companies.

Hydro's Allan Kupcis says, "We have to put much more effort into providing individuals with the development and skills that they need. We have focused our efforts on reorganizing and downsizing, and not much on development. We used to be really good at this, and now we have to put much more effort into training and development again."

Bernard Cormier of Bell Canada agrees that not everyone can be well-versed in all areas. "It's important to get people around the table in a facilitated process way to look at specific issues and address them quickly versus waiting for the traditional organization to come to grips with them. In general," he says, "this calls for more skilled and flexible people."

He goes on to say that the paradigm of permanent employment security no longer exists and the very notion of a career and how it evolves has changed. "We have to be able to redeploy people much more quickly nowadays," he says, "and it is essential that we provide people with a tool kit of skills that enables them to move around."

How HR Can Help

The HR function most often mentioned in connection with providing training to keep up with technological change was developing a competency-based personnel framework; in addition, executives said, they needed HR's help in building and maintaining workplace diversity.

Developing a Competency-Based Personnel Framework

Core competency[1] definitions and their application to hiring and training have been brought into today's organizations by Human Resources. The development of competencies for various positions and job families has become critical; a framework is also needed for identifying those competencies necessary for future success and providing a template for recruitment, training, learning and development, and for promotion and succession planning.

The A.T. Kearney study "Globalizing the Corporation" identified the key competencies for the future as adaptability, technological literacy, and collaborative skills. The study also cited integrating skills as a key competency, as organizations seek to bring together people of different backgrounds, cultures and experiences, who are often working in different time zones.

Searle Canada implemented an organization design initiative in November of 1995. This involves a series of projects that have been extremely valuable in moving people, creating information and preparing and planning for the future. "We've looked at our business areas," says Chris Nelson, "and thought through every department and defined explicitly what kinds of capabilities we want there, and we're very actively managing that. We're also doing a lot of strategic people planning and succession planning. That means, looking at a number of people, their capabilities, future potential, where they're going to fit and who should have our highest priority. Plus, we've invested a lot in training and learning maps so that people can understand what's going on around them."

"At Ericsson," says Bernt Hoegberg, "we are working on a more systematic competence development process and are benchmarking ourselves around the competencies we need. We are using cross-country moves as a means of development; we are putting great effort into leadership development, and making sure all people go through basic training. We recognize the need to continually reevaluate who we are going to advance in the company."

---

[1] Core competencies are defined by Gary Hamel and C.K. Pralahad in their book *Competing for the Future* (Boston: Harvard Business School Press, 1994), as a bundle of skills and technologies, particular to any given organization, that provide the unique competitiveness and contribute to the long-term success of the organization.

"We have to assess the competencies at the leadership and management levels of the company to make sure that they are market-oriented," says Hydro's Allan Kupcis. "We have to bring people into the company when we do not have the right skills, and that is counter-cultural. We can no longer overestimate our strengths and skills in the marketplace. We have to use our brand equity within Ontario to full advantage and capitalize on this in the marketplace. Ontario is proud that they own us and want us to do better.

"But we are lacking solid marketing skills," he continues. "We have to both develop and bring in more marketing competencies if we are to take advantage of the new global marketplace. We have good technical and engineering skills and know how to reliably operate power and distribution systems, and this will be of interest in the global marketplace. We need to get into brokerage marketing efforts with people who are knowledgeable about hedging, financing, trading and future markets. We can partner to bring the technical expertise."

Training and development was seen as critical since employees need to constantly upgrade competencies and embrace lifelong learning. Increasingly employees are expected to take more responsibility for their own learning and development, with HR as a centre of expertise for their use.

At Ericsson, says Bernt Hoegberg, "we have to work on the development of products, and that means having the right skills in place to do that. Our products are now ready for use when they are delivered. Not too long ago, when you built a telephone switch, you literally had to build it on site. The meant that you had to have skilled installers. Now, as electronics have become integrated, the products are ready for use and only have to be plugged in. This means that installers can now be trained to do trouble shooting and technical maintenance instead."

RBC Dominion Securities must also think creatively about training and development, says Ian Hendry, while being careful about getting a return on investment dollars. "We also need to provide a framework for individuals to work on their career development."

Guaranteeing Workplace Diversity

Says Courtney Pratt of Noranda, "One of the things we have recognized is that we are not very representative of the world. Our employee population does not reflect the customer and operation bases in the parts of the world in which we operate. We need people who understand how to do business in different parts of the world. I think the challenge for us is to develop a network of relationships and to ensure that our workforce is representative of these networks."

SUMMARY

In this chapter, top Canadian executives and HR professionals have taken us inside their operations and shared their insights on how organizations are being changed by globalization, competition, and advances in information technology. They have also provided details of the ways Human Resources is already at work turning the challenge of change into directions for strategic growth.

From my research, I identified seven key ways in which HR can contribute to dealing with changes in the marketplace and workplace. They are:

1. Creating a common company-wide value system,

2. Developing a "competency-based" personnel framework,

3. Providing leadership assessment and development,

4. Moving people within the company for best advantage,

5. Guaranteeing the workplace diversity that allows success in a company's varied national and global markets,

6. Handling the question of change, and

7. Re-engineering the corporate Human Resources function as a consulting centre to company management on hiring, training, managing, paying, retaining, and developing an organization's human assets.

In the chapters that follow, we will learn more about the history of the Human Resources function, go behind the scenes in case studies of companies in transition, and follow step-by-step applications of some of the most advanced HR techniques in personnel evaluation, leadership development, and compensation.

Part Two

The Changing Role of Human Resources

As ORGANIZATIONS UNDERTAKE constant, rapid change to meet the requirements of a more competitive global environment, they have found that high performance depends on people. In many cases, the Human Resources function has had to reinvent itself in order to serve the needs and foster the creativity of organization members coping with change.

Chapter 2, *The Changing Role of the Human Resources Function*, describes the evolution of the function from being solely a provider of transactional services to an expert consultant to senior business partners on business strategy, advice and management of change. Transactional services—the administration of compensation and benefits, status changes, and the creation and maintenance of Human Resource information systems—are being re-engineered, automated, streamlined, and sometimes outsourced in order to increase efficiency and reduce costs. The chapter then examines specific competencies required by Human Resources professionals as they take on more strategic roles.

Chapter 3, *The Contribution of Human Resources to Change Management: A Case Study of KPMG Canada*, considers the fundamental changes that are taking place within KPMG, a global advisory and consulting firm. KPMG, along with other major professional service companies, is facing changing client requirements, increasing competitiveness, rapid technological change, and the need to develop specific lines of business.

In order to meet these challenges, KPMG is realigning its operations, creating new culture, investing heavily in technology, and leveraging knowledge to change the performance focus of the firm.

To deliver on these changes, the firm needed to enhance its HR experience and knowledge. KPMG brought in seasoned HR professionals who had the required change management experience. The current HR agenda focuses on creating a competency framework; developing a competency-based reward structure, recruitment and compensation; creating a performance management process to support the business direction; and developing a career advancement and partner admission process.

Chapter 4, *Measuring Human Resources Effectiveness*, is written by Larry Morden, former Senior Vice-President of Ault Foods, who has created and developed ways to measure the effectiveness of Human Resources in an organization. Morden defines three broad categories of measurement standards which have been at various times applied to the Human Resources function. First are the functional measures, those that relate to the efficiency and effectiveness of the Human Resources function by examining rates of turnover, cost per hire, and number of grievances. The second are operational measures, which gauge human asset performance through such statistics as units of output per employee and cost of output per work team or division. The third category is strategic measures, which chart the future, e.g., measurement of intellectual capital.

This chapter also provides a case study of Ault Foods and shows how that organization has over the past twelve years become much more competent at measuring the efficiency and effectiveness of Human Resources.

Chapter 5, *Redefining and Restructuring the Human Resource Function*, provides an example of a large company that redefined the role of its HR function in order to meet its current and future business needs. This case study illustrates many of the concepts and issues discussed in Part Two. It describes the existing HR function of the organization, which was largely decentralized and concentrated primarily on transactional activities. Based on consultation and recommendations, the HR function realigned itself into five primary roles and then organized in order to fulfill those roles. The role of the corporate group and the role of HR in the divisions was redefined. This chapter examines how the new roles and structures were implemented and provides some of the outcomes.

CHAPTER TWO

The Changing Role of the Human Resources Function

Margaret Butteriss

THE PREVIOUS CHAPTER highlighted the macro changes that organizations require to succeed in a more competitive and global environment and outlined the specific initiatives that may need to be taken to improve the effectiveness of people management and the productivity of the workforce. In some instances the role of HR in these initiatives was mentioned.

This chapter focuses on the role of Human Resources in support of changing business requirements. Much of the material in this chapter comes from my own experience in helping a number of organizations refocus and reorganize their HR functions to better support the business as a whole. I also have drawn on an interview with Carrie Shea, a Principal in the Strategic Services practice at A.T. Kearney's Chicago office, who conducted a study on the global best practices in HR management for one of Kearney's clients. The study, entitled "Global Best Practices in Human Resources," was aimed at identifying lessons learned from attempts to improve company performance through the implementation of innovative HR programs, and the ways these drove improvement in workforce productivity.

THE CHANGING ROLE OF HUMAN RESOURCES IN RESPONSE TO ORGANIZATIONAL CHANGE

Given the changing environments and requirements in many organizations, it is not surprising that the expectations of the Human Resources function are changing. Traditionally, HR has been responsible for transactional and administrative activities such as recruitment, employee record keeping, compensation and benefit administration, and dealing with employees' queries. Now, in contrast, the role of Human Resources is rapidly becoming one of assisting in the creation of an organization that adds value to its shareholders, customers and employees.

The Kearney study found that "best practice companies have repositioned their human resources organizations to be much closer to the businesses." These companies consistently made the following changes:

- secured senior level commitment, involvement, and enlightenment;
- reorganized their HR organizations to better deliver their new value proposition;
- upgraded the skills/competencies of the HR function; and
- expanded the role of HR beyond the traditional HR service areas.

"At the highest levels," the study states, "and with the support of the board of directors and senior team, many of these companies have elevated their most senior HR executive to a direct reporting relationship to the CEO, and in nearly every case, the senior-most HR executive is a member of the highest-level strategy or management board. In best practice companies, the CEO as well typically spends between 30-40% of his or her time on people related issues. These CEOs understand the levers they can 'pull' from an HR perspective, and view succession and planning and leadership development to be two of the most important roles they can play as the Chief Executive Officer."

Companies are also seeing a need to redefine what line managers need to do in relation to people initiatives, and what the role and function of HR is. Emphasis is being placed on what functions can be outsourced and what can be automated, in order to increase the value-added of the HR function and reduce the costs of non-value-added areas.

Specifically, CEOs are looking to HR for help in recruiting and selecting the right people, improving the capabilities and competencies of the workforce, managing and paying for results, and maintaining a vital succession of management, professional and skills talent as the business grows. As organizations become more global, they need to have different recruitment, compensation and development systems to suit each country or region, along with a set of core values and principles that hold the company together. Equally, they have to ensure that an individual going to work in another country understands that country's "way of doing business."

HUMAN RESOURCE REQUIREMENTS TO ADAPT TO A CHANGING WORLD

Carrie Shea of Kearney notes that the HR function is having to change as a matter of survival. In many companies it is being required to justify its budgets to the CEOs and to explain why so much money is being spent on transactional HR activities. Such spending does not "cut it" with CEOs, who do not see such processing costs as part of the core competencey of the organization.

The Kearney study found that best practice companies recognized a link between improvements in workforce productivity and state-of-the-art Human Resources programs. "Whether measured in terms of salaried or hourly productivity, they are driving productivity improvements by investing in the key human resources productivity levers." The study defined seven key **productivity levers** as follows:

- recruiting,
- training and development,
- performance management,
- compensation,
- organizational development,
- global programs, and
- diversity.

It also found that companies achieving the greatest productivity gains were increasing their investments across all of the productivity levers. They were realigning service area goals with the needs of the business, streamlining transactional activities, and increasing line management involvement and leadership. They had also set up formal and informal processes and networks for disseminating Human Resources practices across the company on a global basis.

As well as focusing on productivity improvement of the workforce, many HR departments have been given the responsibility for making the organization's core values operational by building them into the recruitment, performance management and learning processes.

MEETING THE CHANGING REQUIREMENTS

In order to deliver on the support and services required by senior management, the HR function has to change in a fairly dramatic fashion. Equally, the capabilities and expertise of HR professionals have to change in response to the need for more value-added services that will contribute to overall business goals. Specific HR competencies will be covered at the end of this chapter; we begin here by considering HR's changing role. One of the best descriptions has been provided by David Ulrich of the University of Michigan.

I heard Ulrich speak at a Canadian Human Resources Planning Professional session that was held in Toronto in the spring of 1994. The material that was presented has been published in *Human Resource Champions* (Boston: Harvard Business School Press, 1996.) Prof. Ulrich has identified four keys to providing specialist HR support and advice on implementing improved roles for the Human Resources function. These are:

- Management of Strategic Human Resources,
- Management of the HR Infrastructure,
- Management of the Employee Contribution, and
- Management of Transformation and Change.

1. **Management of Strategic Human Resources**: HR acts as a strategic partner and is involved in aligning HR and business strategy to facilitate execution of the business strategy. It determines what HR practices are required to support the business strategy and provides tailor-made services in such areas as customized training and development, facilitation of business planning and team initiatives, value-added recruitment and staffing processes, and performance management. It also assists with the streamlining of business processes and productivity-improvement initiatives, and assists in organization and job design in order to provide more value-added to the end customer.

2. **Management of the HR Infrastructure**: HR acts as an administrative expert and re-engineers HR organization processes in order to build an efficient infrastructure, e.g., for staffing and recruiting, training and development, salary administration, maintenance of employee records, processing payroll and benefits, implementing new policies, and listening to employee concerns.

   Re-engineering takes place in order to reduce administration effort and costs, through such things as the introduction of Human Resources Information Systems and the outsourcing of labour-intensive activities.

3. **Management of the Employee Contribution**: HR acts as an employee champion, and listens and responds to employees' needs in order to increase employee commitment and capability. This role of being an employee advocate is one of the more traditional and valued roles that HR has played in an organization.

4. **Management of Transformation and Change**: HR acts as a change agent to manage change and transformation in order to create a renewed organization. HR professionals assist management to make change happen.

Changes in Handling Traditional HR Functions

As Ulrich's list shows, the Human Resources function is expected to become more of a strategic business partner and consultant in the area of change management. It is, however, still expected to manage its traditional transactional activities.

Re-engineering and Automation of Transactional Activities

If the HR function is to deliver value-added service, it must re-engineer and automate many of HR's transactional activities, what Ulrich calls "the HR infrastructure."

   Many organizations are seeking to dramatically reduce the costs of HR transactions by automating and streamlining processes. They have automated such areas as status changes and departmental moves, compensation and benefits administration, and information management.

As well as automating such processes, they have moved towards more self-service by employees and managers, rather than having HR staff perform these functions. Managers are able to access and change information on their employees quickly and easily, and can reduce approval delays. Employees can find out company and policy information quickly and can make changes to their own status information themselves. Queries on such things as health and dental plans, share purchase plans, vacations and leaves of absence, RRSPs and general benefit and policy queries are handled by automated telephone systems. More difficult queries can be put through to people trained to handle them.

The use of kiosks and automated telephone systems results in lower staff overhead and more effective and empowered managers and employees. These concepts also enhance HR consultation services by freeing managers from depending on HR staff.

Other areas that have been re-engineered and automated include: candiditate selection, hiring and salary and merit adjustments, benefits management, terminations, and HR data integrity. One large international consulting firm is setting up a service centre to handle all incoming resumés, put them into a database by means of optical scanning, and allow easy access to the database from all offices in North America.

Some organizations have automated the flexible benefits enrollment process and self-administered investment plans. Others have developed automated tools for job specifications and grading, compensation programs, performance management, and career development. Larger companies have introduced an automated internal staffing process, whereby jobs are posted on-line with the required competencies. Employees apply on-line, with their resumé, to these positions.

A major telecommunications company is in the process of developing an "employee in a box" initiative. When new employees start, they are usually not productive at once, since they have to get phones, office furniture and equipment, security clearance and passes, sign up for benefits, etc. The company is looking at how it can provide all these services and requirements before the employee arrives, thus allowing for immediate employee motivation and productivity.

Outsourcing of Routine, Labour-Intensive Functions

Some organizations are not only re-engineering and automating transactional activities but are also outsourcing some more labour-intensive functions to companies that specializing in these services. Activities that are being outsourced include payroll processing, and pension and benefits administration. Other functions which are not performed as regularly as payroll, e.g., training and some aspects of recruitment and staffing, are also being outsourced or provided by contractors. There are two benefits: first, organizations reduce costs by paying for the functions only as needed, instead of assigning them to full-time employees; and, second, they have the flexibility to obtain the right skills and expertise when required in each situation.

Carrie Shea makes an interesting point regarding outsourcing of the HR function. "The companies in our study found that they were outsourcing to many organizations. In three to five years I predict that a company will want to outsource to only one organization, who will be able to provide all the HR services from one base—this will be like a virtual HR organization."

HOW IS THE HR FUNCTION ORGANIZING ITSELF TO MEET THESE REQUIREMENTS?

Many organizations have already reorganized, or will need to reorganize, their HR function in order to obtain the results now required of Human Resources. The current trend is for organizations to have small corporate HR functions, whose role is to provide overall strategy and policy advice, and to decentralize all other aspects of HR. Decentralizing HR involves having some HR staff reporting to line managers who draw specialist advice and consulting skills in areas such as compensation, recruitment, and organization development. Tasks may be performed by small corporate functions or by external consultants. HR staff at the business-unit level are becoming like account executives, as they identify business and HR needs, contract for the required help, and bill for services they have provided. Such an arrangement ensures that they provide the support a business unit requires in a cost-effective way.

HR reorganization involves new roles and responsibilities not only for HR staff but also for line managers and individual employees. In the sections that follow, the roles of corporate HR, HR staff assigned to operating units, line managers and individual employees will be examined.

The Role of Corporate HR

As noted above, many organizations are moving towards having small strategic corporate HR functions. This is particularly true when an organization has many divisions and strategic business units that operate in very different ways. In order to find out the responsibilities of these corporate HR functions, I recently conducted a survey of 30 large and medium-sized organizations that operated both in North American and globally. Many of the companies are household names throughout the world.

A common theme that emerged was that the corporate HR function is very important both in terms of assisting the implementation of its business strategies, and in reinforcing the corporate culture and values.

The HR function has a very strong link to corporate planning in that HR plays a major role in assisting with the implementation of corporate strategies. In some cases, Human Resources and corporate planning functions report to the same person. Senior HR executives generally have a great deal of influence and usually serve on the senior management team and on the Board of Directors.

The corporate HR function is also responsible for creating the policies and programs which embody the corporate culture. When a policy is created, it is signed off by the senior management team, and adherence is expected. The level of integration and commonality of HR policies and practices is determined by how far the different strategic businesses within the organization need to integrate in order to be successful. A number of organizations are finding that it is necessary to have common executive development and performance management systems so that they can reinforce the company's vision and values. However, there is a move away from having numerous policies towards a few core policies and many guidelines. This allows business units greater flexibility to adapt to local conditions and specific business requirements, while operating within a common framework of fairness and equity for all employees.

Key Corporate HR Functions

The role and function of corporate HR consists of the following areas:

- **Identification and development of core competencies required to support the business**. Once they have been identified, strategies are put in place to develop or acquire the core competencies. The corporate function is also responsible for monitoring the progress of development.

- **Development of executive talent.** Corporate HR is responsible for systems that identify and develop high-potential people throughout the organization, and to prepare them and existing senior management to achieve current and future business requirements, including succession planning.

- **Development of training and development initiatives to support the common culture, values and operating principles**. Many organizations use training and development sessions as a communications vehicle to develop, implement, and sustain the organization's culture and values.

- **Development of standards for employee assessment and compensation**. Corporate HR identifies company standards for hiring, judging and assessing employees. In some companies, people who do not demonstrate the required values are terminated, even though they might have achieved the required business results.

- **Development and implementation of performance management and compensation policies and programs for use in all operating companies**. These are often adapted to meet local conditions and requirements, particularly when a company operates in many different geographical areas; however, the systems still maintain core information and principles.

Some of the organizations in the survey situated such functions as Industrial Relations, Compensation and Benefits, Health and Safety, and Employment Equity at the corporate level. Corporate HR's role was to develop policy and strategy, with execution being done within the various business units and divisions. A few organizations have created common service groups at the corporate level to handle such things as payroll for the whole company, resumé management, and recruitment. Others prefer to keep the corporate function strategic in nature, and have these service areas handled by some of the operating groups.

Internal Consulting Groups

Some of the organizations surveyed have created internal consulting groups that perform such functions as company-wide re-engineering, business process re-engineering, restructuring and change management. These groups, which relate to what Ulrich calls the "Management Transformation and Change," help business units with key decisions, assist underperforming units in turnaround initiatives, consult on the creation of new business units, and identify business opportunities to be developed. They also assist with the development of leadership and organizational skills.

These internal consulting units are usually located within the corporate HR group, but in some cases are located in the corporate or strategic planning function. They are usually staffed by a mixture of internal HR and line people, and people who have been recruited from external consulting firms. They often charge out for their service and behave as though they were external consultants.

Role of HR Business Partners in the Business Units and Divisions

Much of the HR work in the business units and divisions is done by HR business partners who are responsible for working with the management teams of their business division, both to identify specific HR requirements to support the business, and to ensure that they are met. The HR business partners may perform these duties themselves, or use other resources such as corporate HR groups or consultants.

They are usually responsible for such functions as HR planning, localized recruitment and staffing, performance management, implementation of compensation and benefits plans, and training and development. They are also responsible for employee relations, which may also cover industrial and labour relations and health and safety requirements. They are also responsible for the implementation of organization-wide policies and programs, and for identifying the need for new systems and processes.

The Role of Line Management

As HR functions change, line management is expected to perform many traditional HR activities. This is made possible by the increasing automation of tools and HR processes, and the consulting support available both in corporate HR and in business units from HR professionals.

Line management is expected to:

- champion change and assist employees through the process, communicate business vision and direction, explain the need for change, and continually reinforce and support new directions;

- do more interviewing and hiring themselves, rather than rely extensively on HR staff;

- manage performance management systems;

- recognize the need for restructuring and re-engineering and get the process going;

- track required business and HR metrics that measure a strategy's effectiveness of the business; and

- share responsibility for executive and individual development and succession planning with corporate HR, by identifying those with potential for development, and ensuring that all individuals are given the opportunities to develop their skills and competencies.

In order for line managers to contribute in all these areas, HR must provide them with appropriate tools and training.

The Role of the Individual Employee

Individuals are increasingly expected to be accountable for their own and the organization's success. Paternalistic organizations are ceasing to exist, because companies can no longer guarantee lifetime employment opportunities. Equally, as employees become better educated and skilled, organizations can no longer tell employees what to do or how to do it. Individuals will increasingly seek employment in places where they can make a difference and where their skills will be valued and enhanced; they will be responsible for this own career planning. A new kind of employment contract is emerging. It focuses more on a commitment to "employability." Organizations will increasingly have to help people achieve their full potential by providing tools and opportunities for self-improvement. They will also have to ensure that a culture and work environment exists that allows individuals to make decisions themselves.

In increasingly tight labour markets, organizations that do not provide such opportunities will find that their best employees will go elsewhere, where they can realize their full potential.

RATIO OF HR PROFESSIONALS TO TOTAL EMPLOYEES

Increasingly, businesses are asking not only how to re-engineer the HR function and provide better value-added service, but also how many HR staff they should have.

The Conference Board of Canada suggests that in the mid-1990s, the median staffing ratio was eight HR professionals per 1,000 employees, and that this was reducing with the advent of automation and streamlining of the HR function. The data they collected showed that this number varies from an average of sixteen per 1000 for small firms, to ten per 100 for medium-sized firms, and five HR staff per 1000 employees for very large firms.

I collected information on this issue from several of Canadian companies whose total number of employees ranged from 4,600 to 45,000, including firms from the oil, telecommunications, financial and retailing sectors. Some of the companies relied heavily on part-time employees. The ratio of HR staff to total staff varied from one person for every 75 employees to one for every 280 employees. The ratio of HR staff to full-time employees showed less variation, with the range being from one per 50 employees to one per 95 employees.

The variation in ratios seems to depend on three factors:

- the perceived influence and competence of the HR function. When the influence and perceived value was high, there were generally more people in HR, particularly at the senior, strategic levels.

- the degree of unionization. My findings showed that the more unionized companies tended to have fewer HR people, since some of the employee relations activities were performed by union officials.

- the amount of automation of transactional activities. Where transactional activities have been automated, the number of HR people—who traditionally performed those activities—is reduced significantly.

COMPETENCIES REQUIRED BY HR PEOPLE

The changing role and function of HR means that HR's core competencies are also changing.

Prof. Ulrich, in his 1994 talk to the Canadian Human Resource Planners, highlighted several HR competencies being developed in a variety of organizations where he was a consultant:

- knowledge of the business—understands the business that the company operates in;
- business and strategic thinking:
- business and customer focus—understands internal and external customer requirements, and has a results orientation;
- individual leadership—provides leadership in achieving company values and goals, and is able to identify and implement the initiatives required to support business direction;
- knowledge and implementation skills in terms of business re-engineering and process practices;
- change management skills;
- can work in partnership with other functions and divisions of the organization and provide integration with other business systems;
- ability to benchmark HR practices within the organization and in other external organizations.

A 1995 study by the Conference Board of Canada entitled "Adding Value: The Role of the Human Resource Function" identified competencies for senior HR executives similar to those identified by Ulrich.

A number of HR professionals will find it difficult to adapt to these new competency requirements, since many of them have been trained to provide transactional support and still continue to have that mindset. Many organizations are therefore bringing more and more line people to fill senior HR positions, since they already have the requisite business knowledge. Others are using an assignment in HR as part of career development for high-potential executives, which has the dual advantage of bringing business expertise to the function and ensuring that potential executives are grounded in HR strategies and processes.

HR Competencies: A Classification by Type

During various consulting assignments relating to Human Resources Management, I have often been asked to assist with defining HR competencies. A colleague, Pelly Shafto of Shafto and Associates, and I have come up with a classification system complementary to those of Ulrich and the Conference Board of Canada. We group competencies by type: firstly, there are those we call **general competencies**, which relate to capabilities required by all those in leadership positions in any organization; and second, we have defined **HR technical competencies**, which relate to capabilities specifically required to fulfill the HR role.

General Competencies

- Business Knowledge
- Customer Service
- Innovation, Change, Risk Taking
- Supports Organization Change
- Teamwork
- Leadership
- Interpersonal Skills
- Personal Effectiveness

HR Technical Competencies

- Develops and Delivers Training
- Compensation Management and Benefits Administration
- Health and Safety
- Labour and Employee Relations
- Recruitment and Staffing
- HR Information Systems/Payroll

Each of these competencies is presented in more detail in an appendix to this chapter.

Customizing Competencies

Competencies can be useful in recruiting HR staff, describing the requirements of particular positions, and developing individuals for current and future responsibilities. Each organization will need to customize the competencies required for its own HR function, particularly in relation to the development activities. However, these sets provide a good foundation against which to begin to define the required competencies.

SUMMARY

There is a need to change the role of HR from one focusing on transactional activities to one that acts as a strategic business partner that provides value-added services. Transactional activities still need to be done, but organizations are increasingly finding quicker and more cost-effective ways to carry these out, by means of technology and outsourcing.

Performing a strategic role often means that organizations have to look at how their HR function is organized and structured, and the type of competencies and expertise that HR professionals require if they are to fulfill this role.

RECOMMENDED READING

The Conference Board of Canada, "Creating High Performance Organizations with People," Report 164, 1996.

Corporate Leadership Council, *Vision of the Future—Role of Human Resources in the New Corporate Headquarters.* Washington: The Advisory Board Company, 1995.

Hamel, Gary and C.K. Prahalad, *Competing for the Future.* Boston: Harvard Business Press, 1994.

Ulrich, D. *Human Resource Champions—the Next Agenda for Adding Value and Delivering Results.* Boston: Harvard Business Press, 1996.

Human Resources Competencies

GENERAL COMPETENCIES

- Business Knowledge
- Customer Service
- Innovations, Change, Risk Taking
- Supports Organization Change
- Teamwork
- Leadership
- Interpersonal Skills
- Personal Effectiveness

Business Knowledge
Definition

- Understands the business and divisional strategies and uses them to contribute to corporate goals and objectives. Understands the economic, consumer, and social issues facing the organization. Links HR goals with business.

Key Behaviours

- Understands key business issues and opportunities of the company and their client groups. Develops appropriate HR strategies to meet these
- Demonstrates a practical understanding of business fundamentals that impact revenue and expenses

- Works with client group in shaping and influencing divisional strategies to optimize Human Resources

- Benchmarks best practices in the industry and influences clients to manage these standards

- Identifies opportunities for integration in the organization supporting cross functional initiatives

- Works with client group to create individual and organization HR plans and development initiatives

Developmental Activities

- Attend management meetings where the company's past performance and future goals are presented and discussed

- Discuss strategic plans with the division head and the manager. Identify ways in which the division/department's goals support the plan, and discuss how to help to support these goals

- View all videos related to strategy and business plans as a whole, and for the division. Read company and division

- Read publications such as the *Financial Post, Fortune, Wall Street Journal*, and the *Economist*. Identify business trends and developments and assess their implications for the company.

Publications

Hamel, G. and C.K. Prahalad. *Competing for the Future.* Boston: Harvard Business Press, 1994.
Handy, Charles. *Beyond Certainty.* London: Random House, 1995.

Customer Service
Definition

- Proactively understands the customer/client, anticipating needs. Gives high priority to customer satisfaction. Assists customers and clients in resolving their concerns and issues

Key Behaviours

- Continuously analyzes needs of client groups and initiates projects to achieve the required results

- Benchmarks and evaluates service delivery against client needs and best practice in the HR community, ensuring delivery requirements are met

- Defines and evaluates service based on reliability, responsiveness, assurance, empathy and tangibles

- Exceeds customer expectations in delivery of service

- Utilizes customer service feedback to continually improve delivery processes and reduce costs

Developmental Activities

- Survey management team and clients for regular feedback on how well service is being provided. Seek suggestions for closing the service delivery gaps and act upon them

- Ask for feedback on where you have exceeded your customers needs and build on those results and behaviours

- Develop measures and identify standards for customer service

- List the clients/customers with whom you have had negative encounters over the past six months. See if any pattern emerges. Note situations and types of people that are difficult for you to handle and seek coaching from an expert in this area

- Attend a Customer Service course

- Attend a Total Quality Management program, and take part in a related process review in order to identify and eliminate non value-added activities and processes

Publications

Albrecht, K. *The Only Thing That Matters: Bringing the Power of the Customer into the Center of Your Business.* New York: Harper, 1992.
Barry, L. *Delivering Quality Service.* New York: The Free Press, 1994.

Innovation, Change, Risk Taking
Definition

- Develops creative solutions and new approaches, initiates change and takes calculated risks

Key Behaviours

- Experiments with new ways of doing things and challenges the status quo
- Searches for opportunities to do the job more effectively or efficiently
- Takes risks, learning from a cycle of continuous improvement
- Initiates improvements or new ideas
- Works with others to ensure involvement in change efforts

Developmental Activities

- Find opportunities to learn about different situations or approaches
- Volunteer to take on an assignment that requires new approaches, and/or requires working with people from other divisions or departments
- Volunteer to work on one of the change processes
- Investigate practices and techniques for generating new ideas, e.g., brainstorming, nominal group techniques
- Observe a person in the organization who is skilled at introducing innovative ideas. Discuss with him/her what approaches and skills he/she uses
- Attend MICA's "Six Thinking Hats Program"

Supports Organizational Change
Definition

- Understands organization structure and systems, and the impact of social and economic drivers; can influence change through the appropriate use of organizational development methods

Key Behaviours

- Facilitates groups to supporting organization change or problem solving
- Is knowledgeable about and can implement a variety of tools for the purpose of individual, team and organizational development
- Is knowledgeable about change methods and processes and can assist client groups with change efforts
- Implements field research methods, counselling and interviewing for the purpose of diagnosis, feedback and planned change
- Supports alignment and achievement of the company's vision and business strategy through the change initiatives of specific client groups
- Alerts management to future changes in the business and in socio-economic trends

Developmental Activities

- Keep aware of trends in the business
- Work with skilled facilitators to support the change process in the company
- Meet with experts in organization change and discusses their approach and processes
- Volunteer to work on a change initiative
- Attend programs in consulting skills, facilitation skills, and change management

Publications

Galpin, Timothy P. *The Human Side of Change: Practical Guide to Organization Redesign.* San Francisco: Jossey-Bass, 1996.

Kotter, John P. *Leading Change.* Boston: Harvard Business School Press, 1996.

Teamwork
Definition

- Promotes interventions and works with others when it is appropriate to the business, in order to collaborate on problem solving, developing new ideas or opportunities

Key Behaviours

- Utilizes the disciplines of role definition, goal setting, agenda and team purpose, in order to achieve team tasks
- Facilitates effective team interpersonal dynamics, using ground rules, conflict resolution, assessment tools and evaluation to ensure full participation
- Undertakes the various roles of team leader and facilitator
- Provides consultation to team leaders and management on team effectiveness
- Develops opportunities for team projects and teamwork in the organization in resolving problems or innovative solutions

Developmental Activities

- Join a cross functional taskforce or team effort. Use it as an opportunity to practice various styles and contributions to teamwork
- Request specific behavioural feedback from clients, managers, and peers on how you enhance teamwork and help a team achieve results
- Observe effective meeting leaders. Make notes of what they say and what they do to contribute to the success of a meeting. Meet them and discuss the processes and approaches they use
- Attend programs in team building, facilitation skills, meeting skills, and dispute resolution techniques

Leadership
Definition

- Articulates and connects others to the business vision by enabling, encouraging and challenging the current state

Key Behaviours

- Encourages and listens to the ideas of others in achieving the organizations vision

- Involves and recognizes others in planning and making the decision they are capable of making
- Fosters collaboration with colleagues and other team members
- Models behaviour that is consistent with the business vision and values
- Motivates others through example
- Exercise integrity and honesty in decision making and providing advice to others
- Achieves goals by focusing on the key priorities and understanding the larger picture
- Searches for opportunities to do the job more efficiently and effectively, exploring ways to improve the organization

Developmental Activities

- Actively seeks out the views of managers, peers and colleagues in terms of what they are doing to achieve the company's vision and business direction. Act upon these views and ideas to ensure that the vision is achieved in your division/department
- Ask your peers how your leadership style is perceived and solicit behavioural suggestions for improvement through the use of a leadership assessment tool
- Convey a strong sense of direction and objectives by presentation and one-on-one discussions
- Maintain a balance between "big picture" and day-to-day needs by defining roles and overall goals, determining key result areas, identifying indicators of effectiveness, selecting and setting key objectives
- With the help of a manager or an associate known for his/her leadership ability, set up a mentoring process. Encourage your mentor to provide you with feedback and coaching
- Attend the following programs: project management course; Covey's *Seven Habits of Highly Effective People*; Niagara Institute in conjunction with The Centre for Creative leadership program, "Leadership Development."

Publications

Covey, S. *First Things First*. New York: Simon and Schuster, 1991.
Kouzes, J. *Credibility: How Leaders Gain and Lose It*. San Francisco: Jossey-Bass Publications, 1993.

Interpersonal Skills
Definition

- Effective written and verbal communication that gains acceptance of ideas while involving others, building constructive and effective relationships

Key Behaviours

- Is open about feelings and other issues in order to develop trust and openness

- Seeks out and uses the input and ideas of others

- Gains others' understanding and commitment and asks for assistance in solving problems

- Seeks to understand others' points of view

- Negotiates issues based on information and openness to others' needs while achieving mutual gains solutions

- Makes presentations that are clear, concise and persuasive

- Uses a tactful, balanced approach to delivering feedback

Developmental Activities

- Seek specific behavioural feedback from your colleagues about the effectiveness of your interpersonal skills. Seek suggestions for improvement

- Observe people who have good interpersonal skills and ask them to share their approaches

- Take on a assignment that requires good interpersonal skills, and afterwards obtain feedback from those you have worked with

- Videotape a presentation or facilitation that you do. Ask for feedback and suggestions for improvement from colleagues
- Attend the following programs: Colors (Myers Briggs) Personality Types, Negotiating to Yes, and a presentation skills course

Publications

Broady, M. *Power Presentations: How to Connect with Your Audience and Sell Your Ideas.* New York: Wiley, 1993.

McAllister, L. *I Wish I'd Said That: How to Talk Your Way Out of Trouble and Into Success.* New York: Wiley, 1992.

Personal Effectiveness
Definition

- Learns from situations while focused on a vision. Challenges own ideas, assumptions and circumstances, initiates opportunities outside of currant patterns and assumptions

Key Behaviours

- Is able to explain and works towards a vision or purpose
- Learns from problems, finding opportunities that close the gap between received notions and a desired vision
- Develops an accurate view of current situations and uses this knowledge to create opportunities
- Challenges own assumptions about the way things are, deepens awareness of self-limiting beliefs
- Is accountable for the interaction between own actions and results by managing agreements and breakdowns
- Initiates by taking action, achieving goals beyond what it expected
- Maintains a balance between work and personal life, performing effectively when under pressure
- Consistently and constantly measures behaviours against goals and objectives in order to ensure congruency

Developmental Activities

- Utilize results-based team and project management
- Create with your manager a personal improvement/development plan

Publications

Senge, P. *The Fifth Discipline*. New York: Doubleday, 1992.

TECHNICAL COMPETENCIES

- Develops and Delivers Training
- Compensation Management and Benefit Administration
- Health and Safety
- Labour and Employee Relations
- Recruitment and Staffing
- HRIS/Payroll

Develops and Delivers Training
Definition

- Understands and can appropriately utilize methods the facilitate learning and needs assessment, their design, delivery, and evaluation

Key Behaviours

- Develops and implements tools determining training needs at the organizational, work group for individual level
- Defines learning objectives that meets learning needs and expectations
- Designs learning processes based on defined needs and learning objectives
- Creates or advises on materials development in order to satisfy the training design

- Facilitates structured learning events utilizing adult learning principles
- Generates feedback through the design and implementation of evaluation processes
- Actively supports the creation of a learning environment

Developmental Activities

- Identify training needs through the use of a defined method
- Develop a training plan based on identified learning objectives
- Facilitate and evaluate a training module
- Observe an experienced facilitator
- Attend the following programs: Friesen Kay and Associates—Facilitation Skills/Program Design; MICA—Facilitation Skills; and Longevin Learning—Needs Analysis

Publications

Pfeiffer, J. and L. Goodstein, "Developing Human Resources," in *The Annuals—Developing Human Resources*. San Diego: University Associates.
Nadler, Leonard and Garland D. Wiggs. *Managing Human Resource Development*. San Francisco: The Jossey-Bass Series, 1986.

Compensation Management
Definition

- Administrates, communicates and advises of the process of job evaluation, variable and base pay structure, and benefits plans

Key Behaviours

- Facilitates the use and interpretation of job descriptions by management, by reducing issues and ensuring the accuracy and quality of information
- Communicates the base pay plan to management and employees, ensuring a broader understanding of the plan

- Provides answers to employee benefit and pension queries and presents information when appropriate
- Recommends appropriate compensation levels for new hires that are competitive and meet internal equity requirements
- Recommends/advises on appropriate severance arrangements within company policy and legislative requirements
- Promotes a total compensation understanding mindset among employees
- Supports management through the compensation planning process
- Advises management on the use of recognition bonuses
- Monitors the status of modified work/rehabilitation programs for employee, facilitating returns from disability leave or workers' compensation

Developmental Activities

- Attend compensation orientation workshops
- Participate in on-the-job evaluation committee
- Take courses on employee benefits and compensation, for general information rather than in-depth knowledge
- Review employee benefits, pension, and compensation policies
- Review bargaining unit agreements

Health and Safety
Definition

- Understands and promotes a health and safety mind-set, ensuring appropriate committee activity, a proactive workforce, training, and modified work arrangements as required

Key Behaviours

- Understands and communicates key provisions of the Health and Safety Act as required
- Ensures health and safety within the client group through effective safety committees

- Proactively monitors employees on work-related disability
- Puts in place modified work programs for injured employees on disability or those on worker's compensation
- Supports management and unions I due diligence requirements including documentation compliance and understanding of company policies
- Initiates cost reduction through proper claims management

Developmental Activities

- Find opportunities to review all accident investigations and work with *Health and Safety Act* staff
- Attend a health and safety seminar put on by corporate HR
- Participate on a joint health and safety committee
- Attend certification training

Labour and Employee Relations
Definition

- Understands, works with, and is able to advise management on the *Labour Standards Act*, employment standards and collective agreements

Key Behaviours

- Initiates workplace change initiatives within the unionized environment, leading to mutual gain and value-creating negotiations
- Ensures positive employee relations by providing a consultation on performance, workplace, and sexual harassment issues
- Coaches and counsels employees on resolution of workplace issues
- Advises on human rights, company policies and the *Labour Standards Act*
- Keeps management current on the labour code, legislation and jurisprudence as it relates to the client group's business strategies

- Demonstrates strategic labour relations skills resulting in progressive union relations
- Provides advice on human resources initiatives within the context of the unionized environment
- Provides training to management on labour relations
- Understands the internal affairs of the particular unions in client group
- Is current on background issues in preparation for collective bargaining
- Facilitates labour management meetings, resolving issues promptly
- Conducts corrective counseling investigations and grievance hearings
- Provides interpretation of collective agreement provisions

Developmental Activities

- Attend Queen's Labour Relations seminars and programs
- Keep abreast of legislative developments
- Keep abreast of business unit developments with respect to labour issues
- Obtain mentoring from an experienced labour relations specialist

Recruitment and Staffing
Definition

- Manages cost-effective recruitment and selection that places the right people at the right time for the right price based on the needs of the business

Key Behaviours

- Utilizes computerized resource planning processes and models
- Identifies and utilizes critical job dimensions when developing selection criteria

- Writes ad copy and postings that attract qualified applicants that meet the business needs
- Develops recruitment strategies that are cost effective and timely
- Utilizes behaviourally based interview methods
- Undertakes recruitment processes that support human rights, employment equity and diversity-valuing strategies
- Determines appropriate employment arrangement for filling vacancies
- Assists management in the development of recruitment and succession plans
- Ensures orientation and documentation of new employees
- Develops success profiles

Developmental Activities

- Attend the following programs: Behavioural Interviewing Skills—MICA, a human rights course, a managing diversity course, and a course on outreach recruiting techniques

HRIS/Payroll
Definition

- Understands and can work with the HR Information System, ensuring accurate utilization of payroll services when inducting employees, approving status changes or terminating employment

Key Behaviours

- Is able to access key HR data on the HR Information System
- Monitors employee status changes to ensure consistency with company policies and practice
- Reviews data relating to compensation administration and employee status changes to ensure accuracy
- Communicates and implements policy changes
- Assists in identification of improvements and efficiencies

Development Activities

- Attend HR/Payroll orientation workshops
- Review HR/Payroll policies and procedures
- Review bargaining unit agreements
- Training on PeopleSoft system

CHAPTER THREE

The Contribution of Human Resources to Change Management

A CASE STUDY OF KPMG CANADA

*Margaret Butteriss with material provided by
John Ellsworth and Geri Markvoort*

THIS CHAPTER WILL examine the role of Human Resources in Change Management. It will show an industry in transition—namely, the financial and management consulting business—and the ways that HR professionals at KPMG, a global advisory firm with offices in 150 countries, have mapped out a strategy for coping with change. Although the information presented is specific to a professional services organization, it also can be seen as a microcosm of changes taking place in virtually every type of organization. The material has been provided by John Ellsworth, Vice-Chairman of Human Resources at KPMG Canada, and Geri Markvoort, Director of Human Resources of KPMG for the Greater Toronto Area (GTA).

THE CONSULTING BUSINESS: AN INDUSTRY IN TRANSITION

In 1997 revenues of the global management consulting industry reached an estimated US\$35 billion-US\$40 billion (excluding systems design and implementation). The industry has been growing at 12%–15% annually during the 1990s and is expected to maintain this rate through the rest of the decade. The Canadian market (excluding systems) is estimated at Cdn$2 billion–Cdn$2.5 billion, which makes it comparable, for example, to the size of the entire Canadian electronics industry. However, a high volume of top level consulting assignments in Canada are handled by U.S. firms. (The data presented in this section comes from an unpublished research report prepared by Jeremy Butteriss at the Queen's University School of Business, 1997.)

The recession of the late 1980s and early 1990s was a mixed blessing for management consulting firms. Those that specialized in restructuring saw increasing revenues, as re-engineering, restructuring and reorganization became a priority for many organizations, while management consultants concentrating only on growth and systems development programs did not do as well. The recession also affected clients' expectations: they wanted more value for their money, and consultancies were forced to redefine themselves as providers of high-value-added services. This still holds true today and is causing a number of firms to implement contingent fee structures that are tied to bottom-line results.

In the late 1990s, economic growth has returned the focus to growth strategies, especially for global expansion. Globalization and growth are creating a demand for consulting services both from Western multinationals who want to get into emerging markets and from emerging-market multinationals who want to fight off the new competitors, and perhaps expand into the Western markets themselves.

Greater demand for their services is causing the major consulting firms to grow dramatically by increasing both the number of consultants they employ and the range of disciplines in which they have expertise. Increased globalization also means that consulting firms need offices in the world's most important markets. The demands of global business seem to favour large consulting firms. Organizations must solve problems quickly, and many are turning to large consulting practices with a breadth of industry expertise which enables them to deploy a number of services at the same time. A large consulting practice has the advantage over smaller firms in means and resources to expand its intellectual capital.

PRESSURES AFFECTING KPMG WORLDWIDE

KPMG, one of the world's largest professional services and global advisory firms, operates in 829 cities and 150 countries, with more than 78,000 partners and staff worldwide. The KPMG Canada organization has more than 4,700 partners and staff operating in over 50 location across the country. Key areas of expertise are Accountancy and Auditing, Tax, Management Consultancy and Corporate Finance. In addition, KPMG Canada targets key industries with teams called market groups, whose mandate is to provide comprehensive, effective services which are tailored to changing industry needs. Some of the key market groups are Financial Institutions and Real Estate; Information, Communications and Entertainment; and Manufacturing, Retail and Distribution. Like other KPMG global offices, KPMG Canada provides local expertise and service supported by the resources of their extensive international network.

The industry-wide changes in consulting and professional services organizations affect KPMG at both the local and global levels.

Colin Sharman, global Chairman of KPMG, believes that "new challenges demand new solutions. Global competition and information technology are creating a new dimension of client needs that require a new type of business advisor—an integrated team of specialists who combine industry expertise with functional knowledge. KPMG is committed to building this new model of a global professional services firm: integrated market teams of the right people, with the right skills, in the right place—where the clients need them.

"By further developing its growing consultative skills while maintaining its high professional standards, KPMG is well-positioned globally to participate in the accelerating pace of activity as developed countries continue to transform their information-based economies and developing countries enter a new era of consumerism and growth."

Four key pressure points are:

- changing client requirements,
- increasing competitiveness of the consulting industry,
- rapid technological change, and
- developing specific lines of business.

Changing Client Requirements

Clients are demanding that consultants have more expertise and in-depth knowledge of their business and industry sectors than ever before.

The clients themselves are facing rapid change in terms of growth, increasing competition and globalization restructurings through consolidation and rationalization and a greater alignment of Canadian and U.S. businesses and their subsidiaries.

In addition, clients now require business advisors to add value rather than simply provide the traditional assurance support. Although assurance and compliance services are still required, consultants must provide them in a cost-effective manner.

Increasing Competitiveness in the Consulting Industry

The consulting business is becoming increasingly competitive both at the local and global levels. KPMG is not only facing competition from others in the "Big 6 Accounting Firms," but also from large consulting firms such as Andersen Consulting, McKinsey, and the Boston Consulting Group, and from specialized "boutique" firms, all of which operate in both the local and global arenas.

It is important for KPMG to *differentiate* itself in the eyes of the client. To do this, it must design new and different products and services that will provide a significant added value to its clients' businesses.

Rapid Technological Advances

Rapid technological advances are affecting KPMG in two ways. First, the firm is helping its clients use technology to become more efficient in managing and operating their businesses. This is a business arena of increasing importance to KPMG. Second, the firm is using technology internally to become more efficient in the way it provides business advisory and consulting services to its clients. This is especially important when operating on a global basis with different time zones, and requirements for immediate access to information and knowledge among KPMG professionals.

Developing Specific Lines of Business

An internal response to the external challenges has been to increasingly reorganize the firm into specific lines of business, i.e., Information, Communications and Entertainment, and Financial Institutions and Real Estate. This kind of focus allows for more in-depth knowledge of a particular business sector.

In order to develop expertise in specific lines of business and different consulting fields, the firm is changing its recruitment practices. It has traditionally recruited new graduates and trained and developed them in the assurance practice, and has also tended to promote from within the firm. Increasingly it is recruiting experienced people with different expertise and business experience in order to satisfy its clients' broader requirement for business advice.

CREATING THE STRATEGY AND FRAMEWORK FOR CHANGE

The senior management of KPMG realized they needed a change strategy and implementation process to help them address external and internal business pressures. During the initial stages of their work, it became apparent to the senior management that the Firm needed an experienced internal change agent to assist them with the change agenda.

John Ellsworth was asked to join the firm in order to develop and implement the change and strategic Human Resources agenda. He had significant change and Human Resources management experience with large companies in mining, telecommunications and financial services.

As Ellsworth explains, "What I was asked to do was join the firm as the principal catalyst of change to support the Chairman and Management Committee in transforming the firm. The role was called the Vice-Chairman of Human Resources, but I certainly wasn't going to be focused on personnel administration. I've been working on developing the whole strategic management system, which addresses annual and long-term business planning, assessment of business performance, and the development of appropriate compensation and rewards to ensure there are sufficient consequences to support implementation and the desired impact. I have also helped the firm bring in a market perspective, and change the structure from a geographic, functional basis to a market focus."

He continues, "I am in a change agent role in the Canadian firm, and I'm also one of a team of eight that is working on the development of the whole change agenda on a global basis. We have built a framework to bring the global firm up to a standard based on how people are managed around the whole world."

The global team has focused on ten key areas:

1. Human Resources Management and the Human Resources Function,

2. Competencies,

3. Recruitment,

4. Recognition, Retention and Compensation,

5. Communication,

6. Performance Management,

7. Leadership and Development,

8. Career,

9. International Transfers and Secondments, and

10. Partner Admission.

Each key area has been defined, and the global team has set standards for each, along with time lines for their achievement. A definition of one of the key areas, Communications, is given in the box entitled "Communications Standards," together with the standards to be achieved by September 1997 and September 2000. These guidelines are used to assess the stage of development of the HR systems in each of the business units.

COMMUNICATION STANDARDS

Definition of Communication

The strategies KPMG implements to share information multilaterally with its members will build an environment where all members can contribute to its success.

Standards for September 1997

Five standards have been identified with an assessment rating on each standard on a scale of 1-4. Two examples of these standards are:

1. There will be in place effective means to gather and respond to ideas, attitudes and suggestions from KPMG people; and pass information to KPMG people.

---

2. There will be evidence to show that KPMG people are aware of expected standards of behaviour and performance.

Standards for September 2000

Examples are:

1. There will be formal systems of upward communication to ensure that the leaders of the business units are aware of the views and opinions of all their people and can take them into account in action planning.

2. There will be formal means to ensure that people are well informed about KPMG's strategy and activities both nationally and internationally.

DEVELOPING KPMG'S CHANGE STRATEGY

Working with senior management, John Ellsworth identified seven significant areas of change for KPMG if it is to be successful in the changing marketplace. These changes are also relevant for other firms in the audit and accounting industry. The seven implications are:

- realigning the business,
- leveraging knowledge rather than leveraging people,
- moving from generalists to specialists,
- changing the culture,
- collaborating and sharing of information,
- investing heavily in technology, and
- broadening the performance focus.

Realigning the Business

One of the key initiatives the firm is undertaking to prepare itself for a new future is realigning its business and developing a market-focused structure. In order to be the best in the world, Geri Markvoort explains, "You need to have a clearly focused local strategy and know how this aligns with the global direction." For the Canadian KPMG group, this means aligning itself with the overall KMPG global vision. "We see a greater emphasis on how KPMG wishes to position itself globally and what KPMG is requiring of its member companies to raise the bar." The required alignment goes from the local office right through to the national vision for KPMG in Canada, which in turn is in line with the global vision for KPMG.

As part of its main thrust and new global vision, KPMG is moving towards a market-focused structure. In the past, the firm organized itself around functional services such as tax, assurance, audit and consulting. Now it is shifting towards an organization based on the needs of the market. This is an extremely intensive process, says Markvoort, since "it not only means redrawing the organization chart, but it concerns all of the business processes which support a market-focused structure." After answering questions such as, "What are our unique services? Where is our competitive advantage? What should we provide for our customers?" Markvoort says KPMG must to align the structure of the business accordingly.

Therefore, KPMG's major thrust lies in realigning its people and processes, changing the way in which it goes to market, and how it approaches its clients with a market focus. This has serious implications for the lines of business. It is no longer enough that KPMG's professionals simply to have functional knowledge—clients expect that at a minimum. John Ellsworth explains that "in today's environment you have to have more than that. There's a requirement by the client that you know their industry and their business." He goes on to give an example of what this means for the company. "If you service a mining client, you must have a deep understanding of the mining industry as a whole, and you have to understand what's happening in the global market. The client requires that we not only have an in-depth knowledge of their own business, but also their industry. That's becoming very important to the client." This means changing the organization and people skills from simply providing services on a functional basis to creating integrated teams that can assist clients to deal with their business issues.

According to Markvoort, accounting firms have to be more marketing-focused. "In the past, this business and similar businesses in the industry have had a 'firm-out' mind-set rather than a 'market-in' mind-set. I think in today's competitive environment we need to have a 'market-in' mind-set." That is, all consultants need to be more aware of what is happening in the marketplace as a whole. They need to think about what the market needs, beyond delivering their own functional expertise in the tax and assurance areas.

In the past, most of the practices and lines of business operated independently of each other, but now expertise and knowledge bases have to be integrated. As Markvoort reveals, "Consultants in different practices may have serviced the same client, but they wouldn't have worked as an advisory team."

The need for greater integration of the business has prompted a much more significant emphasis on developing and maintaining a strategic and business planning focus. According to Ellsworth, "This firm has in the past always created financial plans. It is only recently that we have implemented a business planning approach. You have to do that if you're trying to align a whole business from a global vision right down to the local practice." This focus has also required that KPMG prioritize which industries to serve. It is tending to focus on industries it has expertise in, and "from that, determine which are the industries where we have a unique market competitive advantage."

In order to respond to alignment based on market requirements, the firm also needs to align its internal processes differently. It needs to "move from time-based pricing to value-based pricing." Currently, customers pay for audit assurance services on an hourly basis. Ellsworth feels that their customers are "less interested in simply buying an hour of our time. Our customers are interested in getting value—getting some value-added services and products." Therefore, the current system is clearly inadequate. Ellsworth describes a shift to a value-based pricing model as "a significant challenge for this business."

In order to realign the business, there is a need for leadership skills to manage the change. In the past, the main focus of attention and success was on the amount of client work that was done, and promotion to the partner level was based on this. This meant that little attention was paid to the development of leadership skills and capabilities, particularly around change and people management. Now, more attention is being paid to enhancing the leadership competencies of more people in the business.

Leveraging Knowledge Rather than People

Realigning the business means that KPMG must move from leveraging people to leveraging knowledge. As Ellsworth points out, "Accounting firms were always leveraging people. They brought in people through their accreditation years to get the Chartered Accountant designation and leveraged them." However, given the clients' need for advice on broad business issues, Ellsworth says, "What we need to do is to move ourselves out of the fundamental model from leveraging people to leveraging knowledge. The challenge is to get people in the firm to see that it's not individual knowledge and their own experience that matters, but rather focusing on the collective expertise and bringing this to bear on the client's business issue. Rather, they have to consider the firm as a global network, and use all the different client experiences from around the world to meet the needs of their client."

Moving from Generalists to Specialists

In the past, consultants were functional generalists who had clients in many different industries, and worked across a number of practice areas. However, in order to provide more value-added services for their clients, they have had to become more specialized both in terms of practice areas and industries they service. As Ellsworth pointed out, "It's a matter of taking their discipline, whether they be an audit assurance partner or a tax professional, and narrowing their market focus. For instance, they can work with global clients and become experts in how to manage tax considerations in the different jurisdictions that the company operates in. They will then need to focus on a particular industry—say the manufacturing industry. This is a tough choice for many of them, as people want to leave their options open."

Changing the Culture

Markvoort states, "A big challenge is shifting the culture. This, in many ways, is a transformation not just of KPMG, but probably of the industry and of the business that it's in. Going through that whole change process and managing that change in transforming the business is a very significant challenge. Our role in Human Resources is to help the members of the firm understand the change, stay the course, bring people along, and help people out who cannot see the new vision and make the change."

One of the main drivers of the culture change will be the recruitment of people with experience, and the development of existing staff to enhance the skills required for the changing market environment. As John Ellsworth says, "We will need more people who have been in different places. We need to be able to bring in people with a lot of different experiences, who can work with the senior management of client organizations. In the past, we hired straight off campus and trained them to be independent accountants. Our business now requires people to work as collaborative members of teams, who together can be a very strong business advisor to clients. We have to train them to work collaboratively and as team members. The diversity of having a multidisciplined team, that knows how to work collaboratively, is a dramatic change. What we need to do is to build a non-hierarchical body of collaborative people who understand the fullness of the business, and not just the financial aspects of the client business."

Hiring people is not the only way to acquire the additional expertise the firm needs. As Ellsworth notes, "We are also acquiring businesses. If we can get the right critical mass in an area, we can catch up with the competition and market requirements. We can offer something that is extremely valuable to a smaller firm and that is a large and tremendously rich client network. As a firm we are able to arrive at the client's door with high credibility, rather than trying to claim we can do something and, over time, proving we can do it."

Collaborating and Sharing Information

The requirement for greater collaboration and sharing of information represents another significant change in culture. Ellsworth points out that "We have people in the firm who pride themselves on independent work. Now we're saying that they have to work in teams and collaborate in order to better service their clients. That requires a whole change in mind-set." Consultants and partners need to share information they have both in terms of knowledge and specific client data. They will be more valuable to the firm and to their clients if they share information both locally and globally.

The partners also have to become more curious and think holistically about the businesses they service. They have been trained to work with only one part of the business, but now they need to build broader relationships in their client base, and become more curious about the

issues that face the business as a whole. This will allow them to identify issues that the client has and to suggest where they might find
resources to help them address these issues.

Investing in Technology

In order to be able to work in a collaborative fashion with consultants
and groups that operate locally and in different parts of the world,
KPMG must invest in technology that facilitates the easy and accurate
exchange of information. Technology must facilitate "real-time" decision making. Ellsworth asks, "What are the most viable approaches to
storage and retrieval of information which allow for real time generation of new interpretations of the information? This in turn becomes
applied knowledge. Those are the large-scale changes that are going on
in this industry."

Ellsworth continues, "The next piece is to develop methodologies
that support where we're going rather than continue with our old
methodologies. We're making millions of dollars in investments in new
assurance methodology that looks at providing value in the audit itself,
and provides greater efficiency at a reduced cost. Clients are getting a
lower-priced audit and added value through benchmarking and other
insights obtained through a comprehensive business analysis stage at
the front end of the audit process."

Broadening the Performance Focus

The final implication that Geri Markvoort identifies centres on broadening the performance focus of the firm. In the past, the firm focused
mainly on annual and monthly profits. However, according to
Markvoort, "You can't lose the focus on financial performance, but in
order to realign your business to become a business advisory services
firm, you need to broaden that whole approach of looking at performance." KPMG is now moving to a "balanced score card" approach that
looks at five dials as a way to measure performance. The five dials are:

- Market—how well they succeed in the marketplace,

- Growth—how well they are achieving their fundamental strategic
  thrust,

- People—how well they support and maintain their human assets,

- Processes—how they perform in the business activities that they must do well, and

- Profitability—how they measure their financial success.

The shift from a purely financially based performance management system to a balanced score card approach represents a major challenge for businesses like KPMG, and of itself will cause a dramatic shift in culture.

Coupled with this broader performance focus is the need to introduce more management systems into the firm. Ellsworth asks, "How do you bring in the right kind of management systems, together with the necessary rigour and discipline that will actually help you do better? How do you sell that constraint which may create a sense of loss of freedom for the people, but will actually be beneficial for them and for the Firm in the long run?"

It is clear that the implications of change for KPMG are quite significant and will create a fundamentally different way of doing business.

THE ROLE OF SENIOR HUMAN RESOURCES PERSONNEL

The global team overseeing strategic change has also redefined the role of senior Human Resources people in the international KPMG organization.

In order to deliver the change and people requirements to the firm, Ellsworth says, KPMG had to add to the existing Human Resources experience. Traditionally, the Human Resources area was the responsibility of one of the partners and was largely transactional. In order to provide the strategic support that was required, the firm has hired seasoned HR professionals who have the required change management experience. He comments, "We want to get seasoned HR professionals to provide support for each of the line executives across the country, and to be full and continuous members of those executive teams. We also have a client service partner in each location who has the responsibility to be the HR partner for that location. The seasoned HR professionals are working with that network to develop them and support them in Human Resources and change management processes and practices."

The Human Resources Agenda

Now that an experienced Human Resources function is in place, it is
working on a number of key initiatives to support the change process,
which are linked into the ten key areas for assessment that were identified by the global team.

The initiatives that have been developed are:

- a competency framework,
- competency-based recruitment,
- compensation,
- performance management, and
- advancement and partner admission.

Competency Framework

One of the critical pieces in the change management process that is
being tackled by Human Resources is the development of a competency framework.

According to Geri Markvoort, "The underpinning of the major culture shift is moving from a progression model based on years of service
to a competency-based one." She believes that the progression model
made sense in the past when the firm was selling technical expertise. As
noted earlier, the firm had a progression system in which people came
in as juniors, became accredited, were trained and eventually became
experts. With the positioning of KPMG as a business advisory firm, that
model must change. The change requires consultants to have both gen-
eral-based business competencies, as well as technical or functional
competencies. This necessitates a move to a broader set of competencies, which will be based on this competency framework.

The first step towards achieving this competency foundation is to
determine what competencies are required. The firm is doing this by
defining the competencies of exemplars by level and discipline, and
understanding what best practices and behaviours look like. The competencies are then used as a basis to redesign almost every people system and business process, including the recruitment, development,
classification, performance measurement, compensation and promotion and advancement processes. "All of them need to be aligned with a
competency-based foundation. This foundation comes directly from

the requirement of the marketplace to have a very different capability within the organization to meet the needs of the client. Every system is being redeveloped." says Markvoort.

Some competencies will require further development, including marketing and selling skills and solving problems for the client's total business. Partners need to do more to sell their own expertise to clients, and they must leverage the expertise within the rest of the organization in order to solve the client's business problems.

The Competency-Based Recruitment Process

The traditional recruitment process for KPMG has been to recruit graduates with a Bachelor of Commerce degree, and then train them to become Chartered Accountants. Now, KPMG is moving towards a competency-based recruitment model. According to Markvoort, "We still go on campus and recruit, but we are also looking for more than academic achievement. We want to hire people who have the right kind of competencies and attributes for the kinds of jobs we're going to have in the future." However, using only this development and growth strategy would take years to reach the desired results. As a result, KPMG is also acquiring experienced people who have the specific competencies and attributes the firm requires. "That means recruiting more professionals at higher levels in the organization," says Markvoort, "and that's a newer thing for KPMG. In the past, we recruited primarily at the graduate level. We rarely recruited into our senior ranks, and very seldom into the partner ranks unless we bought a practice." The use of a competency-based recruitment process allows the firm to acquire the kind of skills and competencies that are required for the present and the future, and to develop the kind of business-based advisory services that they require to meet their clients' needs.

Compensation, Rewards, and Recognition

As a natural extension of the changes, the whole compensation process must also be altered since it, too, was based on a progression model. A more performance-driven system is required, based not on years of service as in the past, but on "role accountabilities" and the related competencies that are required to be successful in delivering against that specific set of accountabilities. Demonstration of performance in relation to key competencies will determine both base pay and incentive pay. This year a formal incentive plan was introduced that replaced a discretionary and subjective bonus plan. Funding of this more formalized plan is tied to the results of the business, and the resulting pool of money is allocated based on the degree to which people achieve their individual objectives, which need to be aligned to the goals of their business unit.

Performance Management

In order to progress to a competency-based pay system, it was necessary to design a performance management system that was linked to both the organization's goals and the setting of individual goals. Thus a new system was designed that required the development and implementation of every step: from goal setting, coaching for accomplishment, providing regular feedback to individuals, and assessment at the end of the year. The assessment will determine consequences in terms of incentive pay, advancement, and development requirements.

This form of performance management requires communication of the business direction to all employees, and two-way discussions of requirements and results. As Ellsworth remarks, "A lot of professional partnerships hold things very close to the vest in terms of where the place is going. You can't have a high performance environment without having people really understand the full picture."

Promotion and Advancement

In the past, KPMG had a simple progression and advancement system: a junior person joined the firm and after acquiring the skills at one level would move to the next level, often based on the length of time in the organization.

A new process has been developed, whereby even some of the leadership roles are defined and posted. While this is commonplace in many large companies, it is quite radical for a Firm like KPMG. As Markvoort says, "We've broken that barrier and some of the most critical roles in the firm have been posted. All of the management positions for the GTA leadership positions were posted. We've had postings for some of the office managing partners across Canada. People have had to apply for these positions, have been interviewed by a panel and have been required to demonstrate their skills, competencies and suitability for the position." Clearly, the competency framework is driving the future direction for external as well as internal selection; however, promotion based on the progression system still prevails in most parts of the firm today.

Admission to partnership process is also changing. A set of competencies for the partner level is being defined and an assessment process will be used to determine whether the people who are being considered have those competencies that are needed for the future. This is a significant change for the firm. They are putting more rigour into the selection of partners and using a broader set of competencies as part of the process.

As Ellsworth puts it, "We are putting far more discipline into defining what a partner is and what the requirements will be for becoming a partner. The partner admission process in the U.K. has an assessment centre and an interview panel process. We are considering the implementation of a similar process in Canada. This means there's more to being a partner than just being somebody's protégé."

SUMMARY

In this chapter, we have followed one company's progress through a period of fundamental organizational change. KPMG's response to external and internal business pressures relied heavily on Human Resources expertise, which both played a significant role in planning the change process and undertook major reworking of many HR processes, including hiring, training, leadership development, and compensation.

CHAPTER FOUR

Measuring Human Resources Effectiveness

Larry Morden

A RECENT ARTICLE in *Fortune* suggested that if Human Resources were "blown up," nobody would even know that it was gone. It then went on to issue a warning: the only way for HR to gain relevance was to contribute directly to an organization's overall business strategy. In the many responses I came across to the article, I found almost universal agreement with its sentiments, if not for the final solution it proposed.

Can Human Resources make a difference to a company in today's business environment? It might be argued that attention to Human Resources is more critical in a service organization, whose human costs (payroll, benefits, staff training, etc.) can account for 70% of the overall cost of sales and whose human assets directly affect performance, than it is for a capital-based organization whose human costs represent only 12%–15% of sales costs, or for a highly automated operation whose human assets only secondarily affect results.

Nevertheless, even the most cursory look at what Human Resources management entails would seem to suggest that every organization's HR is an area with significant impact on profitabilty. Hiring just one employee at $30,000 annual salary is an investment decision worth in excess of $1 million, based on a thirty-year career and discounting future spending at today's interest rates. If that investment were being made in capital, it would receive rigorous analysis regarding rate of return. The Human Resources function today must be prepared to apply a similar rigour to the acquisition and management of our human resources if competitiveness is to be enhanced.

Many recent studies have argued that improved Human Resources management can make a positive difference in company performance. In 1985, a *Wall Street Journal* article by Peter Drucker suggested that the personnel function needed to redirect itself away from its traditional concern for the cost of employees to concern with their yield. Y.K. Shetty and P.F. Buller, writing for *Personnel* magazine in 1990, stated that internal management and HR improvements are the best ways to boost company quality and competitiveness.[1] Dr. F.E Schuster has reported in several studies, including one I co-authored with him on Ault Foods Limited, where I worked from 1985 to 1997, that a strong correlation exists between improved Human Resources management and a company's financial performance.[2]

With so much at stake, why is it that an investment decision about human assets still generally receive much less scrutiny than one about capital? I believe an important factor has been the comparative lack of measurement techniques for assessing the effectiveness and results of Human Resources interventions. In this chapter, we will examine the history of measuring HR performance and provide a case study of the positive effect of new measurement methods on company performance at Ault Foods Limited.

Our findings suggest that the same sort of methods for acquiring and managing other company assets can be applied to human assets as well, with outstanding results. Other researchers report similar findings. The Hewitt consulting organization conducted a survey which compared the financial performance of companies using new performance management HR processes with results of companies not using performance management.[3] For companies using performance management,

---

[1] Y.K. Shetty and P.F. Buller. "Regaining Competitiveness Requires H.R. Solutions," *Personnel*, July 1990, pp. 8-12.

[2] F.E. Schuster, D.L. Morden, T.E. Baker, I.S. McKay, K.E. Dunning, and C.M. Hagan, "Management Practice, Organization Climate and Performance: An Exploratory Study," *Journal of Applied Behavioural Science*, Vol. 33, no. 2 (June 1997) pp. 209-226.

[3] Hewitt Associates Study, "The Metrics Questions, Human Resources and the New Math of the Corporation," *Corporate Leadership Council: CEO Briefing* (Washington, D.C.: The Advisory Board Company, 1996).

income per employee was almost three times higher, productivity per employee was more than 30% higher, and profitability, as measured by such traditional performance ratios as Rate of Return and Return on Assets, on average was 100% higher than for the companies not using performance management. Such results clearly show the potential value in increased attention to Human Resources and in implementation of improved Human Resources methods.

MEASUREMENT OF HUMAN RESOURCES

Measurement of Human Resources falls into three broad areas:

- function measures,
- operational measures, and
- strategic measures.

HR function measures relate fully to the efficiency and effectiveness of the HR function itself, such as turnover measures, cost per hire and number of grievances.

Operational measures relate human asset performance to operational performance of the company. Examples are revenue per employee and operating performances per work team.

Strategic measures are future-oriented and include the Human Resource requirements. These are such things as skills required vs. current skill sets, culture and environment, information utilization, technology utilization and demographics. Strategic measures in Human Resources are just now starting to emerge as a critical element for improving future competitiveness.

My experience has been that no one accepted measure or set of measures exists that meets all the requirements of these areas. In fact, some companies adopt their own measurement processes in some or all of the three areas mentioned.

EVOLUTION OF MEASUREMENTS IN HUMAN RESOURCES MANAGEMENT

Human Resources began to emerge as a separate department in the 1930s and 1940s; its principal role, taken over from accounting, was payroll. Function measures, that is, evaluations of how well Human Resources was carrying out its assigned duties, began almost at once and remain an important area of HR accountability. The principle drawback in function measures however is that they do not establish a clear link between HR and overall company performance. The more recent types of measurement, operational and strategic, both attempt to address this issue.

Function Measures

Function measurements in use from HR's early days started to take on a more scientific flavour with the development of job evaluation systems, which sought to establish equitable pay relationships between jobs. Another function measure, the attitude survey, soon after appeared on the scene as a measure of how well HR was meeting the needs of the employees.

The 1960s and 1970s saw the development of more complete and detailed function measures, e.g., standard HR cost measures. The best listing of these I have found is in Jack Phillips' book *Accountability in Human Resources Management*[4]. His list follows, with some item additions by me:

- Employment Measures: e.g., cost per hire, cost per orientation, cost of turnover;

- Training Measures: e.g., cost per employee trained, training costs, % of payroll;

- Compensation: e.g., total cost, % of operating costs, ratio-staff costs/line costs;

- Benefits: e.g., cost per employee, % of payroll;

- Fair Employment: e.g., # of complaints, cost per complaint, total cost;

- Labour Relations: e.g., cost per grievance, cost per work stoppage;

- Safety and Health: e.g., cost per accident, frequency and severity ratios, total Workers' Compensation Board costs; and

- Overall HR: Costs: e.g., % operating costs.

---

[4] J.J. Phillips, *Accountability in Human Resources Management* (Houston: Gulf Publishing Company, 1996), pp. 186-200.

Jac Fitz-enz, through his work in his own organization, The Saratoga Institute, and on the Society for Human Resources Management (SHRM) Saratoga Institute Measurement Project[5], expanded the number and type of function measures and, for the first time, provided comparable data between companies and industries.

Human Resources Accounting

The 1960s and 70s also saw the development of Human Resources Accounting (HRA), an encouraging advance whose goal was to quantify the value of a company's human "assets" in traditional accounting terms. HRA showed much promise but ran into many valuation problems. Accounting "rules," for example, do not allow for the capitalization of human assets or for the treatment of training costs as anything other than an expense, thereby defeating some attempts to assess them on a "Rate of Return" basis. As a result, these valuable efforts fell largely by the wayside. Fortunately, HRA is once again showing some promise: strict application of accounting rules to human assets has been challenged recently and the use of more flexible accounting techniques is being evaluated.

Human Resources Audit

The 1980s saw the development and rise of the Human Resources Audit, which also drew on the accounting discipline in its attempt to apply audit principles to HR. The goal was to assess the Human Resources function to determine its effectiveness and establish a baseline from which to measure future performance in subsequent audits. This tool, when used properly, is very useful and continues to be used today in many companies.

Activity-Based Costing

In the last few years, Activity-Based Costing (ABC) has emerged as a useful method of determining both the cost and the efficiency of the HR function. As it has for many other functions and processes, ABC has

---

[5] J. Fitz-enz, SHRM/Saratoga Institute Human Resources Effectiveness Survey: 1994 Annual Report (Saratoga, CA: Saratoga Institute, 1994).

particular appeal since it measures the cost of specific activities, not of the global function, and provides information which can be further analyzed to determine function efficiency and to improve organizational structuring and cost allocation.

In the end, however, HR function measures in and of themselves do little to improve the overall performance of the business. They may well improve HR performance, which is important, but we are left to guess whether HR has any significant impact on the overall performance of the business. Operating measures were developed, in large measure, as a way of determining the connection between HR and an organization's overall performance.

Operating Measures

Many operating measures have been proposed for evaluating Human Resources. A company should evaluate its particular needs and adopt a few truly meaningful measures from the many available.

Some measures chosen may be fairly broad, such as F.E. Schuster's Human Resource Index (HRI). Schuster's research was referred to earlier and will be discussed at length in the section below entitled Case Study: The Ault Experience. Another is Phillips' Human Resource Effectiveness Index[6]. Both these indexes purport to link broad measures of effective management of Human Resources to overall business performance as measured by operating performance and financial measures.

Other, more specific measures relate to productivity and profitability. These can be units of output per division, work team or even employee, and cost of output per division, work team and employee. These measures are becoming more prevalent as meaningful measures of how well human assets are contributing to the overall success of the business and hence how well the human resource function is fulfilling its role. In addition, Return on Investment (ROI) is increasingly being used as a proper and meaningful measure of human resource initiatives and projects.

Lastly, there is increased discussion of treating Human Resources as a profit efficiency centre to ensure that the HR function remains a contributor to the operating effectiveness of the enterprise. The argument

6 Phillips, op.cit.

goes that by allowing line management to "buy" HR services either internally or, if it is more efficient, externally, the organization can ensure optimum rates of return or, as a minimum, the lowest cost HR service possible. While the proposal is intellectually intriguing, I think it is not workable in its purest form. If HR must take the lead in advising and directing the use of a company's human assets and be accountable for providing that service in the most efficient and effective way possible, then giving line managers permission to opt out on a cost basis, undermines this accountability and weakens the connection between HR and the overall business strategy.

Strategic Measures

Strategic measurement is an area under development in the field of HR measurement. The impetus for strategic measures comes from the requirements of strategic planning and HR's increasing role in that area. Of necessity, strategic measures are future-oriented, although the measures depend on assessing today's environment and HR capabilities. This assessment then can be applied to the company's future plans to determine what actions must now be started to ensure that the plans can be realized. Climate surveys, such as the HRI, can be used both as a tool to determine if the right environment exists to achieve the company's future goals and as a predictor of the company's future operating performance. Progressive skills inventories related to the current and future needs of the business as well as HR planning information and measures are critical.

Of more recent development is the identification and quantification of intellectual capital and its relationship to the company's current and future plans and goals. The recognition of intellectual capital, it is argued, acknowledges that the future of an enterprise mainly depends on the uniqueness, abilities and experience of the company's employees. The required measurement process catalogues and quantifies a firm's intellectual capital so it can be used as a main input into (or a response to) the strategic planning process.

We would all do well to understand and measure those parts of our HR asset base which have strategic implications for our organizations.

An HR Measurement Checklist

Jack Phillips' book *Accountability in Human Resources Management*[7] lays out three challenges:

- the Human Resources function should be integrated into an organization's strategic planning and operational framework,
- Human Resources staff must build relationships with other key managers, with a particular focus on the line organization, and
- Human Resources staff must improve techniques and processes in order to measure the effectiveness of the function.

We have found the following checklist useful although probably not complete in determining appropriate measures from the three types discussed above.

Function Measures

- Use only a manageable number.
- Measures used should represent the effects of as many aspects of the HR function as possible.
- Use readily available data.
- Measures should provide for internal (if divisional) and external comparisons.

Operational Measures

- Every HR program should be assessed in terms of ROI.
- Each measure must have an accountable person or group.
- Results must be communicated to all concerned, not just the accountable person or group.
- Process measures must be relevant and frequent.
- Measures used must be of value to and supported by line management.

---

[7] Ibid.

Strategic Measures

• Measures must be part of and come from the planning process.

• Measures must be implemented over time.

• Measures must be owned by an accountable person or group.

• Measures must be comparable year-over-year and linked to ongoing plans.

CASE STUDY: THE AULT EXPERIENCE

The Ault Foods organization I joined twelve years ago was much different from the Ault Foods of 1997. Although the company ranked as one of Canada's largest food processing and distribution companies, with $1 billion in sales, it had not developed its internal management processes and systems. HR management was very basic and mostly focused on labour relations. Of the three major areas of measurement described above, only HR function measures were in use, and at a fairly rudimentary level.

Function Measures

In the early years Ault Foods' planning was essentially finance-driven; much focus was given to costs. As a result, the Human Resources function, like other functions, was most concerned about its own costs and efficiencies. In this sense the focus was an appropriate one.

HR function measures were in keeping with the notion of cost and efficiency. Measures in use included:

• the ratio of HR staff to total employees,

• the ratio of training costs to overall payroll costs,

• the ratio of benefit costs to total compensation costs,

• total compensation costs—direct and indirect,

• health and safety—frequency and severity of accidents and injuries, and

• the ratio of overall HR costs to operating costs.

The company was highly decentralized and organized into operating divisions. Measures were applied on a divisional basis and aggregated up to provide an overall company view.

The function measures employed were adequate for the purpose for which they were designed, that was understanding HR costs and efficiencies, both internally and, where possible, externally. We resisted further global development of function measures for the simple reason that we generally could not relate them to company performance.

Some exceptions stand out. Health and safety frequency and severity trend data allowed us to identify negative trends and to direct company operations to take corrective action. A significant improvement both in the cost and efficiency of operations resulted, as it did also from tracking incidents and types of grievances. This data was collected by location, by step level within each location, and overall.

These two measures had an operational focus, while others served only as a measure of HR itself and therefore were only useful for monitoring HR cost control and efficiency purposes.

Operational Measures

The usefulness of the two function measures with an operational focus encouraged us to turn our attention to other measures which connected HR to operational performance. We initially sought a global type of measure which would provide information about the general effectiveness of HR management and its impact on operational performance. Our hypothesis was that if we could determine our effectiveness we could predict whether the company was headed for better or worse operational performance. We knew of no studies that actually confirmed this causality, although we felt it made sense. Most of the proof we had was anecdotal. One such anecdotal incident stands out in my mind.

I met a mid-level IBM employee while on vacation in the mid-eighties. Despite the fact that IBM was viewed as model corporation—this was before its fall from that lofty position—my acquaintance thought otherwise. He articulated a long list of mistakes he thought the company was making, forecast that IBM would lose its place of dominance and enter a period of competition which would threaten its very survival. Obviously this employee was seeing something that others in places of power were not seeing. I was sure that his situation was not an isolated case within IBM. Something was up and that something would eventually affect the company's overall performance.

The struggle of IBM since the mid-eighties has been well publicized and documented. The lesson for me was that if I could measure the sentiments and opinions of employees about how their company was being managed, I would have a clue, if not an outright predictor, of future company performance. Collecting, measuring and understanding the wisdom buried within the corporation could provide an early warning system and enable a company to react in time to affect performance.

The Human Resources Index

We were struck by some of the work that Dr. F.E. Schuster had done in this area, and reported in his book *The Schuster Report: The Proven Connections Between People and Profits*[8]. He described his development of a Human Resources Index (HRI) which measured fifteen broad managerial factors. These factors are as follows:

- reward system,
- communication,
- organizational effectiveness,
- concern for people,
- co-operation,
- intrinsic satisfaction,
- structure,
- relationships,
- climate,
- participation,
- work group,
- intergroup competence,
- first-level supervision, and
- quality of management.

   Employees at all levels annually filled out a standardized questionnaire containing sixty-four statements to be scored on a scale of 0 to 5 and then aggregated into the fifteen factors listed above. There were also two open-ended questions which allowed employees to state what they felt was good about the organization and what they thought

---

[8] F.E. Schuster, *The Schuster Report: The Proven Connection Between People and Profits.* (New York: John Wiley, 1986.)

should happen to improve the organization. The data could be analyzed a number of different ways, including:

- by overall company,
- by division,
- by organizational level,
- by location,
- by gender, or
- by any combination of the above.

The Human Resources Index was used by Ault Foods over an extended period of time. The results were tracked annually and reported to the organization, both for the year and as a trend. This allowed the organization and its component parts to develop and implement corrective action and to maintain continuous improvement in the management of its human resources.

The actions developed and implemented as a result of using the HRI contributed to a significant improvement in the operational performance of the company. These results and their correlation to the management process improvements resulting from the HRI were reported in the June 1997 issue of the *Journal of Applied Behavioural Science* in an article I co-authored with Dr. Schuster entitled "Management Practice, Organization Climate, and Performance—An Exploratory Study"[9].

The operating income of the company rose 66% between the years 1988 and 1992. Correspondingly, each of the fifteen factors showed an increase over that period of time with twelve of the company's fifteen locations showing a steadily upward trend. As stated in the report: "Although it is impossible to prove causality with absolute certainty, the data strongly support the conclusion that improvement in the motivation, morale and commitment of the human organization has led to significantly improved organizational performance."

Costing Human Resources Initiatives

Useful as the HRI was, we required a more direct process of measuring, in an investment sense, the viability of specific HR initiatives, many of

---

[9] Schuster et al, pp. 209-226.

which were suggested by the Human Resource Index. It was hit-or-miss to determine which initiatives were most likely to affect operational performance.

We again turned to the accounting function for an answer. The company was very disciplined in identifying the overall cost of a capital project and, correspondingly, how much the expected rate of return would be on a discounted cash flow basis. Why then, could we not do the same thing with any large HR initiative? We always knew what the overall cost of a project would be. All we had to do was to identify where the savings would come from for the project and how much they were expected to be over a defined period of time, generally established at ten years (our best guess at the useful life of the initiative). We then calculated a rate of return using the same discounted cash flow method which we used for capital projects. This provided us with a decision point based on comparing this rate of return with returns on other projects and our company's required rate of return and taking into account other mitigating factors. As important, however, it also provided us with an audit process for setting goals to be achieved during the life of the investment. For example, if we planned to get a 10% productivity improvement in year three because of this initiative, we were accountable for delivering that improvement in year three.

Redesigning the Organization

An example would be useful here. In 1993 we embarked on a significantly new development in labour relations. Its objectives were improved relations with the unions and greater involvement of the employees in the business. It also involved the redesign of our organizational structure within the plants, enhanced information systems, changes to physical plants and associated training for all involved. The purpose was to lower operating risk and costs and improve efficiency and quality. The cost was considered a major outlay for any plant undertaking the initiative. We began by determining where returns would come from and quantifying how much the returns would be in each area. We were careful to stay away from "soft" benefits at this stage of the analysis and looked only at those areas of change that would affect results in dollars and cents. Restructuring Associates, a consulting firm specializing in this type of analysis and intervention, helped us complete the assessment.

Essentially we looked at a long list of cost areas, including the following:

- management systems,
- product quality,
- product rework,
- product waste,
- technical implementation,
- cycle time—new products,
- employee turnover,
- acident frequency rate,
- accident severity rate,
- management training,
- non-management training,
- grievance volume, and
- arbitrations,

Then we considered where we would likely see an impact from this initiative, and also tried to quantify this impact. For each line item listed above, we tried to determine, in quantifiable terms, what effect the HR initiative would have on these areas of cost. In some areas, it was minimal or non-existent; in others it was significant. The question to answer was whether, in the aggregate, it was significant enough to warrant that level of investment in human resources relative to other areas in which the company could invest and make a return on that investment.

Having quantified both the initiative's costs and expected savings, we were in a position to calculate a rate of return using the same method that we would apply to a capital expenditure (but not including special tax treatments associated with capital expenditures). We prepared a rate of return analysis using both a 10% interest rate assumption and a 15% interest rate assumption over a fifteen-year period. The results are shown in Table 1 on the next page.

Based on Table 1 projections alone, it appears that the investment would be hugely worthwhile if the benefits were likely to continue at the projected level for a period of fifteen years. Further analysis indicates, however, that the actual break-even point for this project is eight

TABLE 1: Rate of Return Projections

In Thousands $ Can.	1	2	3	4	5	6	7	8	9	10	11	12	13	14	15
Savings			2212	2328	2348	2540	2540	2450	2450	2450	2450	2450	2450	2450	2450
Costs															
Conversion	789	1183	588												
On-going	45	464	1499	1487	1493	1524	1524	1524	1524	1524	1524	1524	1524	1524	1524
Total Costs	836	1647	2087	1487	1493	1524	1524	1524	1524	1524	1524	1524	1524	1524	1524
Net Savings	(836)	(1647)	125	841	855	928	928	928	928	928	928	928	928	928	928
Disc. @ 15%	1.00	0.87	0.76	0.66	0.57	0.50	0.43	0.38	0.33	0.26	0.25	0.21	0.19	0.16	0.14
Discounted Cash Flow	(836)	(1432)	95	553	489	460	400	348	303	263	229	199	173	151	131
Disc. @ 10%	1.00	0.91	0.83	0.75	0.66	0.62	0.56	0.51	0.47	0.42	0.39	0.35	0.32	0.29	0.26
Discounted Cash Flow	(836)	(1497)	104	632	584	575	523	475	432	393	357	325	295	268	24

years at a 15% discount rate (six years at a 10% rate). At this point, management can now determine whether the project should go ahead based solely on the merits of the rate of return and break-even data presented. (I don't think it should, for what it is worth!) Management may consider whether the project costs should be adjusted to make this a more viable financial project, or whether there are "soft" benefits that should be considered, in addition to the financial projections. The other considerations may warrant approving the project. The point, of course, is that management now has a measurement method which can be used for decision making and project support or denial.

Strategic Measures

We have also experimented with strategic measures. Like many other companies, we have been experimenting without a lot of historical data to guide us. We had, however, begun to understand that this area of measurement would offer enormous potential for the future of the company.

Strategic measures, by virtue of their focus on the future, must be tightly linked to the planning process of the company. At Ault Foods, this linkage occurred at the very beginning of the planning process; each operating division and the overall company identified their specific areas of business core competency. This, in turn, was matrixed against a financial measure of Economic Value Added (EVA)[10]. This is illustrated in Figure 1.

Core Competencies

The important issue here, of course, is understanding to what extent the business has a sustainable core competency for success. For example, if a business division continually generated high returns on the EVA measure and had sustainable core competencies to maintain that position, the company would be inclined to continue to invest heavily in that business. The challenge for Human Resources here is to ensure that the organization continues to have the skills, knowledge and experience to exploit its core competencies. If, on the other hand, a business

[10] G.B. Stewart III, *The Quest for Value, A Guide for Senior Managers* (New York: Harper Business, HarperCollins, 1991).

FIGURE 1: Ault's EVA/Core Competency Grid

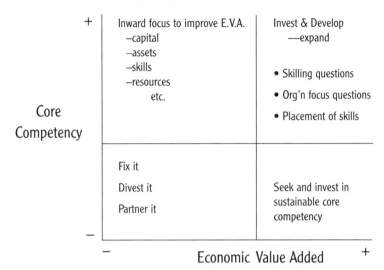

division had a low score on core competency (with or without a high score on EVA), the question to be asked was whether the skills, knowledge and experience of the people was sufficient to develop the necessary core competency to be successful in the marketplace. (A high score on the financial measure of EVA could not be sustained if there was no core competency in the business.)

An understanding of the core competency a business needs to be successful is, therefore, a linking point from planning to Human Resources. These core competencies may be technology, brand management or customer service, but they are all ultimately skills embodied in people.

Skills Inventory

If we accept this premise, then we must be able to collect data and measure the extent to which the quality and quantity of the skills exists within the human assets of the company. It clearly falls to HR to collect, analyze and present measures related to the extent, depth and utilization of these skills. Are they embedded in only a few key personnel or distributed widely throughout the company? Are they bottlenecked at or around one organizational level or centred in the company, or is there a depth of the skills elsewhere in the organization? Are the skills utilized broadly and innovatively to grow and evolve the core competency of the business, or are they deployed solely for maintaining past successes?

A clear baseline inventory is required of the skills that support the core competency of the business. It will form the basis for annual measurement and evaluation of performance. Clear succession plan information is required and must be grounded in skills acquisition and development. This information must be both dynamic and tangible in that it can be tracked and measured over time and related clearly and directly to those areas of core competency that drive the success of the business.

In the case of Ault Foods, this analysis contributed to our decision to sell parts of the company when we determined that the gap between the business core competencies and those of our people was too large. On the other hand, we were also able to confirm our investments in the other parts of our company where the skills, knowledge and experience of our people were highly aligned with the core competencies of the business.

Intellectual Capital

Additionally, the newly emerging process of understanding and measuring "intellectual capital" offers great promise in understanding and measuring how skills can be applied in innovative and pre-emptive ways. Microsoft, I would suggest, keeps ahead of the game by the sheer application of intellectual capital to their areas of core competency, (which are not unique to them). At last count, Microsoft had a value of over $100 billion.

The definition of intellectual capital varies greatly. From an accounting standpoint, it usually comes under goodwill, that "catch-all" accounting term that identifies value between the measurement of physical and financial assets and market value. But what is in goodwill? There are real, albeit intangible, assets such as trademarks, brands and Information Technology systems, but there may also be a market value placed on other intangible assets, such as the ability of a company to learn and adjust goodwill. The challenge, in which the Human Resource plays a vital role, is to measure it.

The companies most recognized for development in this area are Skandia AFS of Sweden and, here in Canada, our own Canadian Imperial Bank of Commerce through the early leadership of Hubert St. Onge.

Measuring intellectual capital has, according to the Skandia model[11], five major components as follows:

- financial,
- customer,
- process,
- renewal and development, and
- human.

Measures are developed for each of these components. Typically, measures for the human component would include employee competency development investment, employee new product training investment, overall training investment in both full-time and part-time employees, etc. The measures for each component would eventually be tabulated and presented in index or ratio form: for example, human focus index .69; customer focus index .71; financial focus .95; and so on, for each of the five components. This tabulation would provide a year-over-year measure as well as a determination of the relationship between intellectual capital components and the overall value of the company.

A more in-depth discussion of this topic is not possible in this chapter. I recommend an interesting and authoritative book on the subject entitled *Intellectual Capital* by Leif Edvinsson and Michael S. Malone[12].

The Future of Ault Foods

Much more work remains to be done in HR management at Ault Foods. As of this writing, Ault Foods Limited has been acquired by the giant Italian dairy company, Parmalat Foods Inc. More development will have to wait until the transition is complete.

CONCLUSIONS

There is no question that measurement in Human Resources is critical. To reiterate, it can be approached on three levels: function measures,

---

[11] L. Edvinsson, and M.S. Malone, *Intellectual Capital* (New York: Harper Business, HarperCollins, 1997).

[12] Ibid.

operational measures, and strategic measures. All three levels must be
addressed if an organization is to be truly in control of both HR and its
contribution to the organization; however, HR must increasingly focus
on the latter two, operational measures and strategic measures. The
evolution of Human Resources management as a contributor to creating organizational value is underway, as illustrated by a chart conceived
and produced by the Washington-based Corporate Leadership Council
(Figure 2).

It is clear that Human Resources is moving from a reactive role to a
proactive one and organizations are demanding that of the function.
We, in Human Resources, cannot adequately assume this accountability unless we can also measure the contribution our efforts make to our
company's performance.[13]

FIGURE 2: Continuum of Human Resources Activities

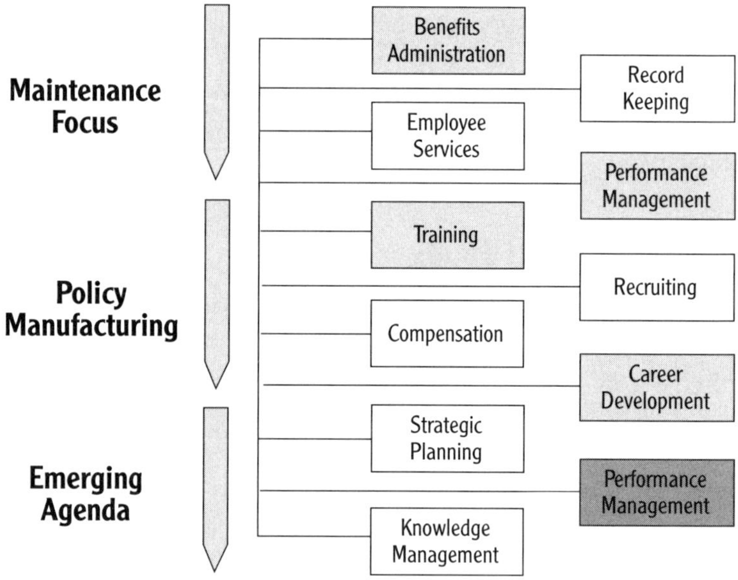

Source: Corporate Leadership Council

[13] Corporate Leadership Council, *Vision of the Future* (Washington D.C.: The Advisory Board Company, 1995).

CHAPTER FIVE

Redefining and Restructuring the Human Resources Function

A CASE STUDY

Margaret Butteriss

THIS CHAPTER PROVIDES an example of a company that redefined its HR function in order to meet its current and future business needs. The company, a well-known business division of one of Canada's most successful firms, consists of several operating units organized by customer segment and regional area. It is unionized and employs a large number of part-time workers. Its growth through acquisition and expansion of existing businesses led to considerable duplication of activities and also to great variation in policies, processes and programs across the operating units.

The company began to streamline various processes and to remove duplication in order to increase productivity and reduce costs. Major efforts and investments went into improving the logistics and distribution side of the business. Plans were made to create one national company out of the regional units, with corporate-level systems for finance, Human Resources, information technology, and some operational activities. Concurrent with the development of common systems and processes, significant effort was put into creating a common company vision and set of values. It was hoped that all these steps would facilitate the integration of future acquistions, and allow the company to focus on customer satisfaction, rather than on financial and other corporate systems.

I was hired as a consultant to assist senior management in evaluating the roles and responsibilities of the HR function in anticipation of the formation of the new corporate HR group. My efforts were aimed at improving the function's standards of service and at connecting HR to the company's strategic direction. My experience on the project illustrates many of the challenges and solutions discussed in the previous chapters of Part 2.

THE EXISTING HR FUNCTION

Most HR activities before the reorganization were carried out by a centralized HR staff which provided services to the line. There were a few exceptions: some of the larger operating units had created their own HR departments in order to better respond to local needs. The role of HR was largely transactional: to hire and transfer staff, to maintain records, and to administer salary and benefits. There was a very strong Industrial Relations function which successfully undertook major initiatives in relation to the company's change efforts. Some centralized training existed; much of the technical training was located in regional offices. Few company polices and guidelines had been developed.

The expertise for consulting on the proposed re-engineering and move to a new culture did not exist in HR. Corporate Development was providing this service, but there was still a need for attention to the people aspects of change management.

Assessing Company Needs

Interviews were conducted with senior management and with HR staff focusing on ways to enable HR to support current and future business strategies. The views expressed focused on a number of key areas which are described below.

Leadership

It was felt that HR needed a clear focus and should concentrate on a few leverage areas to support the business. Equally, there was a need to ensure that there was HR expertise in strategic HR management, as well as in the transactional areas. It was also necessary to develop a few consistent policies, so that people in various divisions received the same treatment.

Capability of HR Staff

It was indicated that HR staff needed to be much closer to their customers in order to have better understanding of their needs. All the people in HR needed to have a much better understanding of the future business direction and the people implications of this direction. Concerns were expressed about the cost and value received from the HR function.

Executive and Career Development

More formal emphasis was required on identifying key organizational and individual competencies, and on developing recruitment strategies reflecting them. Career development and training for all employees was needed to strengthen capabilities that would support the future business direction. Career development tools and processes were needed that would identify individual capabilities and have ways of filling any capability gaps.

Change Management and Organization Development Support

More support was required to manage the major changes the company was undertaking, as outlined at the beginning of this chapter. The view expressed that more consulting support to the various business divisions was needed.

Planning, Recruitment, and Staffing

Better HR planning was needed to match staff size and capabilities with the future business direction. Staff planning was currently done in a haphazard way, with very little information exchange between business units, which led to layoffs in some divisions, while external hiring to fill jobs with similar skills was going on in other divisions.

Processes and systems were needed to ensure that the company was attracting people with the competencies required to support the business. More proactive hiring processes were required, and managers needed more training on hiring processes.

Communications

Support was required to enable all levels of management to communicate issues and business directions to all employees. It was particularly important to have vehicles to ensure common understanding of the company's vision and values, and the part each individual employee could play in reaching this vision.

Compensation

Compensation strategies needed to be better linked to company and divisional performance, in order to ensure that compensation dollars were spent wisely and in ways reinforced the desired business results.

Roles of the Corporate Group

The corporate HR group was seen not to have a clear mandate, and there was little integration of the administrative and transactional processes and actions of the whole business. Improvements were required in the way administrative functions were performed in order to provide service in a timely and cost-effective manner.

Recommendations

Based on staff interviews, studies of the company's strategic vision and values, a thorough analysis of HR costs and budgets, and material from benchmark companies, it was concluded that the company should pursue eight key HR initiatives.

1. A clearly articulated HR philosophy was required to guide and communicate the company's principles, commitment and performance expectations to employees.

2. A Human Resources planning process was needed to forecast future staffing and capability requirements.

3. There was a need for a structured and comprehensive process to develop the capabilities and competencies required by the organization. A career development strategy was also required that included retraining, training and developing capabilities to perform current and future jobs.

4. A comprehensive approach to executive development, succession planning and the development of "talent pools" was needed.

5. A comprehensive and yet customized performance system was needed to link business planning, objective setting, coaching and mentoring, performance appraisal, training and development, compensation and HR planning.

6. Innovative recruitment processes, tools and technologies needed to be developed.

7. Employee feedback mechanisms and communication vehicles needed to be developed.

8. More effective approaches were required to improve the administrative activities performed by HR and to allow line managers more access to employee data and reports.

THE NEW HR

It was recommended that the HR function as a whole should be realigned to fulfill five primary roles.

1. **Baseline services**: HR should continue to provide traditional services, including employee transactions, salary administration, pension and benefits administration, and collection of employee data and provision of reports.

2. **Compliance**: HR should be responsible for ensuring company awareness and compliance with union agreements and relevant legislation.

3. **Development of programs to become an employer of choice**: Activities in this area should position the company as an employer of choice in its industry sector and develop recruitment strategies to attract desirable employees. Career development strategies, tools and programs should to be developed to assist existing and new employees achieve their full potential. More innovative forms of communication should be developed to allow for two-way feedback and followup on ideas and issues.

4. **Development and retention of capabilities and competencies to support company strategy**: Career development strategies and policies were created and aimed at developing and retaining human

resource capital. Strategies needed to focus on the identification and development of core competencies. Greater emphasis is to be placed on executive development and succession planning for senior executives and people with leadership potential. Learning, training and development mechanisms should be put in place. Compensation and incentive systems capable of attracting and retaining employees with key capabilities should be established.

5. **Issues management and policy and program development**: HR must identify and manage emerging issues in relation to current and potential legislative trends and changing employment trends. It should also develop and implement polices and processes to support the Human Resources direction of the company.

Changing HR Structure to Meet the Required Strategies and Recommendations

In order to ensure that the key initiatives and roles noted above were implemented, it was proposed that the structure of the HR function be changed. The existing centralized HR staff was reorganized and given new responsibilities, including streamlining transactional activities and developing HR strategies to support overall company strategy. Each division was to have senior HR staff member who provided liaison between line management and corporate HR.

The Corporate HR Function

It was proposed that a centralized corporate HR group be established whose role was to develop strategies and design various process, systems and policies that would support the company's overall direction. The focus was to be on design of a Human Resources planning process, performance management systems, and executive development strategies. A career development strategy would be created, along with training, development, and recruitment strategies. A total compensation strategy would also be developed to support business strategy. A consulting group was to be created to support change management initiatives, organization development and communication strategies.

Corporate HR was also to be responsible for issue management and the creation of policies and guidelines, and for designing and implementing a combined Information System (HRIS)/HR Payroll system that would streamline transactional and record-keeping activities. These systems would be implemented by HR staff working in each division, as described in the next section.

The Industrial Relations function was split off and expanded at the corporate level, so that it could continue to focus on required initiatives. HR benefited by this separation: it would not be diluted by the company's strong emphasis on industrial relations, and would provide the new HR focus required for the business. However, divisional HR staff would continue to be responsible for both HR and Industrial Relations activities.

HR in the Divisions

Each of the business divisions and functions was to have a senior Human Resources person on its management team. This person would be responsible for providing the necessary day-to-day HR support in areas such as industrial employee relations, the implementation of corporate polices and programs, and staffing and recruiting. He or she would also be responsible for identifying and implementing the strategic HR needs of the division and would draw on resources from the corporate group as appropriate.

The corporate group and the divisional HR people would be jointly responsible for HR planning, performance management, executive development and succession planning.

IMPLEMENTATION AND OUTCOMES

The new roles and structures were accepted and implemented and have begun to deliver the required results. A number of senior and experienced HR specialists and generalists were recruited from outside the company to direct areas such as total compensation and organization development.

A great deal of effort was put into role clarification for both the corporate HR function and the business unit HR heads. A training and development process was developed and implemented in order to upgrade the skills of the existing HR staff. Regular training sessions were held on such topics as the future direction of the company and the required culture and values, employee relations, issues management

TABLE 1: Human Resources Then and Now

	H.R. Then	H.R Now
Role	policing and centralized	decentralized; sit on management teams of each business division
Recruiting and Staffing	place ads, conduct interviews and check references	forecast future staffing requirements and capabilities to support the strategic plan develop programs to become an employer of choice
Compensation	transactional and administratively focused Inconsistent practices across the business	designing equitable, performance based plans that link compensation to company and divisional performance.
Executive and Individual Development	informal and depended on the individual's manager	identification of key organization and individual competencies to support the business; plans to hire and develop these
Employee	erratic and inconsistent	communication plans and action re: vision, values and plans
Policies and Procedures	rigid, but much breaking of the "rules"	guideline linked to business trends and emerging issues

and change management. The sessions were run by HR experts themselves, line management and a few external training consultants.

A combined HRIS/Payroll system is in the process of being implemented and a base salary plan and an incentive system have been designed and implemented. A flexible benefits plan is currently being designed. The compensation and benefits strategy has been put in place which has already aligned compensation with business results, and has produced significant savings for the organization.

A great deal of effort is beginning to be devoted to consulting on organizational change and to the design of executive development, succession planning and career development systems. Such systems

are intended to ensure that both organizational and individual competencies are developed so that the company increases in market share
and return on investment.

Senior management has expressed satisfaction with results to date
and it is perceived that HR is adding more value to the business than it
did in the past. There is a recognition that change of this nature does
not happen overnight and may take anywhere from three to five years
to fully implement.

It should be noted that the changes have taken place without any
increase in costs or in number of employees in the HR function.

Part Three

Managing Change

THE PACE OF change is fast and furious these days. My experience has been that organizations know *what* to do and where they want to go with change. However, few really understand *how* to manage change whether from the human dimension or the business dimension. Part 3 focuses on how to manage change from many different dimensions and highlights the role that the HR professional can play in the change process.

Chapter 6, *Moving from Machine to Network: A Practical Guide for Changing Our Organizational Metaphor,* is a thought-provoking essay that challenges our assumptions about organizations. The old (or Newtonian) assumptions were based on the metaphor of a machine, whose archetype was the clock. This chapter offers an alternative new (or Einstein) view of organizations based on energy and relationships, whose metaphor is the cell and whose archetype is the Internet. This new view of organizations is better suited than the old style of centralized control to a global marketplace. Innovative thinking requires decentralization, and organizations need to build relationships and partner with others to create markets beyond themselves and invent new ways of doing business. This approach of networking and relationships demands that organizations define their core competencies based on knowledge and the unique value that an organization can contribute. Once these competencies have been defined, partnering with others will reduce restrictions of place and cost and maximize distribution of core competencies in a global marketplace.

Chapter 7, *Effective Change Management,* is written by Sherrill Burns, who has assisted a number of organizations in managing change at many levels. This chapter defines change management and the processes that are required to manage change in a thorough and systematic manner. It also provides a nine-step guide for senior executives and managers facing business change, looks at what is required in each of these steps, and outlines the success factors and potential pitfalls at each stage of the process. Burns also looks at time factors for the various stages of change management and defines the role that HR can play in the change management process.

Chapter 8, *Changing and Re-engineering the Information Systems Function in Nortel: An HR Case Study,* focuses on the restructuring of the Information Systems function that was required to meet the changed vision of Nortel as an integrated provider of network solutions moving into a globally competitive environment. It examines closely the communications and involvement strategies in relation to key stakeholders and also defines clearly the change management processes used. It describes how the I/S function reinvented itself and the phases it went through in order to better meet the requirements of its customers while satisfying the needs of its employees.

It also looks at the design and implementation phases of the change process, emphasizing the role the change agent played in working with management and employees to create and sustain the changes. Nortel places great emphasis on both employee satisfaction surveys and customer satisfaction surveys and credits the role these two have played in the change process.

The chapter ends with a look at the business results of the change process. It also looks at the things that have helped and hindered the change in culture, and finally, what could have been done differently.

Chapter 9, *Building Teamwork in a Unionized Workplace: A Case Study of Change at Noranda Inc.'s CCR Refinery,* shows how a union plant responded to the need for flexibility and increased its business effectiveness as a result of changes that were implemented in the plant. Noranda's CCR refinery built a new relationship of trust with unions, management, and employees, and used self-directed teams to create a new corporate culture.

A detailed description is given of the objectives for change, the change process itself, the results of the process, and suggestions from key players on how the change might have been better managed.

CHAPTER SIX

Moving from Machine to Network

A PRACTICAL GUIDE FOR CHANGING OUR ORGANIZATIONAL METAPHOR

Robert Paterson

What form should the industrial system have? That of bureaucratic industrialism, in which the individual becomes a small, insignificant cog in the social machinery, or that of a humanistic industrialism, in which alienation and the sense of impotence are overcome by the fact that the individual participates actively and responsibly in the economic and social process?[1]

UNTIL VERY RECENTLY, organizations have used Human Resources primarily as a kind of lubricating agent to keep the machinery of business running smoothly. HR's connection to business strategy was perceived, by and large, to be an indirect one: the multitude of transactions relating to hiring, compensation, and health and safety issues needed efficient processing. In the best companies, there might also be some scope for training and executive leadership development. Underlying this common understanding of Human Resources was a theory that organizations essentially work the way a machine works, that is, as a system of parts which predictably perform functions as long as the machine's operator directs it properly.

---

[1] Erich Fromm, *On Being Human*, edited by Rainer Funk (New York: The Continuum Publishing Company, 1994).

Today, a review of the Human Resources function is a common feature of business restructuring. Despite all the talk there is about the importance of "intellectual capital" and involving an organization's "human assets" in its future development, Human Resources is rarely treated as an invaluable contributor to planning for the future. What happens more often is that Human Resources is targeted for cost-cutting because of its perceived lack of connection to the company's bottom line; when it is called in, it is expected to deliver, usually on its own, ways to make organizations better, usually by making them bigger.

Human Resources can, indeed, play a central role in rethinking our troubled organizations, but not if it is constrained by old ways of thinking about organizations. In this chapter, we show that a new kind of organizational model is central to success in a global society and a global marketplace and suggest ways for both new organizations and old ones to benefit from this model. In this model, concentration of resources, including workforce, is superseded by decentralized systems of co-operation.

Such decentralization may spell the end of large Human Resources departments which process forms, but HR has a role in helping existing companies and start-up groups implement the new model. In addition, the new model should alert HR professionals to the potential benefits of rethinking the delivery systems they rely on, whether in an internal business unit or an external agency, as expert consultants on people issues. In a world which asks each worker to become his or her own entrepreneur, Human Resources could become the most important source of learning, of career planning, and of new management theory, and therefore the agent on which our success as a society depends.

UNDERSTANDING OUR TIME OF TRANSITION

Most of us feel that there is something wrong with our organizations. Whether they are conventional organizations—government agencies, schools, hospitals, and large businesses, or social organizations—such as nations and families—they no longer work as well as they used to.

We sense that this growing problem of our organizations has something to do with globalization and the new technology. The main symptom that we all experience is cost. Most of our organizations appear to have too much cost embedded in them to be competitive in a global environment. We tell ourselves in the public sector that we do not have enough money to continue to serve the public and maintain our credit rating. In the private sector, we tell ourselves that we are not earning enough of a return on capital to protect ourselves from larger global competitors.

Is Bigger Always Better?

Much of our response to this analysis has been to try and make our organizations more competitive by increasing their scale and by centralizing. We often think that our problem is that we are not efficient enough. This is the "bigger-is-better" model. For a long time, in fact, increasing the scale of organizations worked well. If we wanted better performance, an increase in scale gave it to us. For instance, supermarkets have doubled in size every five years for the last twenty years. We as customers have benefited from this bigger-is-better process. We got more choice, lower prices and more convenience.

But there are limits to this model. As the stores grow beyond a certain size, customers begin to lose convenience and the supermarket chains feel increasing pressure on their net margin. One of the aspects of life today is that we have so little time. Ask yourself what is the maximum distance that you will drive to go to the supermarket? How big will the supermarket be when you spend more time there than you want? For consumers, a retail scale limit is in sight.

For supermarket managers, the strain is on the margin and the balance sheet. They have found that they are required to make a geometric increase in capital expenditure for a linear increase in return. As capital investment increases geometrically, the financial pressure and risks to their business also increase. The capital plant has to be worked harder all the time: any small downturn will create a serious problem.

The bigger-is-better model is to be found everywhere. We have applied it not only to business but also to schools, hospitals, government, and agriculture. We are experiencing what appears to be a relentless process of consolidation and centralization, but just as in the example above, many organizations are showing that there are limits to profitable growth.

Perhaps the greatest risk of the bigger-is-better model is that, as it becomes more difficult to earn a return from the operation of the activity itself, we put pressure on the underlying resource, such as the people, the land, the trees, or the fish. The result is a capital approach to fishing that destroys the stocks, a capital approach to medicine that erodes our ability to deliver healthcare, a capital approach to schools and universities that erodes are ability to educate our children, and a capital approach to natural resources that erodes our environment.

Where should we look to find an alternative to the bigger-is-better response?

Looking for Answers in a New Place— The Importance of New Assumptions and Metaphors

If we surrendered
to Earth's intelligence,
we could rise up rooted, like trees.
Instead we entangle ourselves
in knots of our own making
and struggle lonely and confused.
—Rainer Maria Rilke
"WENN etwas mir vom Fenster fällt"
tr. Anita Barrows and Joanna Macy

I think that it would help us if we re-examined the assumptions that we use to define our world and if we looked for a different metaphor to describe how we all related to each other.

FIGURE 1: The Shift in Context

Our scientific metaphor has shifted from machine to relationships

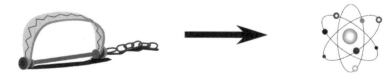

Simple Machine   **Organism**

Newton   Einstein

Fixed purpose   Learns and shifts
Externally driven   Internally driven
Power and Tangibles   Energy & Relationships
Things   Information

Our predominant organizational assumptions are based on the concepts of a Newtonian universe. The Newtonian universe is fixed in space and time and is therefore controllable. The Newtonian universe is based on things. Its underlying metaphor is that the world is a machine.

I believe that a new set of assumptions is emerging that drives a new metaphor. The new assumptions are based on a vision of the universe begun by Albert Einstein. The Einstein universe is not fixed in space or time. Everything in the Einstein view of the universe is relative and hence not controllable. The new universe is based on energy and relationships. Its underlying metaphor is the organism or the cell (Figure 1). As the clock was an archetype for the machine metaphor, so the archetype for the new natural metaphor is the Internet.

Shifts in assumptions and metaphor have happened before. If we can understand how these shifts occur, we can discover what is happening to us now and make informed decisions about what to do. Figure 2 shows the major shifts in assumptions and metaphor since 3,000 BC. The shaded areas represent the periods of transition when two metaphors exist at the same time. The shifts occur whenever there has been a converging change in the power of information technology, how

FIGURE 2: The Creation of Wealth

What are the asssumptions, tools and metaphors

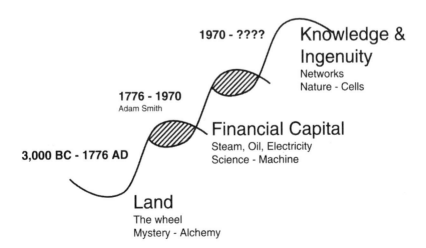

we relate to the cosmos, how we use tools, and how we understand the creation of wealth. The basis of power shifts during these periods, which means that in all organizations, our structures for the collective exercise of power have to be reinvented. Figure 2 on the previous page, for example, makes a crucial connection between the Newtonian machine and a profound shift in Western structures for creating wealth rooted in the work of economist Adam Smith.

Once again, we are living in one of the transition times when all the rules change. The next breakthrough in information technology is here. Our understanding of the cosmos has shifted from Newton's machine to Einstein's relative universe, and we have a new order of tools that will give us the power to form organizations in an entirely different way.

How Tools Affect How We Organize and Live

The most promising faith for the future might be based on the realization that the entire universe is a system related by common laws and that it makes no sense to impose our dreams and desires on nature without taking them into account [2].

We define ourselves and our culture by the tools we use. As we create new tools, they change our metaphors and, therefore, our culture. Our view of the world is largely defined by the relationship that we have with the most important tools in our lives. The stone spear point enabled us to leave the trees and form hunter societies. The discovery of the wheel and the domestication of the horse enabled us to have cities and to structure ourselves as monarchies and feudal societies. The clock and the steam engine enabled us to become industrial democracies.

All these changes in tool sets altered power relationships. We can expect a very significant change in how and where we live as the new tools take precedence over the old. Until now, all tools from stone axes to tractors have been designed and operated on the basis of the application of external energy to move matter. They have all helped us to become physically stronger in the physical world, where bigger is better. Urbanization is a social result of this set of tools.

---

[2] Mihaly Csikszentmihaly, *Flow: The Psychology of Optimal Experience* (New York: Harper & Row, 1990).

The Old Tool Metaphor

Our old tools *extended the power of our bodies*. They moved things. We started with enhancing the human muscle directly, a lever. We then used nature to help us move objects, waterpower or sail. We then used the stored energy of the sun, coal and oil. Our organizing model extended from the human skeleton to the machine. Each stage provided an enormous leap forward in capability, but each stage took the person further away from the natural world and increased the need for financial capital. Eventually only very large organizations, located in developed nations, could afford to use the bigger-is-better model; moreover, as we saw above, their experiences suggest the model has limits.

The New Tool Metaphor

The new tools do not operate in the physical world. They manipulate information. We now have an entirely new type of tool metaphor *that extends the power of our consciousness*. Its focus is to expand understanding and to move information.

Just as the older physical tools set us on a course that causes us eventually to see the whole universe as a machine, so this new information tool will set us on a course that reintegrates us with nature. It will use the laws of nature and life to design tools and organizations. These rules are based on how the brain works rather than on how our skeleton works. The Internet is the living symbol of the application of these new rules. The neural network is the new organizational model.

The New Rules

The Power of the brain is largely a function of number of neurons and the richness of their connections. Colin Rose, *Accelerated Learning* (New York: Dell Books, 1989).

The old set of assumptions is underpinned by a belief that man, through the use of machines and his rational intellect, can and should dominate nature. We use only our intellect to design tools and structures. The purpose of the old metaphor is "progress," which can be defined as the belief that if we only had enough things we would find true happiness. The organizational essence of the old metaphor is control. Strength comes from increasing size and efficiency. The managerial concept is parental. Power and motivation are sourced externally.

The new set of assumptions is underpinned by the belief that man is not separate from nature, and if we choose to understand nature it will provide us with the knowledge we need to live well. The purpose of the new metaphor is "development." Development is the process of finding our full potential as human beings. The organizational essence of the new metaphor is the network. Strength comes from the number and quality of our relationships. The managerial concept is service. Power and motivation are internally driven.

I doubt that much of what I have just told you is news. If we know that the old system does not work very well, why are we not doing a better job in changing it?

WHY CHANGE IS SO DIFFICULT

> *The fault, dear Brutus, is not in our stars,*
> *But in ourselves, that we are underlings.*
> —*Julius Caesar*, I, sc.ii, 140-141

We know intellectually what the new design is. The challenge is putting it into practice. Why is change so difficult? I think that there are two blocks. The first is the power of perception. The second is that all the rules, incentives and punishments that we use to operate the old system are still in place.

Perception

What I mean by perception is that some of us are so immersed in the old way of thinking that we simply cannot imagine, or see, the reality of the new. No matter how hard we look, we see only machines and, hence, machine problems and machine solutions.

If this explanation of two competing realities sounds odd, have a look at the picture of the woman in Figure 3. This image, frequently reproduced in scientific studies on human perception, shows two women: an old woman and a young woman. Here are two competing realities in one picture. Can you see them both? Can you see both at the same time? Can you make them flicker between each other? Can you only see one of them? If so, which one is it, the old or the young?

FIGURE 3: Two Competing Metaphors

This same sort of confusion is what faces all of us today when inter-preting our organizations. We are flickering between two metaphors. Some can only see the old. A few can see the new but the old keeps coming back into view. The result, confusion!

The Battle between Amazon.com and Barnes and Noble

To illustrate the impact of two metaphors existing at the same time, let's have a look at Amazon.com, the new online Internet-based virtual bookshop, and Barnes and Noble, one of the largest conventional "Big Box" booksellers[3].

Barnes and Noble used the bigger-is-better model to become the dominant bookseller in North America. Now it is being challenged by Amazon.com, an organization that is using an entirely new concept based on a natural model. Amazon is using an organizational metaphor based on the neural networks of the brain. It is based on connections and relationships. It uses the new information technology to connect the customer to the value. This design only needs a fraction of the financial capital that the conventional design requires. It directly con-nects the customer to the product using a surprisingly personal service.

---

[3] Michael Krantz, "Amazonian Challenge," *Time* (Canadian Edition), April 14, 1997, p. 38.

It dramatically increases choice—2.5 million titles versus a conventional inventory of 150,000—which is at the limits of the bigger-is-better model. It offers a 40% discount! While Amazon is small now in terms of earnings, it has defined an entirely new way of being a bookseller.

Where Are the Costs?

Amazon.com	Barnes and Noble
1996 Revenues	1996 Revenues
• $15.7 mln	• $2.45 bln
Book Titles	Book Titles
• None in inventory	• 150,000 in store
• 2.5 mln on-line	• 2.5 mln on-line
Stores	Stores
• None	• 1,009
Staff	Staff
• A handful	• Thousands

What can Barnes and Noble do about the capital costs embedded in their branch system? It seems impossible that Barnes and Noble could make its physical branch system efficient enough to compete with Amazon on price, choice and convenience.

Barnes and Noble's initial response to the challenge of Amazon has been to set up an on-line service of its own, but this does not address the apparent obsolescence of its branch system. It has caught itself in a trap. It still believes in the old machine metaphor and is only trying to co-opt the new metaphor. Barnes and Noble still requires a significant multiple of Amazon's resources simply to keep its doors open. It must be very confusing to be working there at the moment. It is probably not confusing to work at Amazon.

There are many organizations like Barnes and Noble whose past success has been based on applying the old rules well. The perception risk is greatest in these organizations. In the traditional insurance business the risk has been in over-investing in their brokerage system. In retail banking it has been in over-investing in the physical branch network. Both the insurance and banking industries have also made a large investment in new direct, technology-based channels. The banks have been conspicuous in their leadership in this field. But I suspect that the sunk investment and the lifetime experience of success based on the old system makes it difficult to see the opportunity inherent in pushing the alternative even harder and the risk inherent in maintaining the emotional and financial investment in the physical plant.

This perception risk exposes an organization to new entrants, like Amazon.com, who have little or no emotional or financial investment in the old. Such an organization may not recognize the risk until it is too late. But even if it does see the new risk, as Barnes and Noble undoubtedly has, there is another powerful block to change, culture.

Culture—The Challenge

Know thyself.

Only revolutionaries, saints and fools operate easily outside their own self-interest. Every culture has a series of rules, incentives and punishments that reinforce its core metaphor. It is not easy for anyone inside a traditional organization to make the changes to a new metaphor, as all these controlling forces will come into play.

It is helpful to look at the power of these forces with fresh eyes. Only when we can see them clearly will we see the value of building new organizations outside the power of the old.

All the rules of the old culture are based on the assumptions that the most important activity is control. The extension of this assumption is that if only we tried hard enough, we could control everything. This illusion seemed to work when we did not operate in a global society. But when we began to operate in a global economy, the complexity of controlling everything has overwhelmed us.

As we talk about being more responsive, more customer-focused and more flexible, let's look at the real rules that govern most of our organizations. They work against these objectives. The budget process is the most important process in the traditional organization. Budgets, not value, determine who has the power. Controlling large budgets, large numbers of people and large physical plants is what gives you power. At a time when the jargon is all about being close to the customer, the traditional reward system values being a bureaucrat. The further you are away from the customer, the more powerful you become. Career success is determined by obtaining and using good bureaucratic skills. The result is a managerial emphasis and a bias against creativity.

The management process is hierarchical with all the key decisions taking place at the centre. Important decisions therefore take a very long time and are based on a narrow slice of information that has been processed by the supporting staff. The feedback response is therefore very poor. This creates the risk that the organization will not see important issues until it is too late to cope without drastic measures. Many of the costs and pain felt in organizations today result from repeated reorganizations which are a sign of acting too late and with too big a response.

Executives, managers and workers are categorized in jobs that are defined by a set of tasks. The money we earn is mainly related to the job and not to the value that we create or the outcomes that we achieve. The risk to the organization in such a course is that its employees are not focused on the key outcomes. The risk to the employees is that they are not connected to their innate capability. Much internal alienation arises from the fact that employees are disconnected by the concept of the job from the true purpose of the enterprise and from their own needs and capabilities.

The external stakeholders, be they investors, bankers or governments, view the enterprise through only one aspect of a balance sheet, financial capital. As the bigger-is-better approach has taken hold, the financial balance sheet has grown geometrically, thus driving up the hurdle rate for earning an economic return. The purpose of the organization tends to become obscured as the pressure to meet the investment hurdle increases. Schools are increasingly evaluated on their budgetary impact rather than on whether or not they are educating our children well. Businesses cannot afford to miss an operational beat because they have to run their system at full tilt all the time to meet the returns on a large capital structure. Executives are being measured quarter by quarter rather than being given a more appropriate time horizon.

Executive management concentrates the wealth created by the organization at the centre. This wealth is largely seen as being financial. Poor management is often hidden by exploiting the true components of wealth creation—the human, social and natural capital on which the enterprise truly depends. This does not happen because the executives are bad people. It is because they are responding to the prevailing performance criterion, which is made up of a series of abstract financial ratios.

The Example of IBM

I believe that the power of the old culture makes it almost impossible to change our organizations from within. The reasons for this failure are not lack of effort or lack of vision but the nature of the cultural reaction to the new. The rules of the old culture operate like an immune system seeking out new and dangerous ideas that threaten the old way of doing things.

What is at issue is power. Think of the recent history of IBM or what is going on in your own Information Technology (IT) division. IBM nearly died as an organization as a result of one of these power struggles. The paradox is that, by its development of the PC, IBM laid the groundwork for the new metaphor. Why, then, did this success nearly cause it to die as a company? It nearly died because it had an internal civil war about two contradictory belief systems, one based on the new organic metaphor based on the PC, the other based on the old machine metaphor based on the mainframe. Anyone who works with a large corporate IT division knows what this struggle is like.

I suspect that what happened at IBM was that the success of the PC division challenged the established culture and the traditional power elite of the company who believed that the really important business was the mainframe. The mainframe represents the old centralizing command and control vision of centralizing the information so that only the elite had access to it. The PC division represented the distributed vision of information. The triumph of the new management of IBM, is that they have overcome this internal battle of belief systems and have been able to use the new culture not only to renew their PC business but also their old mainframe business.

NEW SOLUTIONS FOR EXISTING ORGANIZATIONS

Many organizations are caught in this struggle of competing cultures. How can we still operate in our existing organizations and make the changes that we need?

Visa International—Showing the Way

Someone has put the new organization into practice on a global scale and has designed this organization so that it provides value to the old organizations, thus avoiding the threat of an immune response. You probably use his new organization every day. It has changed the world we live in, but you probably don't know how it works and how very different it is from your normal view of an organization.

Its designer's name is Dee Hock and the organization that he designed is called Visa International. Dee Hock describes his concept as a Chaordic Organization[4]. His intention is to find a structure that has an underlying order powerful enough to hold a very distributed structure together. He seeks to find the organizational balance between order and chaos where the maximum creativity can exist within a set purpose.

Visa International has only been in existence for a quarter of a century. It has grown at a compound growth rate of between 20% and 50% and clears more electronic transactions in a week than the Federal Reserve wire system does in a year. It has 355 million users, 23,000 partners and operates in more than 200 countries but has only 3,000 employees. (In comparison, NatWest has 81,000 and Bank of America has 91,000 employees.) Visa truly operates locally and globally. You can use it in your local corner store or in Ukraine. This type of growth, scale, and small overhead would not be possible in an organization designed like a machine.

Visa is a non-profit organization using a new approach to capitalism; it is a wealth distribution rather than a wealth concentration system. Its role is to facilitate the wealth creation of its partners by connecting them to the world's population of consumers and service providers. The power of the system is that it obeys the rules of success of the brain. It seeks to offer the highest number of high-quality connections. Its distributed and networked design has meant that in spite of its growth and market share, it has not had to use the capital markets to fund its existence. It has mainly used the resources drawn from the intellectual capital of its partners. It is not subject, therefore, to the financial forces that might distract it from its mission of providing service.

---

[4] "The Chaordic Organization: Out of Control into Order," *Perspectives Magazine*, Vol. 9, #1 (1995), pp. 5-18.

In essence, Visa is a network of partners who have agreed to connect to each other for their mutual benefit and who use a small number of protocols or standards, which function as DNA does in an organism. These standards are related to how the partners connect to each other and to how the value of the uniting brand is enhanced and protected. There is no physical controlling centre for Visa. There is a central staff, but they are small in number and their role is to "facilitate" the interests of the partnership and to ensure that the network is running well. The enterprise accepts the fact that the partners all have different cultures. It only asks that partners strictly adhere to the rules of the brand and the rules of performance and connection. The system operates even when the partner nations are at war with each other.

Except for setting protocols, the management process is distributed. The purpose of executive management is to hold the vision for the enterprise and maintain the standards that hold it together. The wealth is distributed to the partners who also evaluate their performance against the design protocols. No one has a say that is not a partner. There are no arm's length evaluators who use only abstract financial criteria for measuring performance. Issues to be managed are connection time, security, fraud, the integrity of the brand, and so on. These issues are self-managed by the partners.

When you think of the Internet, you can see that it operates using many of the same rules in use at Visa International. Who controls the Internet? No one. Rather, the Internet is a co-operative partnership. It works because HTML (the computer language used for writing programs which operate on the Internet), its DNA, has been accepted by all Internet participants. HTML enables the Internet to operate as a "Chaordic Organization."

Facilitating Structures

I believe that Visa also performs the external role of a "Facilitating Structure[5]." A Facilitating Structure is one that is designed to help the old move to the new. It achieves this purpose by allowing adherents to the old culture to meet in a safe new place which enables them to solve the problems of reaching the customer in a much more effective way.

---

[5] Dr. Fraser Mustard, the Founding President of the Canadian Institute for Advanced Research, introduced me to this concept.

Let me explain this idea by looking at the Interac Association, the Canadian partnership of financial institutions, formed for the purpose of creating a Canadian network to link the institution's proprietary ABM and point-of-sale networks together.

It has a similar internal structure to Visa International. It is also non-profit and relies on its own connecting protocols and the brand— its DNA—to hold it together. It also acts as a "Facilitating Structure," because it enables its partner members to jump between the old and the new cultures without creating the immune system response that would occur if it were part of the old host culture.

Interac began as a result of a problem. All the Canadian banks were running at full speed to build their own proprietary networks. They still are to some extent, but they realized that the project was too big for any one of them alone. How could they create the maximum number of connections without bankrupting themselves in the process? The answer was to build a facilitating structure that would act as the "Connector."

Interac is, in effect, only a switch and a brand that is jointly owned by the partners. As such it costs very little to operate but provides enormous value to its owners and to us as users. The switch enables all users from any bank to connect to their home account through a switch that is safe. The brand, Interac, means that we as users are indifferent as to which bank operates the terminal in the supermarket. What we are sure of is that the transaction will go through accurately. The same is true about Visa as a brand. The more the brand is recognized the more value it has to expand the system. Each new terminal that the Royal Bank, for example, puts in adds value to the entire Canadian system. The link from Interac to Visa adds the value of all the connections of all the other banks in the world that are partners in Visa.

Facilitating Structures are "Connectors." They seek to find the standards—appropriate DNA—to connect systems of users. They are cheap to build because they are based on protocols rather than on plant. They are information-based, not financially based.

The initial cash investment in Interac was about $25 million. This is pocket change when you consider a typical bank's IT budget, which is often in excess of $500 million per bank. What was more valuable than the initial investment was the intellectual capital that came free from each bank as their best people designed the new structure and borrowed collective resources.

While there were disagreements, there were no wars. Since Interac is a connecting process and not a process of integration, the banks did not have to change their own culture or IT system. They only had to determine the protocols by which they would talk to each other. This meant that there was no need to use power to force another bank to do it "my way." Doing it "our way" was the nature of the discussion.

In addition, Interac did not threaten any of the internal fiefdoms of the parent banks and therefore did not elicit an immune response. In fact, the opposite has happened; organizations not in the founding group so badly wanted to join that they went to the Competition Board to force entry into the club.

What Does This Mean for You?

Alliances and partnerships are emerging in many parts of organizational life. They are emerging as a response to finding another way of dealing with the costs that are weakening our traditional organizations. Our need to control everything is breaking down as we see the cost involved. The big insight is that what makes us special is not usually the "housekeeping" but our core competency and our identity.

So we see Air Canada form the Star Alliance with a group of other airlines. Like Interac, Star does not stop Air Canada from being Air Canada. It enables Air Canada to deal collectively with the housekeeping costs of global baggage handling, ticketing, local airport staffing, and so on. It does not have to subsume its identity or culture to achieve this. The old approach would have been that one airline would take over the others. This would have blown up the balance sheet and increased the problem. Star is an innovative attempt to find the efficiencies and reach scale but in a new way. Star is a form of Facilitating Structure. The partner airlines use a series of common protocols to connect their housekeeping items so that they can become part of a system that serves all the partners. Star increases the power of each airline while reducing the costs and scale of each one.

E.F. Schumacher got only part of it right when he said that "small is beautiful." The risk of being just small is that small has little power. Small is never powerful, but networks of small units are. What he missed is that with networks you can still have a unit scale that is human but also have the power of scale by being connected to a large group of small units.

Networks paradoxically increase their power as they become larger. Networks can grow to infinite size because, as they become larger, they become more robust. They achieve this by increasing their diversity. Increased diversity means that if parts fail the whole can reroute and continue. Conversely, as machines become larger they become more fragile and the failure of a part can bring the whole machine to a halt.

Our bodies are not machines, they are networks of cells which are held together in a Chaordic way by our DNA. This is the next model for design.

A GOOD PLACE TO START

My advice is to seek partners who can help you solve some of your most pressing cost problems by forming a facilitating structure. Use Chaordic principles and see what connecting network will provide you with the most value.

A good place to start is government. Government has taken too much of our potential wealth-creating capacity. On the other hand, simply cutting may in fact damage our society even more. Most governments are cutting to reduce their costs but cannot offer a better alternative than a loss of service. A large part of their costs are derived from the need of each separate department in each separate part of government to control the housekeeping, or the basic transactions. Just like the banks before Interac, many of the transactions, such as getting a cheque or a license, require us to turn up in the service providers' time and at their place to conduct the basic transaction in the most expensive way possible.

Three competing levels of government deliver many of these transactions. They, like the banks or Air Canada, do not wish to give up their identity or culture. They talk about shifting the burden from one level to the other or even of amalgamation. None of these solutions attack the core problem. They could find a way of forming facilitating structures that would enable them to deliver a better service, keep their identity and reduce their costs.

Healthcare and education are in a vice as well. The users have to turn up in person for every transaction. Hospitals are closing and amalgamating, as are schools. If they were to reconceive themselves as not being buildings and see themselves instead as being centres of knowledge, they too could serve a wider group of users by forming facilitating structures to connect them to the world beyond their immediate locale.

Women's College Hospital, located in Toronto, possesses a concentration of expertise in women's health matched by only three institutions in the world. It is threatened with closure because it is too small in local Toronto terms. But if it were to reconceive itself as a global supplier of women's health knowledge, it could serve billions of women. To do this, it would have to partner with some other specialized centers so that it could afford to build the connections and the network.

Rural healthcare is in crisis just as the central hospitals with all the expertise in critical care are being closed. Is there not an opportunity to create a rural network offering their expertise that extends from these centres into the countryside?

Smaller regional universities are under siege, as are smaller schools. Is the answer really only closure? Is the answer unco-ordinated and competitive attempts to offer courses of distance-based learning? Or is it to create a national network that can extend learning opportunities throughout Canada and later throughout the world? After all, there is only a local shortage of educational capability in the developed world. Billions of people need inexpensive access to learning, which may be possible only if we use networks.

I am not suggesting that our future is only electronic, or that we should spend our lives in front of screens. I am talking about the enhancement of place rather than its extinction. I am talking about being able to have small local schools that work. I am talking about being able to have small communities that have access to all that is best in our culture and infrastructure. I am talking about reducing the costs of our institutions so that they can refocus themselves back to serving us as human beings. I am talking about a much lighter footprint of man on the planet.

The Need to Define Your Core Competency

To thine own self be true.
— *Hamlet*, I, sc. IV, 78

Our traditional organizations compelled us to give up who we really were. In the struggle to fit into the machine, we as people had to become a job rather than a person with unique capabilities. Our organizations also became focused on function rather than creation.

A precondition of being successful in a network means that the components, be they individuals or organizations, have to become clear about who they are. Organizational core competency is based on knowledge and the value you bring. Good management is not a core competency, it is only an important hygiene matter. Being able to accumulate knowledge and to apply it to create value is the main work.

The core competency of Toronto's Women's College Hospital is that it knows a lot about women's health. Such knowledge is globally in short supply. Prince Edward Island's core competency is that it knows a lot about how to grow potatoes in a world that is short of food. The University of Toronto School's core competency is that it knows how to teach exceptionally bright children, the sort of children who are withering away from boredom in our regular high schools. In each instance, the use of the core competency is currently restricted to the place where the knowledge is centred, but there is an enormous global demand for these core competencies. This demand could be satisfied if these institutions partnered with others who had complementary competencies.

There are organizations you can partner with who need the benefit of your organization's core competency. You do not have to do it all by yourself. You can exchange value and cover your own weaknesses by using the offsetting strengths of others. You can borrow rather than have to bear the cost of owning everything that you need. This approach will enable you to reduce your costs dramatically.

This is how nature really works. Organisms do not fight tooth and claw, they find niches and form effective working relationships with each other. For example, the rhino has poor eyesight and suffers from ticks. The tickbird has good eyesight and needs to eat. The rhino allows the tickbird to ride undisturbed on his back thus providing lunch while the tickbird rids him of his ticks and provides him with an early warning system. The two different species have worked out an effective partnership based on their self-interest.

Hewlett Packard needs to be able to operate in a very short product life cycle. One of its core competencies is in designing new printers. If it had a large financial investment in manufacturing, it would not easily be able to make the model changes that it needs to keep up. So it has partnered in Canada with IBM who uses one of its core competencies, large-scale quality manufacturing, to offset a role that HP does not find strategic. IBM gets the line utilization that it requires, while HP gets the quality and the flexibility that it needs.

We all have to become sure of our individual core competencies as well. However, the risk with "competencies" is that we may think of them in the old way. Thinking about them in the old way means thinking of them simply as being collections of technical skills. The most important "skill" in the new model will be relational, how well we can communicate and work with others.

Again, this is not about technique. When I say communicate, I do not mean being slick, I mean being able to connect to others. In the old model you could get away with having only analytical intelligence because you could use positional power to get your way. In a network you have to use "emotional intelligence[6]" because you can only use personal power.

If you saw the film *Braveheart,* you will understand what I mean. The William Wallace character operates entirely by using personal power. The Bruce and the aristocrats use positional power. Wallace knows his own power and is motivated by his vision of a better world. He attracts others to him by his courage and energy. He shares his vision with them and, above all, he walks his talk. The Bruce and the aristocrats use their power based on their titles to order men around. Their main motivation is the fear of losing their position. The strength of Wallace was not that he had better technique, it was that he knew who he was and what was truly important for other men and women.

CONCLUSION: SOLVING THE PARADOX

We have come full circle. We began with the observation that today we commonly see our problems as dealing with increasing costs and the effects of globalization. This is a correct view, but only a superficial one. Our real problem lies deeper, and we need solutions that address it. Too often our response has been to try and make the underlying machine work even harder, but fixing the old in the old way will not give us the relief from our problems. It will make them worse.

A more effective response would be to consider and apply the new rules of networks and partnership. I observe many organizations already beginning to use a sense of their core competency as a basis for beginning to partner with others. I observe some early forms of facilitating

---

[6] See Dan Goleman's excellent book *Emotional Intelligence* (New York: Bantam Books, 1995).

structures that are having a transforming effect on how we do business. I believe that all the technology that we will need to create these facilitating structures is already available.

We live at the dawn of a tremendous change to human society. In 1880, 80% of North Americans lived and worked in rural communities. By 1960, 95% of us lived and worked in cities. This is the speed at which the powerful application of the machine metaphor transformed society once the tools of the industrial age reached critical mass and effectiveness. My sense is that the tools needed to apply the new metaphor have now reached the critical mass needed for transformation.

The buildup for the breakthrough is over. The process of actual transformation has begun. I cannot predict the details of the future, but I can say with certainty that just as the steam engine, electricity, and the internal combustion engine changed everything for our grandparents, so our new tools will change everything for us.

We cannot choose to stop this process: that is beyond our power. Our choice is to decide whether to become a participant or a victim in the change.

To be a participant requires us to have faith in how we fit into the new. It requires acts of courage in the face of the doubters. It requires us to try things that we don't fully understand. It requires us to trust those we don't know. It requires us to stop hesitating and to make a commitment, if not for ourselves, then for our children. It requires that we make a commitment to the new.

If we do, the results can be remarkable. I am reminded of the inspiring words of W.H. Murray, a member of the Scottish Himalayan expedition:

> Until one is committed, there is hesitancy, the chance to draw back, always ineffectiveness. Concerning all acts of initiative (and creation), there is one elementary truth, the ignorance of which kills countless ideas and splendid plans: that the moment one definitely commits oneself, then Providence moves too. All sorts of things occur to help one that would never otherwise have occurred. A whole stream of events issue from the decision raising in one's favour all manner of unforeseen incidents, meetings and material assistance which no man could have dreamed would have come his way.

CHAPTER SEVEN

Effective Change Management

Sherrill Burns

CHANGE HAS ALWAYS been a part of doing business, but the large-scale changes often required of organizations today are complex, difficult and emotionally challenging. To protect the success of major changes, leaders must deal not only with the logistics of transforming systems, processes and procedures, but also with the difficult emotional transitions people endure when they are called on to do things differently. It is only through engaging all members of an organization in the process of change, and not just leaving most of them to deal with its consequences, that leaders can hope to minimize its downside and actually use it to revitalize and renew their organizations.

Business often does a much better job at the structural aspects of change than it does with the people dimensions. The new discipline of Change Management—that is, the process of enabling people affected by organizational change to successfully transition to a new business or work enviroment—lays great emphasis on addressing the emotional challenges brought by business change. A key principle of Change Management is the engagement of every employee, with Human Resources being singled out by Change Management theory as having a key role to play in major change initiatives.

In this chapter, we will make the business case for Change Management and identify the fundamentals of Change Management, particularly HR's role.

WHAT IS THE BUSINESS CASE FOR CHANGE MANAGEMENT?

Even the possibility of a major change sets dynamics in motion which affect individual employees and, consequently, the organization. Listed below are some of the typical responses which occur in individuals when faced with adapting to new work conditions. Once these individual dynamics begin, the whole organization becomes embroiled in a churn of emotional reactions.

Individual Dynamics	*Organizational Dynamics*
• Feelings of betrayal and loss	• Increase in indecisiveness
• Sense of confusion	• Deterioration of communications
• Deterioration of trust	• Decline of teamwork
• Heightened self-interest	• Shift from external to internal focus
• Stalled creativity	• Stalled innovation

Unfortunately for the business, this organizational turmoil negatively impacts the bottom line. Think of it as a predictable loss of time and focus during each day of transition through a change. If each employee is now spending one to two hours per day caught up in hearing what the latest rumour is, discussing their career plans with their peers, not to mention postponing decisions and actions, the productivity can dramatically drop. Productivity and morale can be irreparably damaged, with the result that a company may never recover adequately from the impact of change.

Figure 1 illustrates the dip in sales recorded for a key product of a global pharmaceutical company during a major structural change in the product's sales unit (no other major factors impacted market share during this period). It clearly demonstrates the impact transitioning through a change can have on business performance.

Employing practical Change Management techniques continuously throughout a major change can minimize the productivity impact and can ensure a net gain in overall productivity. Without some specific Change Management activities in place, executives can expect at least a 20%-30% decrease in employee productivity.

FIGURE 1: Market Share Consequences of Transition

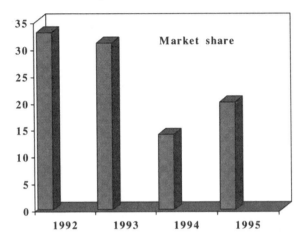

Why Is Transitioning Through a Major Change so Difficult?

A major change starts with a corporate vision, a focused mission and a set of operating principles to guide decisions and actions, but its success depends on attention to two very different aspects of change. First, the changes to systems, structures, policies and processes must be designed and instituted. This is the rational side of the change process. It is easy to see and also easy to track and measure. In Figure 2, this rational side of change is presented on the left side of the model.

FIGURE 2: The Two Sides of the Change Process

Second, major changes usually require substantive shifts in mindsets, attitudes, behaviours and beliefs. For example, people often need to rethink what success looks like in their business, their role and their interactions. It is often much more difficult to deal with these personal transitions, shown on the right side of Figure 2, than with procedural changes.

Failure to deal with transition issues is most often the downfall of large-scale change projects. Organizational productivity and morale are drained and focus on the strategic agenda lags. In addition large-scale change projects frequently suffer delays and set-backs because they have planned time for the *change* side of the project (i.e., process changes, system changes), but have failed to allocate the necessary time to managing the *transition* side of the initiative. For large-scale change projects, 20%-25% of the time should be spent in transition management activities.

THE CORNERSTONES OF CHANGE MANAGEMENT

There are several steps to follow in managing both the *change* and the *transition* sides of a major change; these are outlined later in this chapter. It is vital first to note, however, that these steps depend for success on some fundamental principles of Change Management. These are:

- A concrete Change Management plan must be integrated in the overall project plan.
- Human Resources must take on a key role in supporting the Change Management plan.
- The Change Management plan must be supported at every step by effective, targeted Communication and Consultation practices.
- The goals of Change Management are building commitment to the vision of change, confidence in the organization's capability to achieve the gains required, credibility that the gains from change will exceed the pain, and capability to meet changing job requirements.

A Concrete Change Management Plan

First, a concrete Change Management plan must be put in place and integrated into the overall project plan. It should include the following:

- a clear set of Change Management goals and measures of success, supported by guiding principles for managing the transition;
- a project team structure to sponsor and resource the Change Management work to be completed;
- supporting a set of practices and tools for project teams, line managers and employees who must live through these dynamics; and
- a project management discipline to rigorously track progress both the rational process and procedural changes being worked on and the more emotional transition activities which must be worked into the plan.

There are some common approaches to change which are not effective and yet which continue to be used by executives:

- **A Project Timetable**: Major changes carry organizations into the "world of the unknown." They are complex and difficult. Having a rigid timetable forces people into delivering lower-quality work based on rapid decision making for the sake of the schedule and results in burn-out and cynicism. A rigorous project management and Change Management discipline is far more effective than managing by timetable.

- **A Permanent Project Team**: Line management, not a project team, needs to own the change. Having a permanent project team gets in the way of line management ownership. As well, permanent project teams need relief from the pressure of a change effort. It is far more effective to have a rotational schedule of team participants, mostly from the areas which will be implementing the change. Team members then retain their vitality and, despite the minor slowdown during transition periods, overall progress will move ahead more steadily.

The Role of Human Resources

Although line management must own any major change, and every employee must be involved, Human Resources needs to play a key role in any major change initiative. Human Resources is the in-house centre of expertise on human issues, and, as we have seen, it is the human dimension of change which so often confounds organizations. HR must be present throughout the Change Management process, but particularly in the crucial planning phases. HR's special contributions, which will be alluded to as well throughout the chapter, may be summarized in the following list of roles:

- leadership in the task of developing guiding principles for Change Management,
- expert advice in Change Management,
- expert advice in the principles of effective organization and job design.
- reworking of Human Resources processes to align them with required changes,
- development of internal resources capable of launching and supporting project teams.
- arrangement of specialized external resources to support project teams, and
- design or acquisition of practical tools for use by project teams and line managers (i.e., job role definition, task analysis, stakeholder analysis, and communications).

Communications and Consultation

Communication and Consultation practices help move the organization through both the *change* and the *transition* sides of Change Management. Table 1 outlines a progression of approaches for addressing first the *change* elements of a major organizational shift and then the *transition* requirements.

Table 1: Communication and Consultation Approaches

Level	Communication & Consultation Approaches	Activities and Methods
I	Share Information	Describe vision, plans and programs through one-way presentations: • Manager presentations; 'town hall' meetings • Video, newsletters
II	Gain Understanding	Discussions about the change through two-way dialogue: • Question and answer format from audience questions • Small group meetings with time to prepare questions • Facilitated questioning of subject matter experts

III	Develop Insight	Discussions about implications of the change: • Discussions with people implementing the change about the implications to self, customers and other groups • Meetings to review interaction points and to sort out what is changing
IV	Gain Commitment	Sorting through choices and reactions: • Iterative process of discussing options, approaches and feelings with others in a safe environment. This could be at staff meetings, with managers, alone. • Need to return to topics after reflection and consideration usually in interaction with manager and peers. • Moving from rejection or resistance to choosing to enter into the change process. This is supported by hearing that others are going through the same personally difficult transitions. • Consultation with representative stakeholders to provide input and validation of changes to process and practices to ensure performer requirements are addressed. Barriers to change are minimized and confidence in the integrity of the design process is maintained. • Agreement to changing expectations of job performance.
V	Shift Behaviour	Trying out new behaviours: • Through training or coaching, demonstrating new skills and building capability to perform against new expectations of the job or work environment. • Requires effective feedback mechanisms and coaching processes to ensure behaviours are maintaned over time. • Requires an environment in which the coaches themselves have transitioned through the change.

A successful change project will move beyond the newsletters and "town hall" meetings of Levels I and II to Levels III through V in which people can discuss and reflect on the implications of changes and develop concrete personal action plans. These interventions enable organizations to briskly move through the Productivity and Morale Impact Curve (Figure 1). Building an effective communication and consultation support system for a Change Management project includes:

- developing a set of guiding principles for communication and consultation for the project teams to follow,
- ensuring a structure is in place to support communication and consultation (i.e., a project team with an executive sponsor), and
- providing resources such as a realistic budget and capability to access the talent required to build effective communication and consultation plans and practices (i.e., internal experts or external consultants).

Human Resources is a vital resource for communications and consultation at every stage: designing vehicles of communication, engaging employees, making contact with external consultants, and providing training in new job functions.

The Goals of Change Management

Before going on to chart the specific stages of a Change Management initiative, we summarize here the goals which should motivate a Change Management Strategy. It should be noted that a strong emphasis is placed on "intangibles," the emotional side of a change process. Change Management seeks to build:

- **Commitment** to the vision, mission and strategy upon which plans are being built;
- **Confidence** that guiding principles, values and transition processes are being put into action and that they will result in fair and respectful treatment of people during the change;
- **Credibility** that the gain will be worth the pain, which requires an understanding of the strategies and plans that will become the framework for the new way of working and a highly visible management team ready to respond to the issues these changes will raise; and
- **Capability** so people can be competent in their changing roles, which requires significant investment in developing both management and employee capability and enabling information systems and support tools for enhanced performance.

WHAT ARE THE STEPS IN A MAJOR CHANGE PROCESS?

Figure 3 on the following page outlines some of the typical steps in a major change project. These steps can overlap or be returned to as information is gathered or actions are taken.

We will now outline the key steps in a major change initiative and some of the success factors and pitfalls to be aware of.

Step One: Identify the Project as a Strategic Initiative

The first step in any change process starts with identification of the major change as a strategic initiative by top management. For example, a shift in strategy, change in business model, introduction of an enabling technology or a merger or acquisition might represent a strategic initiative with Change Management implications.

Key Activities:

1. Strategically assess current reality:
   • Ensure the situation is assessed using data, not opinion.
   • Use external and internal benchmarks to build the case for change.
2. Agree on strategic options:
   • Explore known options.
   • Explore new approaches.
3. Agree to the need for change:
   • Each executive should feel a compelling need to make a major break from the current approach.
   • Select from the strategic options the ones which the executive are willing to consider and are the best match to vision, mission and strategy.

Success Factors

• Consensus in the executive boardroom of the strategy underpinning the change initiative.

• Compelling reasons to risk a change are fixed in each executive's mind.

Potential Pitfalls

- Complacency and locked-in mind-sets about how to run the business.
- Covert resistance from parties who will lose power as a result of the change.
- No powerful group of executives standing behind the initiative.

FIGURE 3: Steps in a Major Change Process

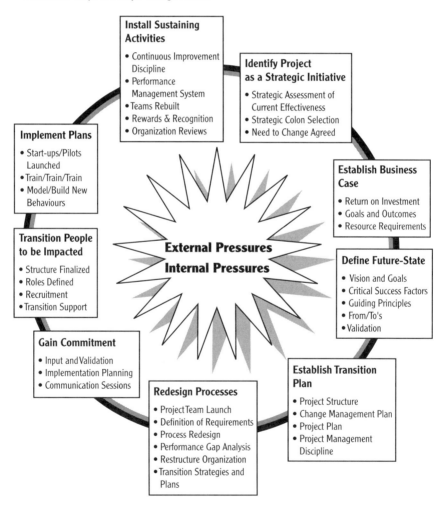

Install Sustaining Activities
- Continuous Improvement Discipline
- Performance Management System
- Teams Rebuilt
- Rewards & Recognition
- Organization Reviews

Identify Project as a Strategic Initiative
- Strategic Assessment of Current Effectiveness
- Strategic Colon Selection
- Need to Change Agreed

Implement Plans
- Start-ups/Pilots Launched
- Train/Train/Train
- Model/Build New Behaviours

Establish Business Case
- Return on Investment
- Goals and Outcomes
- Resource Requirements

Transition People to be Impacted
- Structure Finalized
- Roles Defined
- Recruitment
- Transition Support

External Pressures
Internal Pressures

Define Future-State
- Vision and Goals
- Critical Success Factors
- Guiding Principles
- From/To's
- Validation

Gain Commitment
- Input and Validation
- Implementation Planning
- Communication Sessions

Establish Transition Plan
- Project Structure
- Change Management Plan
- Project Plan
- Project Management Discipline

Redesign Processes
- Project Team Launch
- Definition of Requirements
- Process Redesign
- Performance Gap Analysis
- Restructure Organization
- Transition Strategies and Plans

Step Two: Establish the Business Case

Once the option has been selected, a business case is usually required to establish the expected return on investment. From a Change Management perspective, this is the critical point at which the executive team must be highly engaged in determining whether the "gain will be worth the pain." No executive is willing to risk the organization's health on a potential disruption without adequate return on investment. Human Resources consultation is a crucial source of expertise in the impact assessment for hiring, or training compensation and other enabling processes.

Key Activities:

1. Define the return on investment anticipated from the change.

2. Establish goals and outcomes expected.

3. Determine the resource commitment required.

Success Factors

- Engagement of the minds of all of the executive in assessing the business case.

- Goals and outcomes are clearly defined and resource commitments bought into.

Potential Pitfalls

- Early fears about business disruption eliminate consideration of a major change.

- Allocation of top talent to the needs of the project is not supported.

Step Three: Define the Future State

Once the executive has agreed to the need for change and the strategic option to be selected, it is time to outline the future state anticipated from the change. The executive or top management team generates a description of the future state. Human Resources is usually a key source of expertise in formulating the guiding principles for Change Management (of point 3 below).

Key Activities:

1. Establish future-state vision and goals.

2. Identify critical success factors, for example:
   - "Return on capital employed increased to meet industry standard."
   - "Qualified, motivated and capable franchisees ready for assignment to new locations."

3. Define guiding principles for managing the change. Here is an example from a major pharmaceutical company during an initiative to revamp a core business process:
   - "Ensure employees receive in a timely manner, the necessary information, tools and training to be well-positioned during the change transition".

4. Define what the organization must move "From and To":
   - For each of the major components of the major change, define what the organization must transition "From and To." As an activity, this can unlock old paradigm thinking and generate consensus on major shifts in accountabilities, authorities, values, behaviours and so on.
   - This should be considered a first, high-level view of how things will be different in the end. It should not determine how things will work, but instead what will be at the end of the change. Two examples from organizations who launched major shifts in their businesses are:
   "From: Functional 'tribes' to total customer service process focus.
   "From: Custom product offering to 'Heart of the Market' menu of products."

5. Consult and gain support from key stakeholders.
   - Engage stakeholders in the process itself, either by involving representatives in the activities or by taking the future-state outline to them for input.

Success Factors

- Agreement about what will stop, start and continue in the future-state.
- Involvement of key customers, suppliers and visionary thinkers in articulation of the vision.
- Involvement of stakeholders not married to past practices or power structures.
- Critical mass of supporters extends now from executive boardroom to the senior/middle management levels.

Potential Pitfalls

- Thinking locked in the successes of the past. No sense of urgency to change.
- Future-state definition raises concerns early in the process which activates resistance from stakeholders.
- Organizational 'sacred cows' not addressed.
- Fuzzy vision.

Step Four: Establish a Transition Plan

The next step is to develop a "doable" transition plan which includes Change Management and transition strategies and tactics. Human Resources acts at this point specifically as an internal centre of expertise on Change Management, but accountability rests with senior management, project teams, and line management.

Key Activities:

1. Establish a project structure that includes accountability for Change Management:
   - Hold three groups accountable for Change Management:
     - **Executive Sponsor**: Accountable to ensure needs are assessed and actions taken to minimize the impact of change on the organization and its people. Usually also accountable for delivering the goals of the overall project.

- **Project Team Leaders**: Accountable for integrating into their project plans specific Change Management and transition strategies and tactics.
  - **Line Management**: Accountable for ensuring effective Change Management and transition management in their areas of responsibility.
- Identify resources which the project team(s) can tap into for Change Management expertise.
  - Organizational Development/Human Resources/Training resources from inside the organization; and
  - External consultants, as necessary, who have proven experience and expertise in large-scale Change Management.

2. Develop a Change Management plan which includes:
   - A change capability assessment of how expert the organization is at managing organizational change and what needs to be done to address any change capability issues.
   - A stakeholder analysis to assess the impact and anticipated reactions of stakeholders and to put in place strategies to protect the success of the project and to assist stakeholders in transitioning through the change.
   - Change Management levers to be utilized. For example:
     - communications processes
     - consultation processes
     - capability development/training
     - leadership initiatives
     - transition support such as Change Management workshops for employees
     - selection and job assignment processes
     - job role definition and competency assessment processes
     - enabling technologies (i.e., use of video conferencing)
     - breadth of roll-out (all or parts of the organization);
     - a "rolling forward" view of the critical path. (Beware of a fixed completion time).

3. Develop a project plan and project management disciplines which include processes for:
   - tracking progress to plan,
   - orienting new team members, and
   - issue raising and issue resolution.

Success Factors

- The Change Management plan sets direction for teams who then integrate specific tactics into their plans.
- Proactive stakeholder assessments identify potential blocks and resistance areas and positive plans of action are put in place to manage the issues.

Potential Pitfalls

- The project management discipline fails to bring teams together regularly to understand what each group is working on resulting in lack of alignment, duplication of effort or rework.
- Starting from stratch rather than learning best practices from the industry, other parts of the organization or its partners.

Step Five: Redesign Processes

Teams at this point need to be launched and held accountable for developing the systems, processes and work procedures required to bring about the future state. There are usually two types of teams: a steering team of sponsors and accountable executive, and project teams responsible for execution of the overall project plan. Human Resources expertise must be drawn on throughout Step 5 as job functions are redefined and support documentation and tools are developed, as training programs are planned, and as job realignment makes provision for career planning and job reassignments necessary.

Key Activities:

1. Launch project teams.
   - This includes ensuring they have a clearly defined mandate, mission, goals and project deliverables.
   - Usually, a one- to two-day working session to launch each team is required. This upfront investment in getting organized saves time in the long run. HR can play a key role in this.

- The team needs to be staffed with the right skills: functional talents required, innovative thinkers, mix of experience levels, etc.

2. Define requirements.
    - Each team needs to define the requirements from the viewpoint of the vision, taking into consideration end-user needs.

3. Redesign processes. Teams must then redesign the way work gets done.
    - Process maps are helpful tools to enable people to see the new way work will get done.
    - The development of interface agreements between hand-off points in the process is also effective. These are agreements which define logistically how interactions will take place and what the agreed performance level/quality will be.
    - Procedures need to be written out and provided to performers. Most helpful are job aids and tools which can be handy reference materials during the transition period. This may require the development of new reference manuals.

4. Assess performance gaps.
    - Assess capability of performers to conduct changed processes and procedures at the performance levels required.
    - Define training needs. Pinpointing specific operational training needs and addressing them in a timely fashion is often one of the critical success factors of a major change initiative.

5. Restructure organization. Once the processes have been designed which will deliver the major change, the organization can then be realigned to ensure efficient delivery of the processes.
    - Organizational structure changes are more than just changing the boxes on the organization chart. They require an understanding of where authority and accountability will reside for particular activities.
    - Since changes in structure shift power in an organization, significant barriers to making important organizational changes can arise. External consultants who can knowledgeably assist in designing the organization and handling internal positioning and conflicts can be of value.

6. Develop transition strategies and plans.
   - Plan for transfer of responsibilities from project teams to line management.
   - Plan for selection and placement of employees.

Success Factors

- Top talent is allocated to the teams.
- Common tools and techniques are in place, such as process mapping, job role definition methodologies.
- The conflict between "do it right" and "do it fast" is managed effectively.
- Breakthrough thinking is supported by external benchmarking and visits.
- How interfaces or interactions between groups will now work is reviewed and agreed.

Potential Pitfalls

- Trying to fix everything at once.
- Politics become more important than progress.
- Powerful allies elsewhere in the organization intervene to support units which may be impacted.
- Lack of engagement of "field employees" reduces their feeling of ownership of the change.
- Unresolved conflicts about process changes.

Step Six: Gain Commitment

It is vital that key stakeholders in the organization feel part of the design process for the change. Certainly this is a challenge in large organizations. Building commitment depends on the organization asking for and listening to input, and considering and acting upon the needs and ideas contributed. Human Resources is a logical partner for structuring a system of consultation and recording its results.

Key Activities:

1. Utilize input and validation activities, for example:
   * interviews and surveys,
   * focus groups for specific issues,
   * stakeholder panels for input and validation at regular intervals, and
   * interactive workshops.

2. Design implementation plans with stakeholders:
   * to be developed by line managers for their areas.

3. Hold frequent communications sessions:
   * frequent sessions with leadership teams about changes and implementation plans, and
   * meetings with senior management to raise issues and concerns.

Success Factors

* Opinion leaders positively influenced.
* Rumours managed.
* Attrition anticipated.
* Few surprises for employees.
* Visible symbols that there is no turning back.

Potential Pitfalls

* Powerful groups reject changes due to lack of consultation.
* Too little time to adjust.
* Existing mental models and assumptions are not shifting closer to those required for success in the new way of doing things.

Step Seven: Transition People to be Impacted

Once the process has been defined, attention needs to focus on the performers and the infrastructure they require for successful performance of their roles in the new environment. Human Resources is likely to be consulted both in training line managers to support employees through the transition, and also to set up counselling and retraining for employees affected by the change.

Key Activities:

1. Finalize structural changes.
   - Align organization with design principles (i.e., along processes, market segments).

2. Define roles and performance standards.
   - Develop a tool kit of templates, either paper-based or on-line, to support consistent, effective descriptions of changing roles and standards.

3. Recruit or reassign people to roles.
   - Determine how people will be allocated to roles, taking into consideration the productivity hit resulting from change, balanced by the need to ensure performers with the right skills are assigned to roles.

4. Implement transition support. Support may be required at any point from the announcement of the changes to occur through implementation. It may take many forms such as:
   - Transition workshops with small groups of employees to work through the implications of the change and how people feel about it.
   - Confidential Employee Assistance Programs for one-on-one counseling.
   - Coaching by the manager.

Success Factors

- Employees understand new job expectations.
- People feel selection processes are fair.
- Transition support is trusted as confidential.

Potential Pitfalls

- Managers are not ready or prepared to help employees work through the transition.
- Change is viewed as an event, rather than a process, resulting in insufficient coaching and support systems.

Step Eight: Implement Plans

Finally, the plan must now be executed. Although accountability for implementation rests with management, Human Resources is key because of the crucial importance of addressing the people issues behind the business and organization changes.

Key Activities

1. Launch start-ups/pilots.
   - Make progress visible.
   - Communicate and celebrate early wins and successes.
   - Stage implementation so resources can be allocated to support problem areas and unknown issues that may arise.
   - Ensure adequate support systems are in place such as hotlines, support desks, Employee Assistance Programs, etc.

2. Provide training, training and more training to build capability and confidence.
   - Build competency while overcoming objections and concerns.
   - Deliberately mix participants to influence slow adapters and fence-sitters.
   - Focus on clarifying new job requirements/behaviours.
   - Build capability through role modeling and coaching by leaders.

Success Factors

- Leadership is visible and hands-on during implementation. Leaders role model the change.
- Sponsors remain confident that new processes will work. They support minor adjustments but resist attempts to derail implementation.
- Designers of the work processes and procedures are actively involved in training and implementation.
- Response to implementation issues is rapid.

Potential Pitfalls

- Problems early in implementation as seen as major setbacks. The new processes and the people who designed them are challenged.

- Leaders fail to learn the new processes in sufficient detail to deal with issues as they arise.
- Too much work for too few people.
- The emotional side of transition is not addressed and the rumour mill is not managed.
- Leaders discount implementation issues and needs of people in the field.

Step Nine: Install Sustaining Activities

As line management implements the change, the leadership team, as well as a core group from the original project teams, should be building the infrastructure of processes and practices which will sustain the desired behaviours over time.

Key Activities:

1. Establish a discipline for continuous process improvement.
2. Refine the performance management system:
   - Ensure there is "no place to hide." Measure progress.
   - Build feedback systems to provide timely and accurate feedback on performance at the organizational and the individual level.
   - Keep external benchmarks highly visible to maintain focus on the continuous improvements and innovations required for competitive success.
3. Rebuild management and work teams.
   - Rebuild teamwork and trust.
   - Focus accountability.
   - Build the means to hold each other accountable.
4. Establish rewards/recognition processes.
   - Plan for celebrations of individual, team and organizational success.
5. Install organizational reviews to assess progress of:
   - Outcomes against goals of the change initiative.
   - People capability compared to organizational needs.

Success Factors

- Top talent is retained to develop sustaining systems.
- Measurement and feedback systems ensure everyone knows how organizational and individual performance is progressing. There is "no place to hide."
- Celebrations recognize group and individual successes.

Potential Pitfalls

- Sponsors retreat too early, thinking all the work is done.
- People are rewarded the old way.
- They declare victory too soon.
- Failure to recognize that a relapse to "old ways" is predictable and needs to be anticipated and managed.

How Much Time Should be Allocated to Change Management Activities?

It is difficult to assess how much time any one step may take in a complex change, but experience has demonstrated some rules of the thumb about the proportion of time to be allocated to specific stages of a major change project. Table 2 outlines a schedule based on experience in large organizations. It is important that sufficient time be allocated to Steps 5 through 9.

Table 2: Time Allotment for Change Process

Steps		Time Allocation
1.	Identify Project as a Strategic Initiative	25%
2.	Establish Business Case	
3.	Define Future State	
4.	Develop Transition Plan	
5.	Redesign Processes	60%
6.	Gain Commitment	
7.	Transition People	
8.	Implement Plans	
9.	Install Sustaining Activities	15%

CONCLUSION

We hear a good deal today about "managing for change," but many ineffective techniques are still being applied with disastrous results to organizations in transition. Effective Change Management practices bring all members of an organization into partnership. The stakeholders must be involved from planning through sustainment if a change initiative is to succeed. Accountability must rest with management of affected operations, senior management, and the project teams that direct the change process.

Where does this leave Human Resources? Theoreticians and practitioners have determined HR should be in the role of expert consultant to management on all people dimensions of an organizational change. Since it is the human, emotional side of change which has so often been neglected in past programs for change, with disastrous consequences, HR is clearly a centre for knowledge and skills which must be drawn on as a part of effective Change Management.

CHAPTER EIGHT

Changing and Re-Engineering the Information Systems Function at Nortel

AN HR CASE STUDY

Margaret Butteriss with material from
Jane Graydon, Senior Manager, Change Management

A RECENT SUCCESSFUL restructuring of the Information Systems (I/S) function at Canadian telecommunications giant Northern Telecom Inc. (Nortel) provides an excellent case study of the important role new Human Resources theories and practices can play in change management. Through material provided by former Nortel Human Resources professional Jane Graydon, who acted as Change Agent in the re-engineering process, we have an insider's perspective on the process from conception to assessment.

Analysis of the Nortel experience confirms one of the key points made by Sherrill Burns in her chapter on "Change Management": effective communication with all stakeholders at every step is essential for successful organizational change. In addition, it reflects another key principle of HR theory, that HR and line management must co-operate when addressing the human implications of change in organizational structure, with HR conceived of primarily as a source of expertise being consulted by line management. The relationship between the Project Director and the Change Agent in Nortel's I/S restructuring provides an opportunity to study this interaction.

SETTING THE STAGE: NORTEL IN 1995-1996

Nortel designs, manufactures, and supplies a breadth of products for digital networks of all kinds. Its customers are local and long-distance telecommunications companies, cellular mobile radio and personal communications services providers, businesses, universities, governments, access providers, and other network operators around the world. Nortel is recognized in the industry for its breadth of products, global presence, and leadership in designing, building, and integrating digital networks. In 1996 the company employed more than 66,000 people worldwide and had revenues of US $12.8 billion.

Nortel's Explosive Growth

Although its roots go back all the way to Alexander Graham Bell's first Canadian patent, the modern Nortel began to take shape in 1972 when the company put its first electronic switch on the market. An all-digital switch followed, which was used in small central offices beginning in 1977 and two years later by large central offices.

In a few bold strokes, the company leapfrogged over its competition. The development of the DMS-100 digital central office switch, combined with the break-up of AT&T and the formation of the regional Bell holding companies in the U.S. in 1984, resulted in explosive growth through the rest of the 1980s.

The rapid growth in the United States became a model for further expansion in the Caribbean, Europe, and the Pacific Rim. During the early 1990s, the telecommunications industry faced challenges from the increasing convergence of telecommunications, cable and computer technologies. At the same time, telecommunications was becoming a deregulated, multi-vendor competitive industry. Faced with such challenges, Nortel began to position itself as a provider of network solutions to customers who required integrated network solutions and services to meet their business needs.

The 1995 Transformation of Nortel

By the mid-1990s the company was also becoming an increasingly large player in the global marketplace; for example, in 1996 nearly 40% of revenues came from outside North America. With customers in many countries, Nortel formed joint ventures and strategic alliances with companies in many parts of the world. Senior managers realized that they would have to fundamentally change the way the company did business. It would have to move from being a product-focused organization to one that was more customer-focused. The company organized itself into four network businesses—**Nortel Broadband Networks, Enterprise Networks, Public Carrier Networks, and Wireless Networks**—with support services provided by Nortel Technology.

In 1995, "A World of Networks" was adopted as the company's vision for the future of telecommunications, and a new logo—Nortel—was adopted as a symbol of the company's new direction and organization.

Nortel further refined its business model in 1995 and early 1996. Product and customer accountability was still to be the responsibility of the network businesses, but they would share common processes. Key processes to be shared included market order management, order delivery, global logistics, integrated product introduction, sales and marketing, and a number of corporate services, including Human Resources and Finance. These processes were deemed to need significant restructuring. The company created process owners for each of the processes that were to be re-engineered, and set up other support mechanisms to help these owners succeed. These included the Operations Council, which was chaired by the COO, and the Corporate Process Council, chaired by the CEO. Each of these councils included members from each of the network businesses, and Information Systems (I/S) played an active role in them.

The Information Systems (I/S) Function in 1995

Prior to 1990, I/S was seen as a support function, and a small corporate staff reported together with Finance and Human Resources to an Executive Vice-President. The rest of I/S was highly decentralized, with small groups being located in each business division. These small groups developed systems which were fragmented subject to frequent changes, and costly to support.

In 1990 the various I/S groups began to report to a Chief Information Officer, although there was central funding of the function, but I/S was structured according to line of business and location. This created a high demand for support, which I/S was unable to meet. Some business units created their own I/S organizations, which meant that there was little rationalization and integration of systems and processes.

When the general 1995 reworking of Nortel's divisonal structure moved financial responsibility for I/S back to the business unit level, I/S was faced with a serious image problem. It was widely regarded as only a support function, and one which had proved itself unable to meet the needs of the business in a timely and cost-effective manner.

Despite its poor reputation, I/S was judged by senior management to have the technical expertise required to create the common processes needed to support "A World of Networks" vision. A new head of I/S, Keith Powell, was appointed and given the title of Chief Information Officer and Vice-President Process Engineering.

RE-INVENTING I/S

Powell, a long-time Nortel employee who had worked on the business side of Nortel in manufacturing and materials, realized that I/S would have to reinvent itself: it had to become more integrated and more business-focused. It would also have to improve its credibility if it was to work in partnership with its clients to design new processes and provide the leadership required for the processes to be adopted. He appointed Brad Taylor as Program Director of Reinventing Information Systems (RIS) in July 1995. Brad had worked in several technical and management positions at Nortel since 1984, all relating to the company's global information systems and infrastructure.

In addition, Jane Graydon was appointed as the Change Agent for I/S in late 1995 to assist Powell and Taylor with implementing the required organization changes as they moved from functional silos to client-centred organization . She had previously worked in the Human Resource Development department of Nortel and had the facilitation skills that were required to assist the management team and employees in the change process.

With the Program Director and Change Agent both appointed, the time had come for designing a model for the new I/S. Before going on to describe the design process, we note here that corporate HR played virtually no role in identifying the need for re-engineering I/S or in defining a method for the re-engineering. Nortel did call on HR to supply an expert consultant to act as a change agent who would assist in communicating the process once it is was defined. In addition, although it was recognized from the outset that the restructuring should focus on systems and people, there was a growing realization of the importance of addressing human and cultural issues, and a corresponding attention to the role of the Change Agent.

A key decision made by Powell and Taylor was to use the techniques of business process re-engineering (BPR). This approach to organizational restructuring was developed by Michael Hammer and James Champy and described in their 1993 book, *Reengineering the Corporation* [New York: Harper Business, HarperCollins, 1993]. Hammer and Champy recommend a radical rethinking of every aspect of a company's operations as a necessary prelude to changing any individual component of the operation (cf. Geary Rummler and Alan Brache, *Improving Performance* [San Francisco: Jossey-Bass, 1995]. Several key I/S managers were trained in BPR prior to the beginning of the design phase.

The Design Phase

Planning and design was conducted by eight design teams made up of key stakeholders and I/S staff. Each team had a director, some full-time members, and a BPR practitioner. The teams began by benchmarking other organizations and reviewing industry best practices.

Based on the work of the design teams, a new model for I/S was developed which identified three key processes:

• client management,

• solutions delivery, and

• business support.

Client Management was to focus on determining what clients needed from I/S . This process was to be based on four design principles:

• dedication to client success,

• in-depth knowledge and understanding of the client's business,

• relationship building, and

• knowledge of how processes and technology could be leveraged to achieve significant business results.

Client management was to be separated from solutions delivery, and the role was to be similar to that of a client manager in a consulting firm. Client satisfaction and perceived client value were to be used as measures to evaluate performance.

Solutions Delivery was to focus on the creation and modification of systems to meet business requirements. The four design principles were:

- developing processes that could be repeated and used in other parts of the business, rather than starting from scratch each time a new process was required,

- looking for opportunities to reuse whole or parts of applications,

- developing standard tools, techniques, and technologies, and

- developing a flexible workforce whose members were assigned to projects based on business needs and career interests.

The plan was to move away from designing everything from scratch toward buying off-the-shelf solutions. Performance measures to be used were overall client satisfaction, delivery satisfaction, time to market, and competitive benchmarking.

Business Support was to focus on looking after clients' needs in relation to delivered products. The design principles were:

- clear service level agreements, and

- creating a call centre approach which was used in a disciplined manner. If a complaint had to be escalated to more senior levels, there was to be a clear process and procedure on how to handle these complaints.

These three main processes were to be supported by four enabling mechanisms:

- **financial management**, responsible for charging out the service of I/S;

- **resource management**, responsible for staffing the various project teams and ensuring that I/S staff are fully utilized and charged out;

- **vendor management**, responsible for managing external suppliers; and

- **infrastructure and process management**, responsible for BPR tools and methods, technology and research and the development of architectures

The Implementation Phase

Brad Taylor recognized that implementing the three key processes would be extremely difficult. Although meetings between the senior management and the I/S staff had begun to change the attitudes of many of the I/S employees, I/S people still sat in the various network businesses, and some only paid lip service to the change. In addition, there was not a tradition of working together. Furthermore, if implementation teams were set up that were not responsible for the results and did not have to live with them, they were not likely to have much commitment to making changes.

In March 1996, Taylor decided he would have to develop a new structure for I/S. This would show that Nortel was serious about change, and I/S would begin to accept ownership for the change.

In 1996, Nortel I/S employed 1,700 people in 40 locations around the world. The I/S people in the North American businesses were pulled together from all the various network businesses to create a centralized internal consulting group to provide I/S services. The new organization had three prime functions, based on the key processes that had been developed in the design phase:

- client management,
- solutions delivery, and
- business support.

Client Management is provided by a team of senior managers who work with the various network businesses in a client management and sales function role. They help the leaders of the corporation determine how information technology can advance their business. They then identify what information systems support is required to help them deliver on solutions for their various external customers.

Solutions Delivery: Once the client manager has determined the need for a product or service, the solutions delivery organization teams set up appropriate project teams to deliver the required solution. These teams are staffed with people who have the required skills and expertise to deliver that particular project. In some cases, the solution may be reused from another network business, bought off the shelf from an external vendor, or developed from scratch by the project team. Solutions delivery teams deploy the solution and provide the required training.

Business Support: Once the system is in place, it is maintained on an ongoing basis by the support function. As noted earlier, enabling functions were set up to take care of financial management, resource management, vendor management and infrastructure and process management.

Changing the Culture

Moving I/S people from the various network businesses where they had performed multi-functional and largely technical roles to business-focused consulting groups was not the end of the restructuring. For the new organization to work, Taylor knew a fundamental change of culture was necessary. Not everybody was happy with the change in I/S since it involved the creation of new roles and for employees with the duty of developing new ways of doing business.

There was significant need for explanations of why the new organization had been created, what its purpose was, and how it would help the business as a whole become more effective. Employees needed to understand their roles and responsibilities, as well as learn the performance standards associated with their role. It was also important to understand where there was resistance to change, and to be able to set up ways to overcome this.

During the planning and design phase, Powell and Taylor had already worked hard to communicate the changes to the whole of Nortel and to develop commitment to the changes. During implementation, the CIO sent monthly updates to all I/S employees. Then the next level of senior I/S management travelled across North America, conducting dialogue sessions with small groups of I/S employees. They also received feedback on the proposed changes. These sessions proved to be invaluable: they elicited ideas that were acted upon and made the change in relation to business needs even stronger.

The Change Agent's role was to help design and facilitate the communication and the training sessions held for managers during implementation. These were run to prepare the managers for team sessions they would hold, describing where and what the changes were and what their role was to be in the new function. Graydon also helped design all the other communication and strategy planning sessions held throughout the I/S organization.

Communications tools were created to enable I/S staff to understand the organization and feel part of the team, even when they are situated in many different geographical locations. They include:

- a learning map, a visual representation of the process of change, which was used by managers in training sessions;

- an Internet home page that links all the I/S groups throughout the organization, and includes interactive forums where employees can ask questions and express opinions; the I/S Webpage also has a biweekly employee poll which takes a quick employee pulse on topical issues and concerns;

- a Web-based newsletter which provides in-depth reporting on key areas and issues;

- quarterly, global town hall meetings are held by means of audio conference facilities at which all I/S groups are given information and can ask questions on any kinds of issues; and

- an award of merit employee team, which is responsible for giving out quarterly awards to employees in I/S who deserve special recognition.

Results of the Reinvention

The change was implemented without any lay-offs of I/S people. The business requirements of I/S have grown since the change, so the company was able to incorporate all the existing people into the various initiatives in one form or another. Equally, they have provided a great deal of training to their staff in order to develop new skills and competencies to support the new business.

The success of the I/S restructing in North American organization has prompted Nortel to apply the model to its global I/S organization. Thus, the Information Systems group is responsible for I/S initiatives throughout the whole of Nortel.

I/S has produced a Change Management Website in order to share their best practices with other Nortel groups that are going through changes. It also shows how they have handled issues of employee satisfaction and customer satisfaction.

Employee Satisfaction and Customer Satisfaction in Nortel

It is important to note that Nortel as a whole attributes tremendous importance to employee satisfaction and customer satisfaction metrics. The company has statistical evidence that there is a direct link between customer satisfaction and employee satisfaction. Satisfied employees are more willing and motivated to ensure that their customers are satisfied.

Both annual customer satisfaction and employee satisfaction surveys are conducted, and the results are built into individual managers' performance appraisals. Each manager is expected to act on the key issues and customer satisfaction that have been raised in any given year. The employee satisfaction surveys are completed in October, and results are presented to the total company, and each business and team, in November. The key initiatives that need to be worked on are identified in January, and by February managers are able to set up teams and begin work on the various initiatives.

Employee Satisfaction Teams

In I/S itself, a global Employee Satisfaction Team (ESAT) was set up to address the common priority issues identified in the latest survey. In some areas, local ESATs deal with local facility equipment issues, local community-building events, and case development; however, there are some global representatives on the local ESAT teams to ensure that there is an integration of all issues across I/S.

Each manager is responsible for aligning objectives with the business direction of I/S, and the total corporation is responsible for its own objective alignment and improving employee satisfaction. However, it was felt that if action planning around employee satisfaction was left to each manager, there would be a heavy concentration on local issues and a great deal of redundancy and overlap. Instead, I/S wanted to integrate the initiatives to prevent redundancy, and use the integration as a way to further cement the notion of a professional global I/S organization. To do this I/S has created cross-functional ESATs consisting of employees who can identify issues and ensure that they are addressed. The Change Agent's role is to integrate the work of all the teams and pull the employee satisfaction initiatives together.

Membership of the Cross-Functional Employee Satisfaction Teams

Member of the cross-functional employee satisfaction teams are initially selected by their manager, based usually on the fact that these people are informal opinion leaders. After being appointed, each team member is responsible for nominating a suitable replacement at the end of his/her term. Members of the teams are expected to have demonstrated the following competencies:

- strong customer orientation,
- applied creativity,
- ability to build trust,
- ability to develop others,
- high levels of initiative,
- ability to build relationships, and
- team leadership.

Tenure on the teams is for a minimum of nine months and a maximum of eighteen months. Membership is on a part-time basis, since it was felt that members need to keep in touch with their project groups and know what the current issues are. ESAT members are responsible for analyzing the results of the employee surveys, proposing and implementing actions, and tracking and communicating progress.

Membership on the employee satisfaction team provides an opportunity for members to learn and to develop themselves throughout the process by learning about project management, team building, communications, and other related skills.

I/S Employee Satisfaction Team Initiatives

Examples of initiatives that are currently being worked on by I/S ESATs are:

- creating career development paths and processes for I/S professionals,
- implementing upward feedback processes that help to develop leadership competence in I/S,
- identifying and addressing key desktop technology issues that prevent employees of Nortel from doing their jobs effectively, and

• implementing a compensation strategy to support the current I/S function.

Assessing the Re-engineering Process

When Jane Graydon, the Change Agent, was asked about I/S performance since the re-engineering process was initiated, she named four key changes. These were:

• **Improved client satisfaction and employee satisfaction**: Both client satisfaction with I/S services and I/S employee satisfaction improved significantly on the annual surveys. Employee satisfaction improved 3% each year during the two years of the transition. This is significant since a drop of 10% was expected due to the increased turmoil and levels of uncertainty among employees.

• **Improved ability to manage client commitment and investments**: Prior to the change it was difficult to assess the level of investment in information technology, because there was no consistent terminology in use and no clear measurement tools. I/S has developed a client investment portfolio approach which allows for a forecast of annual investments and allocation to specific projects. I/S is also able to forecast and track investment at the specific phases of a project and can provide skills to enable their client to implement their projects.

• **Improved efficiency through implementation of common processes and tools**: Prior to the change there were twenty or so processes relating to Information Systems that were muddled and ill-defined. For instance, clients contacted call centres for help. It was unclear to the client whether to call the global call centre or the local centre. Different levels of help were available from these different centres, and there were no clearly defined, common timelines for resolving client issues and problems.

I/S has now defined what the various processes are, what to expect and have defined clear measurements for service. Such measures have been defined by site and business unit.

• **Increased flexibility and ability to quickly adapt to changing business priorities**: Increased flexibility has come from defining processes, procedures and systems. By having this type of information relating to all the businesses, the I/S function is able to adapt to new situations quickly, since I/S has access to all the information they required about businesses before it starts a project. I/S can provide help and support more effectively and much more quickly.

Since all employees have been centralized in a resource pool, I/S can quickly provide resources with the right skills to support a new project or business requirement, such as joint ventures. Equally it can reassign resources as projects wind down.

Helps to Re-engineering

Jane Graydon identified the two factors which helped change the culture. First, CIO Keith Powell was unwavering in his focus and vision for the I/S function. He showed that he was willing to do what was needed to reshape the culture and that he was going to manage the short-term pain for the long-term gain. The vision and direction for the function was maintained, in spite of the many changes that have taken place in the business as a whole.

Second, Nortel has a base culture of continual change, which has given employees resilience and commitment to change, whereas in other organizations there may well have been more resistance than was encountered in Nortel. The employees generally understand the relationship between the need for change and the requirement to stay ahead in the global marketplace in a very competitive business.

Hindrances to Re-engineering

Graydon noted three hindrances to the change process:

- Even though employees were generally capable of dealing with change, some were cynical about this change. There had been some failures in the past in this organization and some saw this initiative as "the flavour of the month" that would soon go away.

- There was some lack of trust of management on the part of some employees. They were afraid that re-engineering really meant restructuring and downsizing. Thus they were afraid that they would lose their jobs, and that the function would be outsourced.

- Nortel operates in many different geographical locations, which makes it difficult to communicate with people in different time zones and with different cultures and ways of seeing the world. Also

the cost structures around systems and people costs vary significantly throughout the company, and this has caused change to take
longer in some parts of the world than others.

What Could Have Been Done Differently?

Graydon identified two areas which she felt could have been helped by
a different approach.

First, there was a need for more engagement of the managers as
advocates of the change. There was too much reliance on direct CIO
communications with employees, which was one of the main lines of
contact during the transition. The CIO addressed employees in memos,
open forums and town hall meetings. Employees were very pleased, but
some middle management felt left out of the process. Also, the communications tended to be at a strategic level and did not cover specific
issues on how the change would take place. This specific information
needed middle management involvement.

Second, it would have been helpful to better manage the expectations of employees on the timing of the implementation. The implementation took much longer than expected, because so many
processes and roles had to be redefined. I/S will undoubtedly benefit
from this experience in the future and will know how to change the timing focus.

SUMMARY

This case study shows how the Information Systems function of Nortel
successfully transformed itself to better meet the needs of its customers
and employees. It also illustrates the importance of communications,
and of securing involvement of all stakeholders in the change process.

CHAPTER NINE

Building Teamwork in a Unionized Workplace

A CASE STUDY OF CHANGE AT NORANDA INC.'S CCR REFINERY

Margaret Butteriss

BETWEEN 1991 AND 1997, Noranda Inc.'s CCR Refinery, a unionized copper-refining facility in Montreal East, underwent a very successful reorganization: over a five-year period accidents causing loss of work time were down 55%, productivity was up 50%, costs dropped 16%, and in-process inventories were down by 21%. A study of CCR's years of change shows that improved results were due in large measure to a new corporate culture founded on a relationship of trust between management and all employees, both unionized and salaried. Key to this new culture was involvement of all plant personnel in the design and implementation of new methods, and the use of teams made up of representatives of all groups to plan and institute changes. Human Resources professionals, both from the internal department and from external consulting firms, also played a central role in change at CCR.

The material for this chapter comes from interviews with **Steve Heddle**, President of Noranda Aluminum Inc. and former general manager of CCR; **Yves Meunier**, President of the United Steelworkers of America local at CCR; and **Bruce Hamilton**, director of Labour Relations, Noranda Metallurgy Inc., who was manager of Human Resources at CCR.

NORANDA INC.'S CCR REFINERY IN 1991: THE NEED FOR CHANGE

Noranda Inc. is a diversified natural resources company that operates in three sectors—mining and metals, forest products, and oil and gas. It employs 33,000 people and, in 1996, had total assets of $15 billion. Eighty per cent of its products are sold in markets outside Canada.

Noranda's mining and metals sector, with 21,000 employees and a worldwide network of offices and facilities, is one of the world's largest producers of zinc and nickel; a significant producer of primary and fabricated aluminum, copper, lead, sulphuric acid, gold, silver, cobalt, and wire rope; and a major recycler of secondary copper, nickel, and precious metals. It operates 22 mines, 13 metallurgical plants and 12 fabricating facilities, including CCR Refinery in Montreal East.

The CCR Refinery produces an average of 350,000 metric tons of copper annually, a million ounces of gold, thirty million ounces of silver, and smaller amount of selenium and tellurium. In 1995, the refinery was the fourth largest producer of copper in the world. At the end of 1996, there were 830 employees, with 630 represented by the United Steelworkers of America.

CCR was built in 1931, and over the course of the next forty-five years the original design was copied on a bay-by-bay basis. It still runs largely on the original refining technology, despite significant technological change and investments over the years, including modernization in the precious metals area and installation of a new materials handling process. It is still a very labour-intensive facility by world standards.

First Attempts to Lower Costs and Increase Productivity

Labour costs have always been high and continue to represent at least 50% of operating costs. Traditional management style began to loosen up in the 1980s, but labour relations remained difficult and strikes took place in 1982 and 1986.

Bruce Hamilton says, "I remember my first week at the plant. I wanted to telephone the union president and couldn't find his number on the list. He's not on the telephone list, I was told and that's company policy. I asked why. If his number is on the list, people will phone him, was the answer. I said, well that might not be such a bad idea. Anyway, we fixed that." At the time, this type of climate was not atypical for the industry.

Until the 1980s, profits came easily because of company ownership of the copper supply. As a result, there was no incentive to invest in either people or technology. In the mid-1980s, however, the price of copper declined dramatically, putting the business at some risk given the high cost of refining. Benchmarking exercises demonstrated that significant cost reductions and productivity gains would be necessary to remain competitive.

Quality Improvement Process

In order to address these issues, a quality improvement process was implemented, and the number of layers of supervisors was reduced from seven to four. The process had only passive union involvement, but began to build a common CCR 2000 working language for everyone in the plant.

By the end of the '90s, the company realized that to be successful it had to make investments in both technology and people. It launched CCR 2000, " an investment program which spent $40 million, mainly in material handling and process control. Management then focused more fully on the people side of the plant. Employees received an enormous amount of information about the business, both on operational costs and on profitability. Monthly meetings between management and employees began. This began to develop the trust relationship which provided the key to success at CCR.

Self-Managed Teams for Salaried Employees

In 1991, benchmarking of the number of staff required to run a refinery was done with refineries of a similar size. Based on this information, the company reduced the number of salaried people from 265 to 200, but left the hourly workforce intact.

Management also made a top-down decision to test the concept of self-managed teams. Steve Heddle, who was then production and administration manager of CCR, says "Picture this—we decided we were going to do this, so we sat around in a management team meeting one day and we said, let's do it. Everyone volunteered to put together a team in their respective areas of responsibility and away they went. It became a bit of a free-for-all. Before too long we had about 22 teams! It was an interesting exercise because everyone was doing what they wanted to do in terms of self-management [but] with no real structure."

Heddle continues: "At that time, the unions came to us and said, you guys are driving chaos into this plant. We got to the point where, for example, our steam team made the decision they weren't going to punch time clocks anymore. You can appreciate all these people waiting to leave at the end of the day, with a bit of a line-up, and this group of prima donnas walking out and waving! This created a whole lot of friction in the plant." However, when management explained that the goal of the teams was to improve profitability and create rewarding jobs, union representatives said they were interested in participating.

Summary: Change Initiatives Before 1992 Largely Top-Down

On the eve of 1992 labour negotiations, there were some promising signs that CCR was moving in the right direction to cope with the market pressures which began to impact company profitability in the late 1980s: more communication between management and employees, regular consultation to address concerns, and experiments in new methods such as the self-managed teams.

But these initiatives were still largely top-down, as in the quality improvement process and the self-managed teams. Monthly meetings between management and employees were held, but they were not used for conflict resolution. According to Bruce Hamilton, "We realized that significant change would only be possible if we could develop trust and shared decision making with the union."

CCR IN 1992: PLANNING FOR CHANGE BEGINS IN EARNEST

In 1992, Steve Heddle was appointed general manager of CCR, just before labour negotiations were to begin on the collective agreement with the union.

Work Reorganization Committee Formed

Heddle agreed to the formation of a Work Reorganization Committee. The charter for this committee was the first joint breakthrough in the plant. It stated that the union and management would work together to improve the workplace and achieve the objective of making the company more productive. Bruce Hamilton, manager of Human Resources, was in charge of the Work Reorganization Team and made a significant contribution to the change process. HR's role throughout the change process was significant. HR management assisted the management team to create the new culture by helping to build an atmosphere of trust, so that all employees, unionized and salaried, could participate in business restructuring and cost reduction efforts. Hamilton was involved in every step of the change process, from the formation of the Work Reorganization Committee through implementation of its recommendations. He was the management team's key representative throughout the process.

Hamilton's role was to address all the people aspects of the change, those aspects of change which company initiatives prior to 1992 had tended to ignore, or treat as a low priority. Acting first as a facilitator of dialogue and a source for HR expertise to the Work Reorganization Committee, Hamilton was also vital in communicating the results of the committee's findings to all members of the plant community, in ensuring that all training required by the change was provided, in overseeing changes in the Human Resources function mandated as part of the restructuring, and in monitoring and assessing the restructuring's results.

The committee was made up of twelve individuals: six unionized employees and six managers. The committee's mandate was to come up with recommendations to improve the productivity of the plant. Five key objectives were set for plant improvement by the committee:

- 20% unit cost reduction,
- minimum 20% return on net assets,
- consistently meet customer requirements,
- improve the health, safety and wellness of the employees, and
- environmental protection compliance.

The committee's mandate was also to oversee the implementation of a style of management that promoted individual empowerment, allowing each employee to maximize his or her knowledge, abilities, potential and training. It was also asked to define training guidelines for production jobs. All reorganization initiatives were expected to respect the company's policies, the collective agreement, and labour-related government regulations.

Union Concerns—Job Security Paramount

The union knew there was ample room for improvement, but was not happy at the prospect of a reduced number of jobs. Management had said cost reductions should include a reduction of employees from 950 to 750. Yves Meunier, President of the Steelworkers local, was asked why he agreed to take part in the cost reduction initiatives. He noted that he had had previous experiences with other companies where plant closures had created negative consequences, including job losses. He believed that through participation in the process, the union would be able to maintain job security.

The union obtained a commitment from the company that any consideration of possible layoffs would look at ways to prevent them. As Meunier says, "That was the main reason I decided to get involved. We explained to the company that if you want to reorganize and cut costs, there is no way people are going to participate if they know they are cutting their own job in the end."

The key to success was job security—not necessarily maintaining the same number of jobs, but keeping the people who were already working there. Says Heddle, "In 1992, we didn't make any commitments on job security, but we were able to show them that 750 was an achievable target without having any layoffs." Departures were easy to forecast. By 1995, 160 people had left, of which 110 hadn't been replaced.

The Work Reorganization Committee in Action

During 1993, the Work Reorganization Committee carried out its review. Some of the highlights of its work were:

- a thorough analysis of the business, and the external environment, and why the company had to change in response to changing market conditions;

- the identification of the need to realign the plant into two business units;

- the selection and training of ten facilitators—five from the union and five staff people;

- the recommendation that three design teams be set up, each composed of hourly-paid employees from all functions and two foremen. They would be assigned to a three-month full-time project to redesign the work processes of the refinery; and

- the formation of two other design groups—one for staff services such as purchasing and central maintenance; and one to develop the roles and responsibilities for supervisors and management. The two teams were composed of a cross-section from all levels of supervision and worked on a part-time basis.

Heddle says, "The whole crux of [the plan] was top-down objective setting and bottom-up planning and implementation. I told the employees that, in my mind, the only way I would ever get true buy-in from them, was if they had a say or a role in making it happen." He continues, "We used to talk about the time lines and how long things take; we used to say that a decision to do something can be taken very quickly, but the implementation may take a long time if it's top-down. On the other hand, if you involve your workforce, it may take a long time to get things set up and working, but the implementation will go an awful lot quicker."

Heddle says the expectations on the part of both management and the union were huge; it took a year to resolve the union's expectations, especially in relation to increased pay. Management was prepared to give pay raises if people had increased responsibility, but they were not prepared to give across-the-board pay increases that would make the plant uncompetitive.

In January of 1994, joint union and management presentations were made to all steelworker union representatives, management and plant employees. The company presented the work reorganization plan, including union priorities for the protection of employment, profit-sharing and improved work conditions.

Some of the core recommendations were that functional divisions between operating units ("functional silos") should be removed and services such as safety, process development and maintenance should be integrated into the business units.

THE DESIGN TEAMS

The next step was setting up the design teams recommended by the Work Reorganization Committee. There were to be five teams, three to examine work processes and two to examine service functions and the role of supervisors. "We sat down and decided jointly that the best way to do it was to bring in third-party help," says Heddle. At the union's recommendation, CCR brought in consultants who had assisted in the design of the General Electric Bromont facility in Quebec's Eastern Townships. The consultants convinced CCR that the best technique for rethinking company processes was the "socio-technical approach," described in the next section.

Socio-Technical Approach

The socio-technical approach involves tracing the process flow of a plant on a step-by-step basis and determining where variances are likely to occur. On the social side, interactions are mapped out to see who was involved in each step of the process, and who corrected the variances.

In typical plants, those working on a process do not correct variances. Quality issues, for instance, are addressed by the quality control department. The objective of the socio-technical approach is to set up multi-skilled teams that can work on all aspects of the process, including taking care of processes. This in turn leads to greater productivity, since there is less down time, and greater involvement by the team in preventing and correcting variances. Teams usually deal with the early stage of maintenance, but do not become fully skilled and certified as electrical maintainers, for example. However, team members have to study all the aspects of teamwork, must complete a training program, and demonstrate that they have the required skills.

The CCR plant was broken up into three distinct value-added areas: copper anodes operations, cathodes operations, and the precious metals operating area. A group of fifteen people was selected from each of these three areas to participate in the planning on a full-time basis during 1995.

As Yves Meunier, the union President, explained, "We started the process by putting three teams on a full-time basis to study the whole plant process—people from every area, every job, different seniority, young and old—people working together, checking the process, asking co-workers for ideas. Those people came out with a plan. We thought they wouldn't want to change much, but they did. It was the greatest experience we had here and it cost the company a lot of money.

"Then [we made an agreement] with the company that they could hire people from outside to replace these people [on the line] for three months. At that time, people who were resisting the process and the plan came to the union general meeting saying that they were not being allowed to participate. So we stopped the whole process and took a vote. We started with a survey that showed that 60% of the people wanted us to get involved. Later on, when there was further resistance from some areas, we took another vote, and this time there was 80% support. So we gained 20% within a year and a half."

Recommendations for Change in Work Processes

By the end of the design teams' work, about 80 employees (10% of the workforce) had been involved directly in the consultation process. They produced more than 150 recommendations for change and suggestions for improvement in virtually all areas. The process culminated in a series of recommendations for social, technical and structural changes. The recommendations focused on:

- continually breaking down functional walls through alignment of plant processes with customer needs,

- partial integration of areas such as technical, safety and maintenance within the work teams,

- introduction of responsible (semi-autonomous) teams with accountability for short-term planning, scheduling of hours of work and vacations,

- the need for extensive and enhanced training of all employees, and

- removal of work quotas. Previously when workers reached their quota, they did nothing more for the rest of the day. Instead, continuous work was recommended.

The bulk of the recommendations, 125 of them, concerned technical changes, including where to place equipment, and how to set up the plant floor to maximize production and improve process flow.

Hamilton comments, "Was this a spectacular example of highly innovative results? No, not really—nothing here that you haven't seen before. Was this a radical and pervasive change in the 'how-to?' Absolutely. We had an overwhelming sense of confidence, pride and commitment because we did it ourselves."

Recommendations on Supervisors and Service Functions

The other two design teams also reported their recommendations at this time. The first team recommended that the whole role of supervisors should change; first-line supervisors would work as resource people who helped the teams, rather than as disciplinarians and schedulers. They also recommended that members of the new responsible team take responsibility for safety and scheduling, which had been the responsibility of the first-line supervisor, and that decisions should be made by reaching a consensus among by all team members. The second team recommended several changes relating to the maintenance function, detailed below in the section entitled "Restructuring and Decentralization."

Heddle had hoped that the union collective agreement in May 1995 could be based on the recommendations that had emerged from the design teams. However, since the recommendations were not ready in a completed form, the union and management agreed to take a couple of weeks' hiatus to study the proposals and see what could be done about the collective agreement. Both sides became frustrated, says Heddle, because of the amount of information that was involved in the recommendations, so they agreed to complete the union negotiations and work on the recommendations afterwards.

Training Facilitators

At the end of the summer of 1995, the company started to set the framework for the new structure and work environment. Supervisors and union representatives jointly began to train the facilitators recommended by the Work Reorganization Committee to bring about the implementation of the responsible teams in the plant for hourly and salaried workers.

Early in 1996, training and information sessions began, dealing with the socio-technical issues that had emerged. In the summer of 1996, union president Yves Meunier and a first-line supervisor from the

Work Reorganization Committee were given a full-time assignment for a year to accelerate the team implementation process.

RESTRUCTURING AND DECENTRALIZATION

As a result of the recommendations, the plant was restructured into two business units: one for copper refining and the other for precious metals and by-products. These were seen as two distinct businesses. At the same time, maintenance functions were also decentralized wherever possible. One senior maintenance person in each of the business units would be responsible not only for the traditional technical maintenance, but also for electrical maintenance and instrumentation.

The safety function was decentralized with one co-ordinator placed in each team. "That has been a really positive move," says Steve Heddle. "Safety people always used to be looked upon as threats to the production people, and now they're really looked upon as part of the team."

On-the-job training was decentralized, as was project engineering and process engineering. The central maintenance function (the mobile shop and the central mechanical maintenance and central electrical maintenance) was retained to provide support, knowledge and overall integrity and expertise to the function.

Responsible Teams

Because the union had participated in the planning process of the reorganization, they now had a hand in the makeup of the responsible teams and how they would work. As Heddle says, "The key is to involve your employees in the process. There is no magic recipe to this. You need confidence and faith in your people; you need to add resources and see what your people can do."

Meunier comments, "On the trades side we have trade teams and on the production side we have multi-function teams. What we did was we picked up natural groups – we didn't want to change anything to start with. We took the people that were working together and we put them as a team so we didn't make any new setup."

The first responsible team began operating in March 1997. As Heddle says, "It takes a long time for things to happen quickly! Moving from a traditional style of management and building trust takes a long time."

The company wanted to ensure that the integrity of function was maintained as it was decentralized. The decentralized maintenance group, for example, reported up through the business unit manager, to make sure that the maintenance and engineering manager, who still managed the central groups, also had an overall responsibility for ensuring that the areas were properly staffed and that the appropriate expertise was there. The same thing happened on the technical side. Technical functions were decentralized, but the technical manager still had an overall responsibility for the technical agenda of the plant.

RESULTS OF THE WORK REORGANIZATION

The results of the changes became apparent when measured over a five-year period. By January 1996, lost time accidents were down 55%, productivity up by 50%, costs down by 16%, in-process inventories down by 21%, and quality improvement index, or the price of non-conformance, was down by 50%. Heddle says that much of this was due to more involvement by employees in the workplace and to technological change.

Yves Meunier believes that at least half the productivity improvement was because of the change in attitude, and the development of trust. In other words, the attitude change improved productivity by 25% even before the teams were actually put in place. Meunier comments, "We're working on the things we can influence. The attitude has changed a lot over the past two years. We communicate the same message repeatedly but in different ways. Almost every morning we have one or two groups meet and you can see and feel the attitude change." If the union makes a decision, workers have a chance to explain it to management. Once management learns the facts, they are better able to understand and accommodate the decision.

Redefining the Vision and Core Values

In the spring of 1996, Heddle and some of the members of the plant took a study tour of a number of companies in the United States that were at various stages of innovative HR practices. He says it was a big eye-opener both for management and the union. "I had a new realization when we toured the facilities in the States. I got excited about the concept of balancing priorities and the use of the balanced scorecard."

The visit to the Saturn plant was pivotal. Saturn was going through interesting times because the plant was built around handpicked people from other GM plants and from the UAW. Their hiring procedures were impressive. What also impressed Heddle was the vision, values, and guiding principles used to manage the business, and the common focus on those priorities that make the business run well. Heddle decided after this visit the management team would sit down with union representatives to revisit their mission and vision statement. He saw a need for establishing core values that expressed how the company wanted all employees and management to behave and articulated the guiding principles for managing the business.

The vision statement that was produced reflected the expectations of the four prime stakeholders—customers, employees, shareholders, and the community in which they operated. The company initiated a balanced scorecard which set up key results areas and measures in relation to the four stakeholder groups. Heddle remarked that establishing the vision, values and measurement process was done in a collaborative manner. "You have to make sure that everyone feels that it is theirs. You have to tailor this to the culture of the organization."

REFLECTING ON THE CHANGES

I asked both Steve Heddle and Yves Meunier what they would do differently if they had to start the process again, and what they learned from this process.

What Would You Do Differently?

1. *Establish the vision, values and principles and tie them in with the balanced scorecard approach.*

Steve Heddle moved from CCR in 1996 to become President of the Aluminum Products group in New Madrid, (Missouri). He took what he learned from the CCR experience to his new position. He moved quickly to work with the management team to establish the vision, values and principles for this location. The team also developed the key results areas for the business and set up a balanced scorecard to measure how well they were meeting the results required by their key stakeholders.

The process is called "Shaping Our Future," and the plan and the required results have been fully communicated throughout the plant.

2. Consider omitting the socio-technical approach.

Heddle is not sure that he would use the socio-technical approach to reorganization again. He prefers the concept of decentralizing into business units and setting up the appropriate processes and work environment within that framework. He would continue to use action teams to develop recommendations relating to the processes and the environment.

3. Gain wider involvement by taking more time.

The union perspective is that the company should have taken more time to study work processes and to involve more people in this phase of the change. This would have allowed for a greater commitment and buy-in to the changes by a lot more people.

Says Meunier, "The consultants recommended that we work on the process for two days per week, and take a year and a half. Instead we said that we would do it for three months working on a full-time basis. The change in attitude would have been much greater if we'd done it one day a week and allowed people to go back to their work area and exchange information. The three months changed the attitude of those forty-five people, but it didn't change the attitude of the plant. I wouldn't change the process, but I would change the way we did it."

What Did You Learn from the Change?

1. Change takes a long time.

Both Heddle and Meunier noted that the process of change goes more smoothly when many people are involved, but it does take longer. However, by getting greater buy-in and commitment, the implementation phase goes much more smoothly than it would have without widespread involvement of all those affected by the change.

2. Senior management should remain in place for the whole change process.

One of the difficulties Heddle faced with the employees was when his HR manager, Bruce Hamilton, moved to another part of Noranda at the end of 1994. Heddle himself left for his new position eighteen months later. "That upset the union," Heddle says, "because they are consistent and have strong leadership year in and year out, but management changes and that's a real problem for them."

3. It is difficult to initiate change when there is no immediate threat or crisis.

Creating change when there is no crisis is difficult and requires constant communication.

Yves Meunier says union members accepted the need for change even though there was no crisis, no threat from outside that indicated that people were going to lose their jobs or the company was going to shut down. However, says Meunier, the company "explained how we make a profit here and some of the things that we cannot influence. For example, we talked about the impact of when the Canadian dollar is low and what happens as we sell our product outside Canada.. If those things change, there might be a threat. We had better take the time to make the best decision now rather than waiting for a crisis when the fastest thing we can do is cut people or salaries, and we don't want to do that."

4. Communication is an essential part of the change process.

A key component of the change process is changing attitudes and this requires significant communication. Yves Meunier says that the previous management team at CCR were only concerned about communicating with the unions in relation to the collective agreement. Therefore, it was hard to solve a problem unless it was covered by the agreement.

The new management team led by Heddle and Hamilton was open to sharing information on all aspects of the plant, including the financial position. This process had begun with the former plant manager, and meant that everyone had the same information and would be able to draw similar conclusions and understand the need for change and the ideas that were being proposed.

Initially the new managers were able to solve problems that were raised by the union, such as pension and insurance issues, and that led the union to trust management and to agree to look at the subject of work reorganization. Now the unions are an integral part of the continuous communications process.

5. There is a need to involve supervisors with the same intensity as the union representatives and employees.

Heddle recognized that he did not pay as much attention to the supervisors as he did to the union members and their representatives. The supervisory role was changing and becoming more that of a mentor and coach, a significant difference from the traditional role. Also, supervisors were being asked to give up privileges, such as reserved parking, and to remove things that distinguished classes of employees. This caused resentment among some of the supervisors.

In retrospect, Heddle says he would have spent more time communicating with the supervisors and would have involved them more in the process of change.

6. Commitments to employment security are needed.

Heddle and Meunier agree that it is important to make agreements in which no one is going to lose a job through participating in the change. Everyone recognized that the number of jobs would be reduced through the change process, but that this would be achieved through such things as early retirement and not filling vacancies. Once this commitment was made, people were willing to participate in the change process.

7. Once change has been implemented, it can cause unionized employees to question the way their union is managed.

For Yves Meunier and the Steelworkers local, the biggest change that happened in the union was an increased participation in union management. Through involvement in questioning and changing everything in the company, members in turn wanted to know more about the structure and workings of the union itself. "A lot more people got interested and learned more about the union," says Meunier. "People are interested in participating in elections now. So far every election we have lots of people running for jobs." As members upgrade their skills, they are choosing better people to represent them in the union.

8. It is essential to build an atmosphere of trust.

From the union's perspective, the process of solving problems as they came up, and the willingness of people like Steve Heddle and HR Manager Bruce Hamilton to involve the employees in the decision-making process, built up a feeling of trust in the workers. The company was perceived as caring about the human problems of the workplace and showed that it was prepared to listen to the workers. This went a long way to building trust and to the success of the project. Says Meunier, "If we don't believe the people that are in front of us, then we can't deal."

SUMMARY

In Chapter 1 the need for flexibility was highlighted as a key to competitive advantage in the global economy. This chapter has shown how a unionized plant environment responded to the need for flexibility and increased its business effectiveness as a result of the changes the plant initiated. It described how Noranda's copper refinery in Montreal East used total employee involvement and team co-operation to create a new culture and make the organization more effective. The key to success was the development of a trust relationship between union, management and all employees.

Human Resources Systems and Processes to Create the High-Performance Organization

PART FOUR COVERS the Human Resource processes required to improve business effectiveness. Today's high-performance organizations need HR processes that support them in achieving responsiveness, speedy delivery, and quality customer satisfaction. Above all, HR must place greater emphasis on upgrading the skills of organizations' people in order to deliver on these requirements.

Chapter 10, by Nancie J. Evans concerns *Executive Leadership Development*. It looks at components of executive leadership development, including the required infrastructure, the process of talent identification, and the selection and resourcing of candidates to fill vacant leadership positions. The chapter also includes an organization self-assessment tool based on the best practices of executive leadership development.

Chapter 11, entitled *Escaping the Performance Management Trap*, is written by Anne Stephen and Tony Roithmayr, who both have significant experience in developing and implementing performance management systems. They discuss why most performance management systems are either questionable or fail to reach the required objectives. They propose that the problem is not with the design and components of performance management processes but rather with their execution.

They argue that performance management systems were designed to support rigid and slow-moving organizations and are not necessarily relevant in today's rapidly changing business environment. They have designed a peak performance model that helps management focus on employees knowing what to do, being able to do it, wanting to do it, and being equipped to do it. They also provide a case study of the model in use.

Chapter 12, *Achieving Strategy Through People: Integrated Competency Based Human Resources Management* is written by Rick Lash and Mark Jackson of Hay Management Consultants, who have developed the Hay/McBer Competencies Process. They define competency and examine the history of competency theory and practice.

The chapter also examines the development of competencies and competency scales, both in individuals and job families. It discusses the various ways that competencies can be assessed and then details the application of the competency framework. It describes the three most common applications of competency models: recruitment and selection, performance management, and development of all employees. The chapter ends by looking at organizational initiatives required to implement the competency approach, claiming that for change to be successful, all aspects of the organization must support the change.

Chapter 13, by John Lewis, is called *Developing a Compensation Strategy*. It defines the underlying principles necessary for a compensation strategy that supports business direction in a changing business environment. These include determining what a job is, how much it's worth, and setting pay structures based on market data. The chapter looks at how individual pay is decided, whether it be on the performance of the individual, the division or department, the team, or the entire organization. Employee benefits are then discussed within the context of total compensation. It then examines differentiating factors that determine compensation strategy, such as technology and expertise, price, and delivery speed and responsiveness to customers.

The final chapter, *Paying for Competencies that Drive Organizational Success: The HB Group Insurance Study*, defines competencies and payment for competencies throughout the example of the HB Insurance Group, formed in 1980, which recently began paying its employees based on competency and enhanced skill and knowledge applications. HB is a highly successful organization and is considered a benchmark leader in the operation of calling centres.

HB simultaneously developed pay and performance management processes to ensure linkage between the programs. Development used a strategy-based approach and a design team made up of a cross-section of people from the organization. The concepts were constantly tested with employees by means of focus groups. Different scales of performance were developed, and a competency-based pay system was initiated which reflected employee achievement as measured by the new performance scales.

CHAPTER TEN

Executive Leadership Development

Nancie J. Evans

Rᴇsᴇᴀʀᴄʜᴇʀs, ᴘʀᴀᴄᴛɪᴛɪᴏɴᴇʀs ᴀɴᴅ academics point increasingly to the fact that the only sustainable source of competitive advantage in a dynamic and complex environment is an organization's people. Technology can be duplicated, marketing plans can be replicated, and financial clout can be created. What is unique in an organization is the sum of the capabilities of its members.

Leadership, perhaps the rarest and most valuable of human capabilities, is essential for every organization. Leaders provide innovative thought—the engine of renewal and reinvention. Effective leadership optimizes the performance of other core competencies, such as distribution networks and marketing plans.

Fortunately, it appears that top decision makers increasingly recognize the need to promote leadership skills. Increasing numbers of surveys and research studies highlight leadership development and succession management as key strategic challenges facing organizations[1]. In addition, Boards of Directors are becoming more involved in leadership succession, primarily in response to shareholder pressure

---

[1] A.T. Kearney, *The Executive Agenda: Corporate Turmoil or Enthusiasm for Change* (Chicago, IL: A.T. Kearney, 1994).

and the growing attention being given to governance issues and responsibilities[2].

CORRECTING SOME MISCONCEPTIONS ABOUT LEADERSHIP DEVELOPMENT

It would appear that the only reasonable course is for organizations to view executive leadership development as a key source of competitive advantage; some researchers suggest that it should always rank in a company's top five strategic priorities[3]. And yet, even today, some companies lack any formal program for cultivating leadership skills. A reluctance to embrace such a program may stem from a number of common misconceptions about leadership itself. Four, in particular, are worth considering, and refuting, here.

- Leadership is an innate quality, rather than a learned skill.

- Executives in a position to benefit from leadership training already possess the capability of leadership.

- A lack of executive candidates inside an organization can be remedied easily by external recruiting.

- Historically many organizations have had less than wonderful results from their attempts at executive leadership development.

First, it has often been suggested that leadership is an innate quality and that leaders will emerge, usually by natural selection, in an organization. Proponents of this view often cite their personal experience as corroboration. "Indeed, given that leaders are born, not bred, why waste valuable resources on leadership development?," as I was asked by the CEO of a large multinational during a 1993 interview. Strong evidence exists, however, that many leadership skills are learned, such as the techniques needed to direct a turnaround situation or to manage people of diverse cultural backgrounds. Personality alone will not a

[2] M.S. Van Clieaf, "Executive Resource and Succession Planning: Re-Engineered for the Twenty-First Century," *American Journal of Management*, Vol. 1, no. 2, pp. 47-56.

[3] M.W. McCall, Jr., "Executive Development as a Business Strategy," *The Journal of Business Strategy*, January–February 1992, pp. 25-31.

leader make! In fact, research has shown that it takes ten to twenty years to develop general management skills[4]. In today's business climate, natural selection is too slow and. too vested in the past to be depended on to create leaders.

Second, it has also been argued that executives don't require leadership development. They already have the capabilities they need, or they wouldn't be where they are. Although this assumption might be true in a static environment, the current rate of change and increasing complexity demands constant upgrading of skills and knowledge, especially at top levels. There is evidence that failing to continue executive development can be very costly both in financial terms—a 1988 study of a large international organization found that the cost of an executive "derailing" was at least US \$500,000[5]—and in the potential negative impact on customers, employees, suppliers and other stakeholders.

Third, there is a lack of internal attention to leadership development in the belief that leadership talent can be brought into the organization from outside. However, this expectation has its drawbacks. For one, finding qualified leaders with the right set of experience and capabilities can be very time-consuming and expensive. Furthermore, there are no guarantees that the individual will be successful.

> Hiring executives from outside the organization is risky. Knowledge of the business and knowledge of the people involved in the business are crucial components of effective leadership, and people who successfully lead a particular organization in a specific industry usually have spent significant time in it.[6]

The alternative is to engage in practices that target the continued development of executive leadership talent. The remainder of this chapter describes these practices and provides an Organizational Self-Assessment checklist, which can be used to assess the reader's own organization and identify opportunities for improvement. A note of caution: assess whether a practice is operating as it was designed to work. If it is not, further analysis is required to determine the source of the problem.

---

[4] J.P. Kotter, *The General Manager* (New York: Free Press, 1982).

[5] M.M. Lombardo, M.N. Ruderman, and C.D. McCauley, "Explanations of Success and Derailment in Upper-Level Management Positions," *Journal of Business and Psychology*, Vol. 2, pp. 199-216.

[6] McCall, op. cit., p. 26.

DIMENSIONS OF EXECUTIVE LEADERSHIP DEVELOPMENT

Executive leadership development may be defined as the identification and development of employees to lead an organization toward its short-and long-term goals. It includes familiar HR processes, including succession planning. Four key steps will be examined in detail in this chapter:

- designing an infrastructure,
- identifying talent,
- tailoring individual development plans, and
- selecting candidates for vacant leadership positions.

   The first and perhaps most important step is designing an infrastructure which creates the conditions necessary for executive leadership development. It includes the design of the process, its interfaces with other business processes, its owner/champion, and the roles and accountabilities of key stakeholders. Of particular interest is how executive leadership development is linked to the goals and strategies of the business.

FIGURE 1: Dimensions of Executive Leadership Development

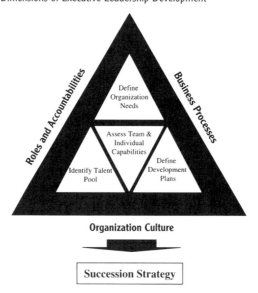

The second step is talent identification, which involves identifying individuals with the potential to assume greater responsibilities in the organization. Third, these people are targeted for development tailored to their individual strengths and weaknesses and to the capabilities required by the organization. Both of these steps apply, with minor modifications, to existing executives who are also assessed for their strengths and weaknesses with a view to creating targeted development plans for them as well.

The last phase is the selection or resourcing of candidates to fill vacant leadership roles. This step has two key dimensions: 1) identifying the needs of the organization in the context of the overall capabilities of the leadership team, and 2) identifying the best candidate for the role.

Executive Leadership Development Infrastructure

Executive development and succession planning processes have traditionally been owned and implemented by Human Resources. This ownership has presented several difficulties for the effective development of executive leadership capabilities. For example, executive development activities such as training programs, run the risk of being treated as annual HR programs or, even worse, events that are forgotten as soon as the forms are completed and filed. Many people today can recall succession planning exercises that resulted in succession charts and detailed employee profiles which were rarely, if ever, actually used for filling job openings later in the year.

The problem is exacerbated by a lack of clear linkages between executive development, including succession planning, and overall business strategy. In the majority of organizations, it is difficult for line managers to see how the two are connected, except perhaps at a structural level, i.e., new tasks create new positions to be filled.

Making the connection requires rigour and discipline which historically many executives and Human Resources professionals have been unwilling to undertake. A vicious circle results: a lack of understanding of the capabilities and "mix" required to execute the business strategy negatively affects the talent identification and development processes, which in turn installs individuals in executive roles who do not appreciate the importance of investing in leadership development.

Correctly structured, the executive leadership development process should be:

- owned by the CEO,
- supported by the organization's culture and philosophy,
- designed as a dynamic process,
- interfaced with the organization's long-range planning processes,
- defined in terms of clear roles and accountabilities for key stake-holders, and
- linked to other management processes.

Ownership by the CEO

Direct, hands-on involvement by the CEO is required in all phases of the process. For example, in defining the requirements for the executive team, the CEO plays a key role both in planning and confirming both accountabilities and the capabilities required for success. In many cases, CEOs "push the envelope" by challenging the status quo and looking longer term to the future requirements of the business. They also can play an important role in holding line managers, rather than HR, responsible for the process. This can be done by involving senior managers actively both during the early stages and in the actual implementation of development plans and selection of candidates. The most effective way to achieve this involvement is to explicitly define the roles and accountabilities of line managers as active participants. Such definitions build line manager commitment due to the value gained from increased understanding of the business, its challenges, and its capabilities.

Culture and Philosophy

Effective organizations strive to create an environment in which learning and growth are valued and fostered. They may choose to invest more in people who are perceived as having greater potential or talent, but this is done within a broader development context which makes opportunities available for all to learn and grow. A common flaw to be avoided is the tendency to create "haves" and "have nots" in executive development and succession planning. In the case of "have not" development, including participation in training programs, access to key projects and assignments, and other initiatives, is limited to those designated as being possible successors. Although cost-effective in the short term, such a plan can, and frequently does, lead to morale problems, including the loss of capable people.

Designing a Dynamic Process

The executive leadership development infrastructure must be flexible and adaptable to the conditions and needs of the business and its external environment. Processes that are rigid, administration-intensive and individual-focused are less likely to meet the long-term, changing needs of business. Effective organizations focus on developing the capabilities of the overall executive team, as well as its individual members, thereby building flexibility. They steer away from paper or electronic administration tools to track people, and rely more on the intelligence of the management team supplemented by a minimum amount of documentation. Furthermore they implement multi-purpose operational methods, such as 360-degree feedback systems. They are, however, disciplined in their commitment to these activities as an annual activity with clearly defined deliverables and standards of performance.

Interface with Long-Range Planning

In effective organizations, dynamic executive leadership development interfaces with long-range planning. This is critical due to the importance of identifying the future needs of the business and the capabilities required for success. For example, if an organization is planning on a major strategic shift, such as a merger, or a global expansion, it will need new skills and knowledge. Not everyone has to have the new skill set, but the requisite knowledge and experience should be included in the overall capability profile of the executive team. As strategies emerge and directions shift, the organization needs to review its capability and succession requirements in order to re-position itself.

Roles and Accountabilities

Particular roles and accountabilities must be clearly defined for all stakeholders involved in the process, including the role of Human Resources as process consultant and facilitator, the CEO as process owner and active participant, the executive team as active participants, and the Board of Directors as the final approval voice for executive positions. These roles are defined in terms of specific accountabilities which are linked directly to consequences, such as bonus pay-outs and other incentives.

Links to Other Management Processes

Finally, an executive development infrastructure must tie into other HR processes, such as compensation and performance management. To be successful all of these processes need to be part of a broader integrated system. The executive development infrastructure must not be developed and maintained in isolation otherwise, it will undermine, or be undermined by, other processes.

Carefully designing the executive leadership development infrastructure with these elements in mind will increase the likelihood of success. Each of the other three steps discussed below depends on the infrastructure for their effectiveness.

FIGURE 2: Organizational Self-Assessment Checklist, Step 1

Best Practices in Executive Development 1.0 Infrastructure	Current Practice (Y/N)	Opportunity to Improve (Y/N)
1.1 The culture of our organization fosters and values the learning and growth of all employees as illustrated by its broad development strategy.		
1.2 Leadership and executive development is viewed as a strategic source of competitive advantage.		
1.3 Our CEO is directly involved in executive leadership development in our organization by: • Providing input to and validation of both individual and team accountabilities and capabilities. • "Pushing the envelope"—challenging the status quo. • Holding line managers, rather than Human Resources, responsible for the process.		
1.4 Succession planning and executive development focuses on developing the capabilities of the overall leadership team.		

1.5 The organization is disciplined in its commitment to these activities as an annual activity with clearly defined deliverables and standards of performance.		
1.6 As strategies emerge and directions shift, the organization reviews its capability and succession requirements to ensure it is positioned appropriately.		
1.7 Execution of related accountabilities is linked directly to consequences, such as bonus pay-outs and other incentives.		
1.8 HR operates as process consultant and facilitator rather than as process owner.		
1.9 The Board of Directors is involved in the succession planning process.		
1.10 Executive leadership development is part of a broader integrated Human Resources system.		

Talent Identification

A typical talent identification process requires managers to identify which of their direct reports have the potential to progress within defined time frames, such as "promotable one level within two to three years," "promotable within one year," and "ready now." Identification guidelines tend to vary widely from little or none to the increasingly popular use of competency models.

Unfortunately, this typical process is often fraught with problems. First, few immediate bosses are good judges of performance, let alone of potential to do something they have personally never done[7]. Second, it frequently results in an "in my own image" identification pattern that may not address future leadership needs. In fact, it may very well promote the "good and the gaudy" instead of the "best and the brightest[8]."

Assessing leadership potential needs to move beyond input from the individual's immediate manager. This can take the form of a senior

[7] M. Sorcher, *Predicting Executive Success* (New York: John Wiley, 1985).

[8] M.N. Ruderman and P.J. Ohlott, "Traps and Pitfalls in the Judgement of Executive Talent," Report no. 141 (Greensboro, N.C.: Centre for Creative Leadership, 1990).

management committee, a multi-rater assessment process, and even a talent "scout." The key is to ensure a breadth of perspective that addresses future long-term needs and charts progress towards the desired goals in the context of building and strengthening the capabilities of the executive team as a whole, rather than the individual. In addition to leadership and learning ability, any assessment of executive ability must also include performance measures, experience such as managing turnarounds and start-ups, team skills, and technical competence.

Competency-Based Talent Identification

Competency-based systems for identifying talent can be a problem if they are constructed on past success behaviours with insufficient attention to the future needs of the business. They can also lend themselves to what is called the "halo effect" if the immediate manager is the only person to complete a competency-based talent identification tool; if the scale used to determine the level of competence is not clearly defined; or if examples of how the competency has been demonstrated are not included in the data collected. There is even the danger that the existence of the competency model lends credence to the findings and thus, blocks the investigation of possible process defects.

An even greater risk may lie in over-dependence on competencies which may result in insufficient attention both to the individual's performance record and to the context within which the competencies are applied. Specifically, an individual may have the competencies to perform a given role, but does he or she know how to apply these skills, knowledge and attributes in a variety of situations to achieve desired results? The question of "to a variety of situations" is important. We can all think of people who are terrific in start-up roles but unhappy and relatively ineffective in maintenance roles. Attention to the context within which the competencies were demonstrated can be critical to success and yet many competency models and assessment tools fail to provide this type of information.

A further interesting paradox also exists with competency models. They tend to represent a desired end state that drives selection based on who best fits the model. However, if we truly believe in development, we would identify the qualities necessary to achieve this desired end state through a series of developmental experiences. Instead of competencies, such as the ability to create a shared mind-set or to make tough decisions, we would identify people who have the ability to learn how to do these things. This might include knowledge of one's strengths and weaknesses, ability to seek out and use feedback, recognition of one's limits, ability to learn from experience, a passion for learning, and demonstrated growth. "The bottom-line: *identifying potential means assessing progress toward meaningful end states.*[9]"

Effective Talent Identification

To summarize, effective talent identification pays attention not only to competencies but also to the individual's performance track record in a variety of situations. The specific competencies take into account the skills, knowledge and attributes required to effectively fulfill the responsibilities of a given role, the ability to learn and develop, and to add to the overall capability of the executive team. They are tested against the organization's long-term goals and strategies to ensure a future focus. This is complemented by clear expectations in terms of the type of work environment and business conditions within which the individual is most effective, as well as proven accomplishments that are relevant to the challenges in the new role. Furthermore, several sources of information are consulted to get the most accurate picture possible of the individual's capabilities.

By implementing these tactics, talent identification expands to include bench strength assessment, or recognizing people who have the capability and the track record to back it up. It also provides valuable information on an individual's strengths and areas for development that can be targeted for action through aggressive development planning.

Why not take a holistic approach?

Question: Why bother doing talent identification at all? Is it not possible to simply engage in a holistic development philosophy that allows all employees equal access to assessment tools and development initiatives, thereby maximizing the resource base from which succession candidates will emerge?

---

[9] McCall, op. cit., p. 29.

Answer: In an ideal world this might be feasible. However, most organizations have access to limited funds and other resources. Therefore, they want to target these resources to get the greatest possible return on their investment. Hence, "hedging your bets" through a talent identification or bench strength assessment process is a viable alternative. This is, however, usually done within a broad development context in which opportunities are also provided to others in the organization but usually without the higher financial cost.

Figure 3: Organizational Self-Assessment Checklist, Step 2

Best Practices in Executive Development **2.0 Talent Identification**	**Current Practice (Y/N)**	**Opportunity for Improvement (Y/N)**
2.1 Measurement of potential includes the ability to learn and demonstrate progress towards development/learning goals.		
2.2 Identification includes input from a variety of sources using varied instruments and approaches.		
2.3 Assessment focuses on future long-term requirements versus solely the here and now.		
2.4 Capabilities include a "situational" component, i.e., skills and knowledge required to manage in a turnaround versus start-up operation.		
2.5 Assessment includes the individual's performance track record within a variety of situations.		
2.6 The capabilities of the overall executive leadership team are considered in addition to specific role requirements.		

Development Planning

Few companies effectively manage the development of their talented people over time. In fact, various research studies have uncovered some disturbing facts, including:

- 30%–50% of "high potentials" never reach their expected potential[10],

- less than a third of "high potentials" are still high potentials within two to three years of identification, according to research conducted by a well-known Toronto industrial psychologist over the past 25 years,

- one of the most common causes of talent leaving an organization is a lack of significant developmental challenges[11].

Once talent has been identified, the work really begins. Since, as stated earlier, it takes ten to twenty years to develop a general manager, a long-term development view is required that emphasizes the growth of the individual as well as his or her performance.

The primary vehicle for development is challenging on-the-job experiences which is supplemented by training/education at critical points in the development process, as well as coaching, regular feedback and recognition of accomplishments. According to M.W. McCall, "…research has shown that it's what a person has to do, not what he or she is exposed to, that generates crucial learning. It is simply not the same to be exposed to customers as to have to deal directly with an irate customer who has just taken his business elsewhere[12]."

Each job assignment has both a clear contract for performance and specific learning goals, including defined accountabilities. Managers must take the risk of hiring someone who requires development to be successful in a new role rather than choosing a candidate whose previous related jobs guarantee success. A job should "stretch" an employee. Of course, it would not be good to promote someone who would have an unrealistic stretch in a new role. Throwing someone into a stretch assignment without providing a clear understanding of what is expected is risking failure, or at least a wasted growth opportunity. In fact,

---

[10] Lombardo, Ruderman and McCauly, op. cit.

[11] Ruderman and Ohlott, op. cit.

[12] McCall, op. cit.

research suggests the optimal amount of stretch is 50%[13]; this level provides enough new challenges to make the assignment developmental without an unacceptably high risk of failure.

Vehicles for Development

Participation in training and education programs should be carefully selected to fit both the development needs of the individual and the organization's requirements. One of the most effective structured forums for executive development is involvement in an action learning initiative. These forums are designed to bridge formal learning with real-life situations by having individuals work in teams to solve business or societal problems. Often these forums extend outside an organization by involving members of other organizations in and outside the industry. Other forums that are targeted at specific development needs may also be beneficial, such as university programs in marketing or finance, or specific skill development workshops.

Another effective development vehicle for executives, and executives-in-waiting, is the personal coach. These highly trained professionals use a variety of means to understand an individual's strengths and weaknesses and then develop and implement a plan of action to address specific needs. They monitor progress through observation and feedback, and provide ongoing coaching until both parties decide the assistance is no longer required. Personal coaching can be very attractive to many executives who find it difficult to take the time away from their responsibilities to participate in other development initiatives. It also has the benefit of being a longer-term process with increased likelihood of positive results. The key is to find the right match of coach and executive, so that an open and honest relationship develops.

Finally, the need to monitor progress over time is a difficult but important aspect of executive development. It requires resources and a commitment by the executive team to be personally involved in monitoring the progress of talent in the organization. Frequently, "talent pool managers" assist the executive team in developing learning and performance contracts, and monitoring progress. They are coaches to the executive team, not actual participants in the process.

---

[13] R.W. Eichinger (1993).

FIGURE 4: Organizational Self-Assessment Checklist, Step 3

Best Practices in Executive Development 3.0 Development	Current Practice (Y/N)	Opportunity for Improvement (Y/N)
3.1 The organization views executive leadership development as a long-term (minimum ten years) investment.		
3.2 The primary vehicle for development is challenging on-the-job experiences.		
3.3 Those directly involved in the development of individuals and teams have the skills required for success including giving feedback, coaching, mentoring, goal setting, development planning, etc.		
3.4 Each job assignment has both a clear contract for performance as well as learning outcomes, including defined accountabilities.		
3.5 Hiring managers take the risk of selecting someone who requires development to be successful in the new role rather than a guaranteed success based on previous related job experience.		
3.6 Developmental assignments are chosen to provide approximately 50% stretch.		
3.7 Participation in training and education programs is carefully selected to fit the development needs of the individual in the context of the organization's requirements.		
3.8 Training programs involve action learning.		
3.9 Personal coaches are used strategically to supplement on-the-job development.		
3.10 Executives are personally involved in monitoring the progress and growth of talent in the organization.		
3.11 Talent pool managers coach the executive team through various phases of the executive development and succession planning process.		

Selection of Candidates

Although many organizations have succession charts, these are often used in a cursory manner. Typically, the organization determines what is needed in the job and does an on-the-spot assessment of internal resources. If there is a lack of confidence in the readiness of internal candidates, the next step is an outside search. At first appearance, such a step may seem unsatisfactory, but in an organization where executive leadership development is practised effectively, senior management has the knowledge and insight needed to make rapid decisions. Critical, however, is the dialogue these situations inspire, the opportunity presented to share knowledge and build understanding. This dialogue centres on the short- and long-term needs of the business, the capabilities of the internal candidates, and the need to develop the overall capability of the executive team.

FIGURE 5: Organizational Self-Assessment Checklist, Step 4

Best Practices in Executive Development 4.0 Selection of Candidates	Current Practice (Y/N)	Opportunity for Improvement (Y/N)
4.1 Senior management has the knowledge and insight needed to make rapid decisions.		
4.2 Selection process emphasizes the sharing of knowledge and building of understanding of the strengths and weaknesses of the organization, the short- and long-term needs of the business, the capabilities of the internal candidates, and the need to develop the overall capability of the executive team.		
4.3 The selection decision focuses on putting together a capable group of people who, as a whole, can lead the organization.		

The team concept is important in that it both recognizes and accepts that people have different strengths, and the key is to put together a capable group of people who, as a whole, can lead the organization versus trying to develop individuals to be all things to all people. This is particularly important as organizations contemplate business strategies that require new leadership capabilities and experiences, such as acquiring or merging with another organization, expanding into overseas market, or becoming a publicly traded company. In any of these scenarios, the organization will need experienced and skilled people who can lead it through the transition and can transfer their knowledge and expertise to others. This transfer of knowledge and skills applies equally to executive peers and to others in the organization.

REALITY CHECK—A LOOK INSIDE ORGANIZATIONS

Although I have worked for several years with many organizations on succession and executive development initiatives, I have yet to discover one that has been successful in executing all of the best practices identified in this chapter. The reasons for this are varied, but the most prevalent is the tendency to compartmentalize the steps of the process. Some organizations go so far as to separate these structurally, and to assign accountability to Human Resources rather than to the executive team. For example, one large telecommunications organization has assigned the accountability for the selection and/or design and development of executive development training programs to the training organization. Succession planning is the responsibility of another part of Human Resources, while career planning—their vehicle for identifying developmental job assignments—is left as a functional role (Finance, Marketing, etc.) also managed by Human Resources. The challenge here appears to be to convince executives to accept stewardship and ownership of executive development and succession planning.

I find most executives regard succession as one of their core responsibilities; however, they also believe that Human Resources is the appropriate owner of the process. The one example that I have encountered that differs from this is a Canadian financial services firm which has clearly articulated executive leadership development as a top five strategic issue, and defined the role of Human Resources as that of consultant to the senior team.

In this organization, the succession planning and executive development process was designed by Human Resources working with outside experts but with a significant amount of direct involvement by the executive team. In its current form, it is integrated into the organization's planning and review process, which is owned by the CEO. For this reason, executive leadership development is built into the organization's strategic plan, and is continually addressed as an agenda item at operational reviews, where the progress of succession candidates and other related issues is discussed.

In this organization, executive leadership development is truly a dynamic and flexible process with all dimensions of the process— except for the initial start-up and transition phase, which ended after approximately three years—constantly in operation. For example, talent pool identification is an ongoing responsibility of executives versus a once-a-year exercise. Rather than being selected, developmental assignments are crafted and customized on a continual basis through the regular operational review process. Hence, when a talent pool candidate is ready for another assignment, all concerned parties have been involved in the process and are prepared for the transition. Candidate progress is reviewed regularly, with executives expected to discuss specific accomplishments and provide feedback including an assessment of the individual's developmental progress. Those who fail to meet expectations are placed on a watch list, with a plan to remove them from the talent pool if circumstances fail to change within a reasonable time frame. The role of Human Resources is clearly that of facilitator and consultant. The Vice-President of Human Resources assists in the planning and organization of discussions of leadership development and participates in the ensuing dialogue, but the sessions are run by the CEO or his designate. Human Resources may intervene, as an advisor, if there is disagreement; however its other role is to facilitate the resolution of the issue not to make decisions.

One concern some may have is that a strong focus on future leadership might cause the organization to lose track of its bench strength, especially in light of rapidly changing external forces. This concern has been addressed in two ways. The first is that a matrix is maintained documenting talent pool distribution across the organization; it is reviewed and updated regularly by the senior team with the assistance of Human Resources. The actual decision criteria themselves are formally reviewed during strategic plan development discussions and, if necessary, a formal bench strength assessment occurs. This organization has chosen to contract an external third party to conduct such assessments. However, discussions are currently underway regarding the merits of having the internal Human Resources organization take over this responsibility. The primary reason for the external focus was concern over HR's ability, both with respect to skills and resources, to complete the exercise in a manner acceptable to the rest of the organization. Both skill and resource gaps have recently been addressed, and the only remaining issue is the confidence of the executive team.

CLOSING COMMENTS

Creating and sustaining an executive leadership development infrastructure requires time, money, and resources. It is a long-term commitment for the whole company and often involves risk. It is also the only way to ensure that an organization will have the leaders it needs for its future.

Of course, if an organization does not view leadership as a key source of competitive advantage, or does not believe leadership can be learned it is unlikely to produce a meaningful executive leadership development infrastructure. This also involves risk. Executive leadership development is one such process that is critical to competitive success.

CHAPTER ELEVEN

Escaping the Performance Management Trap

Anne Stephen and Tony Roithmayr

Performance management, is a set of practices through which work is defined, reviewed and rewarded, and employee capabilities are developed. It has been a staple of Human Resources research and practice for more than half a century, and the bane of HR professionals for roughly the same period. As internal and external HR consultants, we have often found ourselves in the awkward position of fiercely promoting performance management processes while privately fretting about their failure to work.

Many line managers get so frustrated they wash their hands of the problem and tell HR specialists to "fix it." Human Resources seems to be trapped in a never-ending cycle of refining or relaunching performance management programs which have fallen into disuse, due to manager and staff dissatisfaction. Despite this cycle, most organizations maintain performance management processes of questionable value. Employee surveys indicate that satisfaction levels with performance management are dismal[1].

---

[1] Studies which attest to dissatisfaction with performance management practices include: Towers Perrin, "The 1997 Towers Perrin Workplace Index"; "Performance Management: What's Hot—What's Not?," *Compensation & Benefits Review* (May/June 1994) pp. 71-75. M., Cameron, "Rewarding for Performance-Any Real

In our forty years with a variety of different organizations, we have authored our share of performance management processes that have fizzled. The problem, we've decided after a review of several models, is not with the processes themselves, most of which are built on a sound philosophical and managerial foundation with many features in common. Rather, the problem is with execution. We have failed to provide the proper tools for implementing performance management, leaving line managers and staff marooned in the day-to-day challenges of running a business.

In this chapter, we will argue that performance management *IS* about running the business. It is not a peripheral issue, but central to the *everyday* work of managers. Equally important, we will argue that we must shift from the traditional performance management focus of managing people—in effect, trying to gain some control over their activities to elicit suitable performance—to concentrating on managing the work context so that staff can be free to perform at their best. This may seem a subtle point, but it is crucial to success in the changing landscape of modern organizations. It also leads to some clear conclusions about improving the execution of performance management processes.

We will also offer a simple tool, the Peak Performance Model, to assist managers in achieving superior performance. The model is rooted in four basic conditions which maximize peak performance necessary for employee effectiveness, efficiency and trust. We are at organizational Ground Zero, clarifying what makes people able to perform. If organizations can manage everyday performance well, and leverage it, the result is likely to be powerful *and* sustainable. Measurement studies are demonstrating that better deployment and use of HR practices correlates with higher business results[2].

Progress?," *Journal of Compensation and Benefits* (March/April 1995), pp. 60-63; and Tracey, Weiss and Franklin, Hartle, Franklin (The Hay Group), *Re-engineering Performance Management-Breakthroughs in Achieving Strategy Through People* (Boca Raton, Florida: St. Lucie Press, 1997).

[2] Studies which indicate the positive impact of progressive performance management practices: D. Kravetz, *The Human Resources Revolution* (San Francisco: Jossey-Bass, 1988); M. Huselid, "The Impact of Human Resource Management Practices on Turnover, Productivity and Corporate Financial Performance," (New Brunswick, N.J.: Rutgers University, 1995) *Academy of Management Journal*, 1995, Vol. 38, No. 3, pp. 635-672; Hewitt Associates, "The Impact of Performance Management on Organization Success," 1994; and Dave Ulrich, "Measuring Human Resources: An Overview of Practice and a Prescription for Results," *Human Resource Management* (Fall 1997), v. 36, no. 3, pp. 303-320.

Some Definitions

Management: The process of managing employees to maximize effectiveness (achieving goals, and realizing plans and strategies) efficiency (doing this at the lowest human resource cost possible) and trust (doing this in a way that leaves employees feeling safe, physically and psychologically).

Performance: Achieving profitability, customer satisfaction, loyalty, and employee productivity through effective strategies, structure, process management and people management.

Manager: An individual held accountable for subordinates' output, exercising leadership, building a team and ensuring continuous improvement.

Source: Based on material in *Requisite Organization: A Total System for Effective Managerial Organization and Managerial Leadership for the 21st Century*, by Elliot Jaques, Arlington, VA: Cason Hall and Co., Publishers, Sept. 1996, and "Performance Management and Assessment," a course prepared and presented at York University by Herb Koplowitz, Ph. D., and Brian Beiles, C.A., M.B.A.

PERFORMANCE MANAGEMENT, PAST AND PRESENT

Typically, performance management includes the following components:

- Planning: setting performance objectives,
- Measurement: determining the "yardstick" to measure results,
- Development: establishing individual development plans,
- Reviewing: evaluating achievements against objectives and expectations,
- Coaching: giving positive and constructive feedback, and
- Rewards and recognition: compensation for contribution to both short- and long-term goals.

In addition, the components of performance management are typically thought of as recurring in a cyclical pattern (Figure 1).

FIGURE 1: Typical Performance Management Cycle

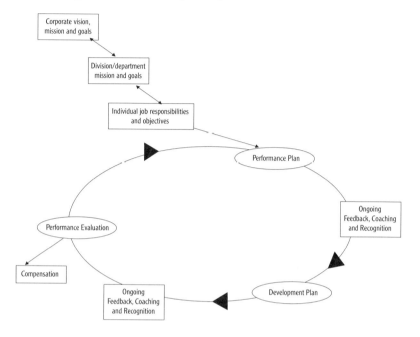

Performance management is a relatively recent term but the concept probably dates back to Frederick Taylor and his scientific management breakthroughs at the beginning of the century. Taylor set out the ideal way to discharge work and then to instruct and monitor employees. The modern rise of performance management processes began over forty years ago with George Odiorne, whose pioneering work on management by objective[3] inspired measurement of managers' performance in the white-collar world.

Despite breakthrough theory and good intentions, traditional performance management often faltered due to execution problems. The essence of management by objectives was supposed to be joint goal-setting by managers and their subordinates, although too often "joint" meant a manager told subordinates what was expected. Discussion of performance was generally confined to an annual review, and precious

---

[3] George Odiorne, *Management by Objectives* (New York: Pitman Publishing Corp, 1965).

little talk about performance occurred at other times. For too many organizations, a once-a-year glance back at performance during the cycle depended on only hazy memory and conjecture. Participants inevitably remembered best, and highlighted, what happened in the previous month, and little was said about the other eleven.

Inevitably, subordinates made a distinction between their daily performance and their evaluated performance. The specific elements of their performance appraisal plan were not integrated into daily routine and tended to be focused on the end of the fiscal period. Feedback from the manager, generally confined to annual bursts, too often was negative. Employees felt dumped on and, in reaction, adopted a defensive stance, closed to feedback. Frustration grew when their perception of personal effectiveness and the manager's perception didn't mesh. Worse, compensation was often tied in to this bundle of imprecision and negativity.

Overall, traditional performance management was plagued by the following execution problems:

- The employee's objectives were set in a vacuum and not linked to the larger business context for the department, division or company;

- Employee's objectives were not representative of the whole job;

- Objectives were often kept a secret and not shared between individuals and teams to give people a better understanding of relationships, hand-offs, and overlaps;

- Feedback, to the extent provided, was usually one way only, from manager to subordinate;

- The key components of the process were not aligned to operate interdependently as a whole system; and

- Development planning was at best secondary, and often forgotten.

The Changing Context

Today, the changes in society and within organizations demand new approaches to performance management. Organizations are experiencing rapid, unrelenting change. The marketplace, consumer demands, and the economics of business are all changing rapidly as globalization, mergers, and intensified competition become more pronounced. Companies are no longer competing just with their neighbours around the corner but with organizations on the other side of the globe, leading to a vastly more complicated workplace. Practices that worked well in a more predictable environment and in an era of abundance need to be revamped for today's world.

Performance management was designed to conform to a hierarchical model which treated organizations as pyramids. Thinking took place at the pinnacle, the control mechanism was stationed in the centre, and the mass of producers were at the bottom. With very skillful communicators in charge, a relatively stable and predictable environment, ample time for scanning, planning, and passing directions through various levels, such an organization can work well.

Today, however, in an age of paradox and lean organizations, we must manage dichotomies, dilemmas, and dissonance—all in a super-charged time frame. The pressure is enormous. The only way to survive is by changing our paradigms and revamping our systems, including performance management. A manager may supervise thirty subordinates, and in that framework no longer has the time, let alone the capacity, to decide everything that must be done and then designate specific activities for those subordinates. The speed at which events now move, the wider span of control and organizational complexity have created a demand for a new system. Thinking, planning and control must all happen where the day-to-day action is, at Ground Zero. And performance management must enable that thinking, planning and control.

THE POTENTIAL OF PERFORMANCE MANAGEMENT

A paradoxical feature of today's corporate environment is that employees are loyal, or want to be loyal, but they are also simultaneously disengaged[4]. As a result, their performance is far from optimal. A variety of research suggests that organizations are failing to capture over 50% of employee performance potential. The same studies indicate that as many as 80% of employees in large North American corporations believe they are not working at their full potential[5].

---

[4] Towers Perrin, "The 1997 Towers Perrin Workplace Index."

[5] M. Huselid, *Human Resources Management Practices and Firm Performance* (New Brunswick, N.J.: Rutgers University, 1995), Vol. 38, No. 3, pp. 635-672.

Research also suggests that organizations perform better if they don't treat people and productivity issues separately. In *The Human Resources Revolution,* Dennis J. Kravetz showed that among Forbes 500 companies there was a strong correlation between progressive Human Resources policy and financial performance[6]. Highly progressive companies had 64% greater sales growth than less progressive companies. Those increased sales translated into much higher profits: highly progressive companies had four times the profits of less progressive organizations. Finally, highly progressive companies were increasing their equity base nearly 80% faster than their less progressive counterparts.

Kravetz, by the way, dismissed the possibility that better financial performance allows companies to be more progressive in their Human Resources policy. He pointed out that successful companies don't change the practices that led to their prosperity. Companies only change techniques that don't work. As well, many of the measures Kravetz used to calculate HR progressiveness—such as management style and company culture—don't increase corporate costs and, therefore, aren't dependent on better financial performance to be enacted.

In another study, Hewitt Associates Ltd. linked performance management processes to higher financial performance.[7] Sales per employee were a third higher at companies with performance management processes than at companies without them. Operating income as a percentage of total assets was 45% greater at companies with performance management processes. The stock return to market index—a measure of the company's wealth creation—was 40% better at corporations with performance management processes. Given these results, imagine what could be achieved with improved implementation of performance management.

This research suggests many organizations are suffering a huge opportunity cost because of faulty management practices. They are failing to take full advantage of their employees' potential—according to those employees. They are losing out on sales, profits and share price.

---

[6] D. Kravetz, *The Human Resources Revolution* (San Francisco: Jossey-Bass, 1988).

[7] Hewitt Associates, "The Impact of Performance Management on Organization Success," 1994.

OUR PERSPECTIVE: THE PEAK PERFORMANCE MODEL

We believe in the value of performance management. We believe if performance systems are executed well, they will reap huge dividends. And the problem with execution, we hasten to add, lies with line managers *and* with HR: we share the problem, the vicious cycle of dissatisfaction and redesign, *and* the solution.

The Peak Performance Model offers an escape from the trap. This simple, four-element tool captures the natural rhythm of successful management, integrating performance management into the daily work at Ground Zero. It helps managers to focus their energies on managing the context and conditions of work, so that employees can thrive in the performance partnership (Figure 2).

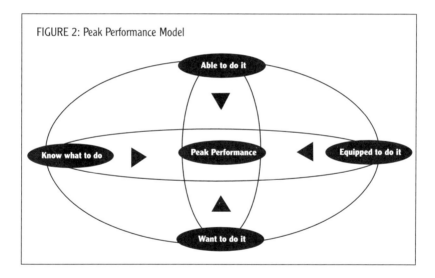

FIGURE 2: Peak Performance Model

Successful performance occurs, we have observed, when people:

- Know What To Do
- Are Able To Do It
- Want To Do It
- Are Equipped To Do It.

When these four conditions are in place, and supported by feedback, coaching and communication, employees can achieve peak performance. Managers can assign tasks without expending undue time in task-specific prescriptions. Together with the employee they ensure the right conditions are in place, and then, like *Star Trek*'s Capt. Jean-Luc Picard, can confidently proclaim, "Make it so, Number One!" Such an approach can be very liberating for both manager and employees.

We illustrate the model as interlocked circles to indicate that the conditions are connected and interdependent; in the daily routine they are all working simultaneously, reinforcing each other. At the same time, managers must isolate the four conditions to ensure they are all being addressed. We recommend using a checklist, e.g., the "Peak Performance Questions" set out in the accompanying box. Good performance is like good health. All elements of our body must be working well. If one deteriorates or is neglected, the problem must be addressed or other elements are also affected and overall well-being declines.

Peak Performance Questions

Know What To Do

- Where is my company going? What is the plan for getting there?

- How does my work unit fit into the big picture?

- What contribution will I make to the overall goals of my company and work unit?

- Do I see the connection between my work plan and the vision and/or goals of the organization? Do I understand how I fit in?

- Do I know what success looks like? Will I know when I've achieved it?

- Am I clear about how I should conduct business, what is valued in this organization?

- Do I know what I am being held accountable for?

Able To Do It

Do I have the "intellectual horsepower" to perform this level of work?

- Do I have the knowledge and skills needed to deliver on the commitments I've made?
- Do my innate traits and characteristics match the needs of the work I'm taking on: is there a good fit between me and the job?
- What work in the organization might better capitalize on my strengths?
- Do I have the knowledge and skills for the work I aspire to in the future?
- Have I provided for the coaching and learning support I need to guide my success and growth?
- Am I taking care of my physical, mental and emotional well-being so I can stay healthy and productive? Am I keeping my life balanced?

Equipped To Do It

- Do I have the authority to pursue the accountabilities and priorities defined in my work plan?
- Do I get the information I need to do my job effectively?
- Do I get the measurement data I need regarding my progress and the effectiveness of my efforts?
- Do I have the tools, equipment, job aids and other resources I need to succeed?
- Are there effective and efficient work processes to follow? Are there clear procedures?
- Do I have sufficient time to successfully deliver on my commitments?

Want To Do It

- Do I feel valued in my work?
- Do I value the work?
- Do I receive the recognition I need to stay energized and excited by my work?

- Am I challenged with meaningful tasks? Do I make a difference?
- Have I discussed and provided for timely sources of helpful feedback and positive reinforcement?
- Do I feel the rewards I'm getting are fair for what I'm contributing?
- Am I happy with the nature and extent of my contributions?

The Four Conditions

Employees in an organization are impacted by all of the conditions of the Peak Performance Model simultaneously! None of the conditions should be dealt with in isolation—*performance can only be optimized when all these enabling conditions are considered, planned for and managed interdependently!*

Aligning Employees

Peak performance starts with framing the business context: providing employees at all levels of the organization with an understanding of business direction so they know what to do. What is the organization's strategy? Why has that strategy been chosen? How does that strategy translate down to the specific work unit and the people in it? Context is much larger than the twists and turns, reversals and roadblocks of normal corporate life. Context is also larger than the boss. It's the organizational North Star. It may evolve a bit during the year but is essentially fixed for long periods.

Here, communication is critical. Managers must have full responsibility for communicating the context, so the relevance is always being underscored. At every staff meeting, and in individual chats, the manager should be looking for opportunities to highlight the connection between overall strategy and day-to-day activities. Employees should be encouraged to look to the context for guidance when they encounter dilemmas in their work. Over time, everyone will become more proficient at understanding context and aligning specific activities with it.

In *Leading Change*, Harvard Professor John Kotter[8] studied why change initiatives failed and found under-communicating was a com-

---

[8] John Kotter, *Leading Change* (Harvard Business School Press, 1996).

mon error. He contends organizations under-communicate their corporate goals by a factor of 10, or 100, and even more in some cases.
We've all seen it happen. The bosses head off to a retreat, return with a
sexy new strategy that's now obvious to them, and after a reassuringly
flamboyant series of kick-off meetings wrongly assume everyone is on
track.

Regular communication is required on all issues and to all employees. During one downsizing exercise, a corporate leader asked, "Why
would I invite the guys in the warehouse to the communication session? They wouldn't understand." That's a terrible undervaluing of
employees and a dangerous misconception about people's need for
context. Generally, the warehouse staff are committed to the company
and have a good feel for the business. It's dangerous to compartmentalize individuals based on role; surveys illustrate that by doing so managers lose out on employee potential.

Employees need information about the significance of each task
for the whole organization; communication enables managers and
employees to view projects in the context of company objectives.

Enabling Employees

After ensuring the employee knows what to do, a manager must ensure
the subordinate is able to perform the job. A good fit should exist
between the employee and the job; if it does not, the job should be
modified or a more appropriate job assigned. Feedback, coaching and
resources for learning must be available so the employee can grow.
Mechanisms to determine development needs must be accessible to
employees. Concern should also be devoted to the employees' physical
and psychological well-being so they can stay healthy and productive.

Equipping Employees

Next, the employee must be equipped to do the work. Clear and effective work processes and procedures need to be in place and communicated in order to guide completion of tasks in an efficient and quality
manner. Employees need adequate information, measurement data,
job aids and other tools to accomplish their tasks. Decision-making
authority and scope must be clear and priorities understood, with sufficient work time to deliver on commitments.

Motivating Employees

Finally, the manager must support the employee's will to do quality work that adds value. The process starts, obviously, with valuing the contribution of employees and ensuring they receive the recognition that will continue to energize them. Employees must feel challenged, consider their workload reasonable, and be fairly rewarded. A serious deficiency in any of the other conditions will often have tremendous impact on motivation. A lack of skills, a lack of confidence, or confusion about what's expected can and will erode the motivation to work.

PUTTING THE MODEL INTO PRACTICE

To see how the Peak Performance Model can be applied, let's study the ABC Consumer Products company. The company has recently redesigned its marketing and sales process and restructured its organization. There are significant changes in jobs and performance requirements. Each retail outlet is served by two positions: the retail business advisor and the merchandising representative.

The merchandising representative helps dealers in a geographical area achieve business goals through detailed merchandising of their stores. Responsibilities include co-ordinating new product introductions, maintaining in-store displays, organizing promotional events, monitoring shelf stock, and providing product training.

Several performance issues have arisen with the merchandising reps. Displays are often set up late, limiting customers' exposure to promotions. Planned schedules are not adhered to: the reps are missing appointments with retailers. Merchandising activities are out of step with the retailers' own business plans. Finally, retailers' staff have insufficient knowledge of ABC products.

Using the Model for Analysis

We analyze the situation by exploring *each* of the conditions for peak performance with the merchandising representatives. We first confirmed what should be in place within each condition to achieve desired performance. We then identified gaps the representatives experienced. These gaps are significant *barriers* to the representatives performing as they should. Listed below are the items identified by the analysis; *barriers* are marked with an (x).

To ensure the merchandising representatives **Know What To Do**, they answered two questions: "Do I understand how I fit?" and "What can I do in my job to contribute?" The answers are summarized in the following list. The reps should:

- understand the strategy and goals of the restructuring and their role in the new marketing/sales process;

x work with retail business advisors regarding the business plans of their retailers and gear their merchandising to support them;

- conduct all in-store merchandising activities on time and in a quality manner, consistent with agreed-upon standards; and

- set up displays, introduce new products, conduct special promotions, monitor stock, train retailers' staff on product features and benefits.

To ensure the representatives are **Able To Do It**, the pertinent question is: "Do I have the knowledge and skills to deliver on my commitments?" For that, they need:

- thorough knowledge of company products;

- skill in merchandising procedures;

x skill in product training;

x knowledge of retail business planning and the specific business goals of retailers in their own area;

- skill in co-ordinating with retailers and retail business advisors regarding plans, schedules and in-store events; and

- skill in using the company's Sales Record System.

To determine if the reps are **Equipped To Do It**, the question asked was: "Do I have the information, tools, and time necessary to be successful?" In this case, we found some glaring needs:

x point-of-sale merchandising material available on time and in good condition;

x efficient system in place for entering and retrieving sales information;

x status information regarding retailers' plans delivered in a timely way; and

- appropriate density of sales territory.

Finally, in checking **Do They Want To Do It**, the critical question was: "Am I energized about my job?" Each should:

- receive feedback on personal activities;
- be recognized and rewarded for efforts and value being generated;
- have a reasonable balance between workload and personal life; and
- x feel good about the work and the conditions under which I do it.

The performance management process, as typically implemented, would at the planning stage emphasize the merchandise representatives' performance goals and measures and perhaps at the reward stage penalize them for poor performance. With ongoing vigilance for all the conditions of peak performance, HR professionals and line managers can focus quickly on issues as they occur and give the key stakeholders a common perspective on what constitutes successful performance.

Conclusions from the Analysis

The above brief summary points to some important ways to improve performance. The merchandising representatives *know* what to do to support merchandising in stores but are unclear about their responsibilities with respect to the retailers' business plans. They have merchandising *ability* but are not able to train others nor support retailers' in achieving their business goals.

They feel very frustrated with respect to the support they receive for merchandising on a tight schedule. The material they need is often late or shipped to wrong destinations, which completely disrupts their routes and scheduling within their territory. The disrupted schedules impede co-ordination of meetings with the retail business advisors. The company's Sales Record System, which requires them to key in information on their computers, is very time consuming.

The merchandising representatives are beginning to feel stressed and unmotivated because they don't understand and can't perform the activities which have been identified as having the biggest leverage potential. Notably, they are having trouble working directly on the retailers' business goals and can't support ABC products through retailer training. Clearly, the dilution of motivation (**Want to Do It**) is due to problems in other conditions, particularly in "**Equipped to Do It**."

Our example, in which we viewed ABC as consultants, isolated current issues. When in use by an organization, the Peak Performance Model would be used in the day-to-day flow of activities. It works just as well as it did in the ABC Consumer Products "macro" application when focusing on the performance of one individual. It allows managers to regularly undertake due diligence, to monitor and adjust conditions instead of waiting for events scheduled in the performance management cycle.

Implications for Managers

Initially, managers might assume using the Peak Performance Model demands a lot of extra work. In fact, it's quite the reverse. The approach can be used to promote and guide self-leadership and self-management by employees within a performance partnership (see the accompanying box entitled "Organizational Outcomes"). With the tools for change in the employee's hands, employee and manager share the responsibility for the conditions that enable performance. The employee is encouraged to assume responsibility for creating peak performance. The organization, of course, still holds the manager accountable for the end results but accomplishes objectives by delegating more responsibility for thinking, planning and doing (see the accompanying box entitled "Responsibilities in Peak Performance Model"). The manager acknowledges that subordinates are fellow adults, worthy of trust and capable of high performance.

At the start, adopting this new approach to managing will require some extra effort by the manager. Fairly quickly, however, time is saved when other work evaporates. Fewer fires need to be fought. Fewer tasks need to be repeated. Performance is smoother and the manager is liberated.

Organizational Outcomes of Performance Management System

To sustain peak performance, a management system should produce these outcomes for the organization:

- Clearly understood organizational context for performance (vision, values, goals and strategies) and individual expectations aligned within that context
- Learning and growth in collective capability to perform

- Employees mentally and emotionally engaged
- Climate characterized by mutual trust, respect and support
- Superior business results

Responsibilities in Peak Performance Model

For The Individual

- Understand organization and work unit vision, goals, strategies and plans
- Develop performance and development plan that is clearly aligned with the needs of the business
- Measure and seek feedback and counsel regarding own performance
- Identify and remove barriers to performance, or enlist help to remove barriers that are outside their own control
- Deliver on commitments and hold self accountable
- Conduct oneself in way that fosters and sustains mutual trust and respect, professionalism and collaboration
- Stay informed about business plans and progress and adjust personal priorities to meet changing needs

For The Manager

- A manager has the above individual responsibilities as well as the following:
- Facilitate the communication and understanding of the organizational context for individual performance (vision, values, goals and strategies)
- Guide the development of individual performance and development plans that will lever organization goals
- Facilitate the removal of performance barriers that are beyond the control of individual employees and teams
- Allocate appropriate resources and reconcile any conflict between performance expectations and resource allocations
- Coach individuals in overcoming difficulties, building skill and applying learning to new opportunities

- Foster and maintain communication that creates alignment and facilitates implementation
- Deal directly and sensitively with issues of inadequate performance and inappropriate behaviour
- Support and guide, as needed, the measurement of individual and group progress
- Recognize progress toward and the achievement of desired results

It should be noted that the manager's role emphasizes communication, facilitation and coaching without being relieved of the final accountability to the organization for results. The focus is very much on helping employees to become self-managing.

Something Old, Something New

Traditional performance management processes, have tended to emphasize planning and assessment, and pay far too little attention to monitoring, feedback and guidance. By focusing on execution, we pay more attention to the critically important conditions for performance. The Peak Performance Model requires a shift in mind-set about performance management and provides managers with a thinking framework to help focus their attention on day-to-day feedback, coaching and communication.

Our model dealing with the conditions for performance is not necessarily a new perspective, a new invention! In fact, our model reflects the way things actually happen when people are producing excellent results. We have simply observed the phenomenon and described it in an easy-to-remember way![9]

This perspective is well tuned to today's organizational environment of leaner management, quicker response times and competitive pressures. If the company loops compensation back to performance and profits, it can cement the relationship, as the employee knows a direct payback will be forthcoming for improving shareholder value and

---

[9] Peak Performance Model is based on the "Performance Diamond" created for Petro-Canada by Tony Roithmayr in collaboration with Cam Graham.

corporate strength. As a result, shareholder value becomes important to the employee; rather than an abstract, or anger-provoking, concept.

Some managers might feel our approach is too simple. We haven't even mentioned record-keeping, which for many is synonymous with performance management. In our view, it's preferable to emphasize the outcomes of performance management and to view record-keeping as a tool used only to the degree needed to support decisions and agreements. Managers must develop a workable system for recording employee data which takes into account the model's emphasis on feedback and coaching, the number of employees they manage, and their own capacity to remember details. (To relieve the burden on managers, many organizations are shifting responsibility for recordkeeping activity to employees.)

And, of course, other elements of traditional performance management don't disappear. For example, the exercise of good judgement is still required—a little simpler with good tools but still a responsibility. Ultimately, the manager must decide: good, bad or indifferent. Poor performance needs to be confronted and improved. Judgements have to be made about allocating the organization's compensation dollars. These become less difficult, of course, when good groundwork has been laid throughout the year.

HR's role in performance management should be to enable an organization to live up to its promises. HR must be a facilitator, supporter and advisor; but it doesn't operate the processes, management does. HR should scout out managerial tools—simple, understandable, easy-to-use tools that can help line managers to improve performance. The Peak Performance Model is such a tool, helping managers but also enabling the individual employee to become self-managing.

This performance management tool can help organizations obtain desired outcomes. It also helps to avoid the problems of past performance management processes. The employee's objectives are no longer set in a vacuum; they are linked to the larger operational context. By placing performance management in the mainstream of daily activity, organizations bring objectives into the open and allow them to be routinely shared between individuals and teams. And everything is now aligned better and operating more interdependently. And, with appropriate recognition and rewards in place, the process of achieving superior results becomes self-reinforcing.

SUMMARY

We close with a summary of key themes, or principles, that are hallmarks of the perspective we espouse:

- Performance management is about managing the context for performance, not about controlling people.
- Performance can only be optimized when all the enabling conditions are considered, planned for and managed interdependently.
- Performance management is a partnership aimed at increasing self-direction by employees (ownership is important).
- Organization alignment is an ongoing task achieved through communication: achieving a "clear line of sight," monitoring and coaching.
- Performance management happens in relationship—it's a people process requiring mutual trust and respect.
- Performance management is a core business process—it *IS* about running the business.

CHAPTER TWELVE

Achieving Strategy Through People

INTEGRATED COMPETENCY-BASED HUMAN RESOURCES MANAGEMENT

Rick Lash and Mark Jackson

It comes as little surprise that organizations are undergoing rapid, unprecedented change unparalleled since the advent of the Industrial Revolution almost two centuries ago. To illustrate the profound impact of change on the way we work today, we can take a lesson from natural history. Twelve thousand years ago the Irish elk, a giant deer with specialized 12-foot antlers, happily roamed in what was then the tundra of Northern Ireland. As the Ice Age drew to a close and the climate warmed, the environment, which had remained stable for tens of thousands of years, began to change rapidly. Trees began to appear in what was formerly open space. Unfortunately for the Irish elk, 12-foot antlers were not well adapted for forests and as a result it quickly became extinct.

The lesson? In stable environments specialization is usually the key to success. When that environment undergoes rapid change, however, those same keys to success can kill you. In changing environments, success hinges on the ability to develop and apply new knowledge and behaviour across many *different* environments. This translates into the ability to be goal-directed, work within more complex social relationships, rapidly seek out and make sense of new information, and influence those around you: in short, the need for competencies.

DEFINING COMPETENCY

A competency is an enduring, underlying characteristic that defines a pattern of behaving or thinking which enables a person to deliver superior performance in a job role or situation. Competencies fall into broad categories:

- **Skill** is the ability to do specific physical or thinking tasks, for example, the ability to program a computer or complete a tax return.

- **Knowledge** is the information a person knows within a content area, for example, a client service representative's knowledge of investment products.

- **Social Role** is the image one displays in public, for example, whether one sees oneself as a leader, an expert, or a family person. It is closely linked to personal values and plays a significant role in the behaviours one projects to others.

- **Self-Image** is a person's sense of identify or self-worth. It is the individual's belief in his/her ability to be effective.

- **Traits** are the enduring characteristics of an individual and can be related to physical abilities, for example, good reaction time, and to personality characteristics, such as being introverted or outgoing.

- **Motives** are the unconscious thoughts and preferences that drive behaviour. Motives include one's desire to set and achieve challenging goals, and one's need to form relationships.

Competencies can be likened to an iceberg. Only a small percentage of an iceberg lies above the waterline and is visible. The majority of the iceberg lies under water (see Figure 1).

Likewise, competencies can be thought of as "above the waterline" and "below the waterline." The competencies above the waterline are those that are most easily observed: technical knowledge and skills. Most organizations focus on the technical competencies, the most visible and easily assessed. Independent research, however, shows that it is the "below-the-waterline" competencies that differentiate between average and superior performers. While technical competencies can be trained for, below-the-waterline or "behavioural" competencies are more difficult to develop. Competency-based Human Resources management therefore focuses on identifying the necessary technical skills and developing those below-the-waterline competencies that will produce superior results.

FIGURE 1: The Hay/McBer Model of Competencies

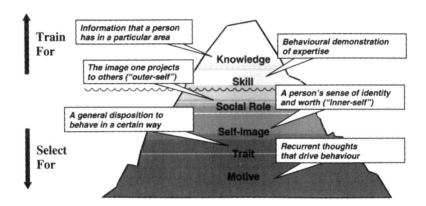

Using competencies as the basis for HR management increases the probability that the competencies people were hired for are the same ones that they are developed and managed for in the job, and that these capabilities are the foundation for taking on future leadership roles.

THREE WAVES OF COMPETENCY THEORY AND PRACTICE

One way to understand competencies is to put them into an historical perspective. In this century competencies emerged in three major waves, each building upon the other and culminating in the current use of competencies as a catalyst for strategic organizational change.

Wave I: The Search For the Outstanding Performer

Competencies are not new. They have been around in one form or another for at least thirty years. In the late 1960s, Dr. David McClelland of Hay/McBer Consulting was engaged by the U.S. State Department to study the hiring of young Foreign Information Service Officers (FISOs). At the time, the U.S. State Department was using a combination of a content-based exam, a standard intelligence test and grade point average to select candidates. The difficulty was that the State Department's own research showed little correlation between these factors and how well someone performed as a diplomat in a foreign country. In addition, almost all young FISOs were white males.

McClelland's approach was simple. Instead of assuming a test or grade point average could predict how well someone would perform on the job, he posed the question "What do people actually do when they are being successful?" McClelland first asked the State Department to identify two groups of FISOs—a group of clearly superior performers, as well as a contrasting group of average or "solid" performers who were just meeting job expectations. By conducting detailed interviews (now called Behavioural Event Interviews) with individuals from both groups, focusing on what they actually did in past job situations, and then analyzing the transcripts, McClelland identified competencies that differentiated the two groups. The resulting competency model was then validated with another group of FISOs to ensure the competencies really did predict successful job performance.

McClelland's approach to finding competencies that would predict job performance included:

- use of Behavioural Event Interviews to focus on past behaviour;
- use of criterion samples (i.e., contrasting average and superior performers); and
- validating the competencies to ensure they accurately predict job performance.

These methods have proved highly successful in identifying competencies and are the foundation of Hay/McBer's competency development methodology. It is both an elegant and a conceptually simple approach that emphasizes past behaviour as the best predictor of future success. The approach relies on identifying what successful people *actually do* on the job and comparing that to average performers (criterion samples). What people actually do can include both visible actions and the underlying thoughts and feelings that lead to actions. In this way, insight is gained into the hidden intent that drives behaviour.

Wave II: Integrated Human Resources Management

The second wave of competency implementation was marked by the move from a primary focus on identifying outstanding performers to a more integrated approach to competency-based HR management. For the first time, competencies provided organizations with a method for bringing together what were often separate management processes and systems into an integrating framework. Competencies provided a common language for bringing together all HR applications, from recruiting and staff selection, to managing and developing people's performance once they were in a job, to career and succession planning, and, finally, to how people are rewarded.

Wave III: Strategic Management

The third wave of competency implementation has been marked by the increasing pace of change as this century rapidly draws to a close. Increasing deregulation in the utilities, financial services, and telecommunications industries, the merging of technologies, corporate de-layering, and the continuing trend to global markets have demanded integrated solutions which would dramatically increase the economic return on strategic investments. If sustaining change characterized the first half of this decade, acceleration of change has defined the second half.

To add strategic value, competencies must be placed within a broader integrated framework of change (Figure 2).

FIGURE 2: Hay's Integrated Change Framework

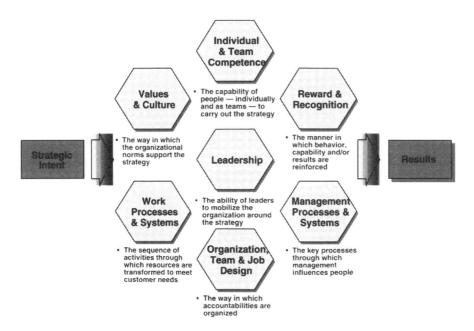

THE VALUE OF SUPERIOR PERFORMANCE TO AN ORGANIZATION

In a study published in the *Journal of Applied Psychology*[1], the researchers asked a simple question: "What is the value of superior performance for an organization?" The answer was somewhat surprising. After reviewing a number of published studies comparing average to superior performers across different jobs, organizations and industries, the authors found that productivity tends to fall into a standard bell curve. That is, about 60% of people are in the middle range of performance. People in this group are meeting the job expectations they were hired to accomplish. What interested the researchers was the approximately 15% of people who represented the top performers—those people who were significantly outperforming their colleagues.

In comparing this group to those in the middle range, the researchers found that differences in value-added output vary according to the complexity of the job. For low-complexity jobs such as administrative support positions, the difference in value-added output between average and superior-performers is approximately 19%. For example, a superior-performing administrative assistant produces approximately 19% more memos or 19% fewer errors in documentation than his or her average-performing counterpart. As one goes up the scale of job complexity, however, the differences become more significant. For moderate-and-high complexity jobs such as managerial, professional/technical and sales positions, the differences in output ranged from 32% to 120%.

The implications for organizations of this research and other studies like it are profound. If superior performers can make such a significant impact on key business results, it is in an organization's best interest to clearly identify what superior performers do to achieve those results. The objective is not to make everyone a superior performer, but rather to "shift the bell curve" to enable all people to perform at higher levels.

Competency Scales

Through the development of literally thousands of jobs throughout the world, Hay/McBer has identified similar competencies that emerge as

---

[1] J.E. Hunter, F.L. Schmidt and M.K. Judiesch. "Individual Differences in Output: Variability as a Function of Differences in Output," *Journal of Applied Psychology.* 75 (1990).

predictors of successful job performance. They tend to fall into broad categories or clusters of related competencies as detailed in Table 1.

TABLE 1: Sample: Managerial/Professional Competencies

1. Self-Management Cluster

- Self-Confidence
- Self-Control
- Flexibility
- Organizational Commitment

2. Cognitive (Thinking/Problem Solving) Cluster

- Technical Expertise
- Information Seeking
- Analytical Thinking
- Conceptual Thinking

3. Achievement Cluster

- Achievement Motivation
- Concern for Order
- Initiative

4. Influence Cluster

- Impact and influence
- Organizational Awareness
- Relationship Building
- Interpersonal Understanding/Responding
- Customer Service Orientation

5. Managerial Cluster

- Directing Others
- Developing Others
- Group Facilitation
- Leadership

Each competency is defined by a title (e.g., "Impact and Influence") and a definition. A major innovation was the concept of rating scales within a competency, or the "Just Noticeable Difference Behaviour Scale," in which each competency is defined in a progressive or cumulative scale of capability (Figure 3).

FIGURE 3: Behaviourally Based Competency Scales

Team Leadership is the intention to take a role as leader of a team or other group. It implies a desire to lead others. Team Leadership is generally, but certainly not always, shown from a position of formal authority.

1. **Informs People**: Lets people affected by a decision know what is happening. Makes sure the group has all the necessary information. May explain the reasons for a decision.

2. **Promotes Team Effectiveness**: Uses complex strategies to promote team morale and productivity (hiring and firing decisions, team assignments, cross-training, etc.).

3. **Takes Care of the Group**: Protects the group and its reputation vis-à-vis the larger organization or the community at large; obtains needed personnel, resources, information for the group. Makes sure the practical needs of the group are met.

4. **Positions Self as the Leader**: Ensures that others buy into leader's mission, goals, agenda, climate, tone, policy. "Sets a good example," models desired behaviour. Ensures that group tasks are completed. Is a credible leader.

5. **Communicates a Compelling Vision**: Communicates a compelling vision that generates excitement, enthusiasm and commitment to the group mission.

Each behavioural level on the scale denotes a higher level of sophistication or difficulty within the competency. The scale is also cumulative; that is, if one can demonstrate Level 3 in Team Leadership, he or she should also be able to demonstrate all the behaviours listed in Level 1 and Level 2. This innovation made for a more precise way to measure people against the competencies and ushered in a new era of competency-based HR management tools. It now became possible to establish target levels of performance within competencies for specific jobs, measure an individual's demonstrated capability against those targets, and identify "competency gaps" as illustrated in Figure 4.

FIGURE 4: Job/Person Performance Analysis

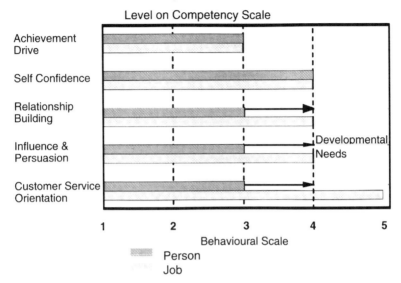

Having a more precise method to assess competencies provided a powerful tool for recruiting and selecting people ("How much of the competency has the candidate demonstrated in previous job situations?"); managing incumbents within a job ("What is his or her current level of performance?"); developing superior performance ("What are the biggest competency gaps?"); and succession planning ("How well does the individual perform against the target competency levels for future roles?").

COMPETENCY MODEL DEVELOPMENT

Any competency initiative, to be successful, must clearly link competencies to the strategic intent of the organization. Many competency initiatives have failed because the project champions failed to answer the question, "How will competencies support our mission and values and provide a competitive advantage?"

The first decision is where to focus competency model development activities. Will competency models be developed for specific jobs within the organization, by job family (that is, by a group of closely related jobs that share the same competencies), or by a job level or band that cuts across functions? Alternatively, some organizations begin their model development efforts by developing core organizational competencies that describe the key behaviours required by all jobs that reinforce and support the organization's mission and values. There are advantages and limitations to each approach, summarized in Table 2.

TABLE 2: Where to Focus Competency Model Development

Emphasis of Competency Model Development	Advantages	Limitations
Individual Job or Job Family	Competencies related directly to the requirements of specific jobs	Can reinforce territorial boundaries between individuals or teams
	Ideal for recruitment and selection of applicants to fill specific job vacancies	Potential for lack of consistency in competencies between job families
Role or Level	Identifies the key competencies required across a role or level versus the function or job	Requires a role-or level-based organizational structure already in place
	Provides the basis for linking competencies to job evaluation and pay	Potential to lose the uniqueness of individual functions or jobs
	Encourages movement across functions within a role or level	
Core	Emphasizes the core behaviours required for all positions in the organization	Does not focus on individual job or role requirements
	Reinforces and supports organizational values	Limited use for recruitment and performance management applications unless combined with other approaches

Many organizations have used a combination of approaches, for example, including the development of core organizational competencies with role- or job-specific competencies.

The Expert Panel

Once the focus, intent and primary applications of competency development have been established, the next step is to convene an expert panel. Participants in an expert panel include job or role experts who have an understanding of the current and future key accountabilities and competencies required for successful performance. The output of the expert panel is then used to develop a draft competency model, including target performance levels within each competency required for superior performance.

Depending on the primary focus for competency development, organizational resources and the level of precision required, there are a wide variety of competency model development approaches available. Experience has shown that expert panels can identify approximately 50% of the competencies that define superior performance.

Auxiliary Methods

For less critical job positions or roles, an expert panel alone can be sufficient to define a competency model; however, for most applications, additional processes are required to validate the competency model. These can include:

- **Behavioural Event Interviews (BEI):** This approach uses the same methodology pioneered by McClelland and Hay/McBer. A group of average and superior incumbents are identified and then interviewed. The BEI focuses on recent critical events in the incumbent's work, and precisely probes how these events were handled. Each interview is recorded and transcribed to capture behavioural details and competency themes. The data are then "coded" (i.e., scored for evidence of competencies) and analyzed for trends and differences between average and superior incumbents to determine what top performers are doing to help them be successful in the job or role.

- **Competency Assessment Questionnaires:** Another method is to use competency assessment questionnaires completed by managers about the performance of their direct reports along a number of competency dimensions based on the preliminary competency model developed by the expert panel. Analysis of the results reveals the competencies necessary for superior performance on the job. In addition, incumbents can also be asked to complete a questionnaire that asks them to rate which competencies are most important for their job or role as well as indicate the level of a competency needed for effective performance.

- **Focus Groups**: Focus groups with job or role incumbents can be used in conjunction with BEIs and/or questionnaires to further validate the competency model with incumbents. The focus groups test the importance of each competency to the job or role and confirm the levels of behaviour for each competency scale for average and superior performance. Focus groups are also useful in broadening the base of employee participation in competency model development and enhancing people's understanding of the process and its outcomes.

APPLICATION OF THE COMPETENCY FRAMEWORK

Once competency models have been developed and validated, they can then be used for specific Human Resources applications. Three of the most common applications for competency models are:

1. Recruitment and Selection,
2. Performance Management, and
3. Developing Superior Performance.

1. Recruitment and Selection

A central issue for HR professionals, including at least a generation of organizational psychologists, has been how to predict who will be successful in a job. Selection and staffing involves matching an individual's capabilities and job requirements with the expected benefits, including improved job satisfaction, higher productivity and reduced turnover. Yet for many organizations these expectations are only partly realized.

Competency-based selection systems give organizations a competitive advantage by providing a disciplined, valid approach for assessing individual capabilities that are directly related to job success. They have been shown to:

- significantly reduce turnover by increasing job satisfaction through better person/job matching—satisfied employees are less likely to leave;

- reduce the learning curve and improve the productivity of new employees by as much as 30% 50% since these individuals already possess the critical competencies to do the job; and

- increase the objectivity and legal defensibility of hiring decisions by clearly showing how selection methods assess the job competencies that lead to success in the job while not discriminating based on an individual's background, gender or age.

Steps in Designing a Competency-Based Selection and Staffing System

1. **Develop Competency Models**: The first step requires the development of a competency model for the target job(s) or role(s) using one of the methods described earlier (i.e., by specific job or job family, job level or band, or core organizational competency).

2. **Develop System Architecture**: Before any selection tools are developed, many organizations begin by answering basic design issues associated with the new process. A distinction should be made between "recruitment," which includes the activities for seeking out potential job candidates, and "selection," which includes the process assessing suitable candidates once they have been identified. Table 3 outlines the key questions that should be answered at this stage. Clearly, the answers to many of these questions will depend on the number of job openings, the expected number of applicants, and the internal resources available to manage the process.

TABLE 3: Guidelines for Developing a Competency-Based Selection System Architecture

Design Issue	Key Questions
1. Purpose of the System	Why does the organization need a new selection system? How does the selection process relate to mission and values? Who are the key stakeholders and what criteria will they use to determine the success of the new selection system?
2. Strategy for Recruitment	What are the organization's current recruitment needs for specific jobs/roles? Should recruitment be an ongoing process throughout the year? Who will manage the recruitment process (e.g., HR or managers)?

Design Issue	Key Questions
	Who will be accountable for ensuring candidate representation from designated groups (e.g., gender, age, ethnicity)?
3. Application and Pre-Screening	What are the ratios of applicants to available positions? What criteria will be used to screen candidates at the front-end (e.g., competencies, technical skills, certifications)? How will these criteria be weighted? Who will manage the application and pre-screening process? Will it be locally or centrally managed? How will the pre-screening process differ for internal candidates?
4. Assessment Process	Which essential competencies should be assessed and at what target level of performance? What methods will be used to assesses "above-and below-the-waterline" competencies? What feedback will applicants receive and when will they receive it? Who will administer the process (internal versus third party)? How will ongoing effectiveness and validity be measured?
5. Final Selection Decisions	Who will have input to final selection decisions? What is HR's versus management's role? What is the process for offers of employment?

3. **Select Assessment Tools**: Once the system architecture has been confirmed, methods for assessing key competencies are chosen. Competency assessment methods generally fall into several broad categories:

   - **Standardized Tests** can be used to assess mental ability and personality characteristics and provide a valid and accurate method to assess individual competencies. Like the Competency Assessment Questionnaire (described below), standardized tests can be a cost-effective method for reducing the total number of candidates at the early stages of the assessment process.

   - **Competency Assessment Questionnaires**: This is a cost-effective method that consists of a self-scoring questionnaire containing sets of behaviours relating to specific job competencies, for example,

Analytical Thinking or Customer Service Orientation. The candidate checks off a behavioural statement within the set (e.g., "I tried to do the job well or right") and then provides a written example of when he or she demonstrated that behaviour. This approach provides applicants with a "realistic job preview" and reduces the initial pool of candidates before they apply. Candidates who complete the questionnaire tend to be of higher calibre and are often better prepared for a Behavioural Event Interview.

- **Behavioural Event Interviews**: This is essentially the same interview method described earlier for developing competency models. For assessment purposes, open-ended questions for each competency are developed, providing an opportunity for the candidate to recall past situations where he or she had an opportunity to demonstrate the competencies required for the job.

- **Job-Relevant Simulations**: These exercises provide an opportunity to observe candidates demonstrating critical on-the-job competencies. They are particularly useful for assessing a wide range of thinking and interpersonal abilities. Different types of simulations that can be used to assess competencies include in-basket exercises, leaderless group tasks, role plays and business cases.

4. **Design the Assessment Process**: Most competency-based selection systems contain several assessment stages or "hurdles" successful candidates must pass through. The challenge in this step is to sequence the assessment methods so that broad, less labour-intensive methods, such as tests and self-assessment questionnaires, can be used to pre-screen candidates, reserving the more specific, resource-intensive approaches, including Behavioural Event Interviews and simulations, for candidates more likely to possess critical competencies.

2. Performance Management

Using competencies to match candidates with jobs is often only half the battle. Once incumbents are in the job, the burning question becomes how to continue to support individual competencies to ensure future success in the role. Yet for many organizations, performance management remains a cumbersome administrative activity executed annually with the enthusiasm of a visit to the dentist.

Looking at the progression of performance management across many organizations, a range of approaches emerge (Figure 5).

FIGURE 5: Range of Performance Management Approaches

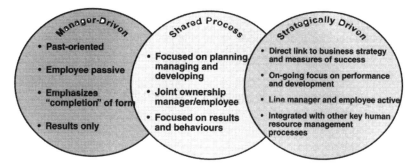

Strategic alignment and performance improvement

- **Manager-Driven Approach**
  The primary focus is on "performance appraisal" of past results and typically does not include competencies. The employee takes a more passive role ("It's my manager's job to tell me what I'm doing right and where my faults are."). In organizations using this approach performance management tends to be an annual activity with an emphasis on the completion of the "form," with HR playing the primary role for administration, management and quality control of the process.

- **Shared Process Approach**
  A second approach makes performance management an ongoing process throughout the business cycle. The emphasis is on planning and managing performance and weighs both achieved results as well as the competencies used to get there. It is more of a jointly shared process between manager and employee; input on performance is provided not only by the manager but by the employee, peers, subordinates and even customers. The manager and the employee together develop consensus on appraisal results.

- **Strategically Driven Approach**
  Over the past several years, a trend has emerged in performance management that is characterized by a strategic linkage to short- and medium-term business results across a wide range of balanced

scorecard measures, including operations, external stakeholder satisfaction and financial results. In these organizations, performance management is viewed as central to enhancing business effectiveness and is fully integrated with other business processes. Employee development is central in these organizations; ownership for the process rests with line management, with active involvement from employees.

Elements of all three approaches may be present in any one organization, and each has an important role to play. The extent to which one predominates, however, will help to determine the direction performance management needs to take for the future.

Solving Design Issues

Competency-based performance management uses a "mixed model" that assesses both performance results and competencies that predict successful job performance. In designing a process that integrates both the "what" and the "how" of performance, a number of design issues should be considered:

1. **What is the purpose of performance management?** Although it may seem like an obvious question, the answer can significantly impact the direction of performance management. Is the primary purpose to assess past performance in order to make compensation decisions; is it to provide developmental feedback so people can improve in their roles; is it for career/succession planning, or all of the above? Where the emphasis is placed has profound implications for how the new performance management approach will be communicated to the organization and the resources and systems required to support it.

2. **What performance data will be gathered?** In a mixed approach, information on results as well as competencies is gathered. Questions that must be considered at this stage include:

   • How many objectives should be set and how will they be established?

   • What relative weightings will be given to objectives and competencies in the overall assessment?

   • Will competencies impact reward decisions?

- What are the linkages to promotions, incentives, succession planning and development?

Given that competencies represent a significant change for people, many organizations take a gradual approach in linking competencies to pay. For the first year or two, competencies are often used solely for developmental purposes, to allow staff and managers to develop a common understanding of the competencies and rating scales before they are used for compensation decisions.

3. **Who will be involved?** Managers, employees, peers, subordinates and even customers can have a role to play in performance management. The key questions that must be answered are:

   - How many source groups will provide input for an individual employee? How will they be selected?

   - Who manages the information and gives feedback to employees and managers?

   - Who maintains quality control over the process?

4. **When will it happen?** Typically, performance management can be viewed as a continuous cycle of four phases.

   - **Planning**: Establishing objectives for the coming year and developmental activities to enhance job competencies.

   - **Coaching**: Maintaining ongoing contact between the manager and employee to provide developmental support and ensure priorities are aligned with changing circumstances.

   - **Reviewing**: Determining gaps between desired and actual performance.

   - **Rewarding**: Answering the question "what's in it for me?"

When these activities occur during the business cycle and how often (e.g., annual versus quarterly reviews) needs to be determined.

   During the design phase it is often helpful to convene a task group to answer these key questions and prepare an architecture document that serves as a blueprint for the performance management system as well as a powerful communication piece and sounding board for the organization. The architecture document would contain a statement of guiding principles and objectives, a description of the system components, and a schedule of performance management activities with the business cycle.

3. Developing Superior Performance

Competency-based HR management challenges the current thinking on how organizations approach the development of superior performance. Using competencies to develop superior performance requires more than just another training program. It is about understanding that superior performance is not a plateau one achieves, but rather a process that people engage in over and above their normal day-to-day activities. Whether people are just learning a new task or have been doing the same job for years superior performers learn differently. Using this perspective, individuals and organizations can begin to view superior performance in terms of how we learn as we approach our daily work. Superior performance, then, depends on helping people acquire the competence to learn.

Stages of Learning

In any field, whether learning to play the piano or to run a business, people go through several progressive stages of competency development (Figure 6).

FIGURE 6: Stages of Learning

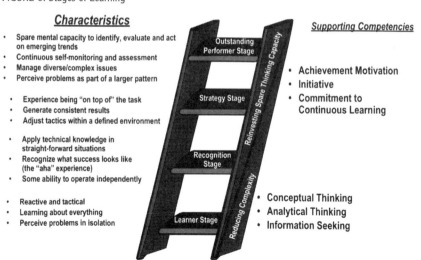

Characteristics

- Spare mental capacity to identify, evaluate and act on emerging trends
- Continuous self-monitoring and assessment
- Manage diverse/complex issues
- Perceive problems as part of a larger pattern

- Experience being "on top of" the task
- Generate consistent results
- Adjust tactics within a defined environment

- Apply technical knowledge in straight-forward situations
- Recognize what success looks like (the "aha" experience)
- Some ability to operate independently

- Reactive and tactical
- Learning about everything
- Perceive problems in isolation

Outstanding Performer Stage

Strategy Stage

Recognition Stage

Learner Stage

Reinvesting Spare Thinking Capacity

Reducing Complexity

Supporting Competencies

- Achievement Motivation
- Initiative
- Commitment to Continuous Learning

- Conceptual Thinking
- Analytical Thinking
- Information Seeking

The beginner or "learner" stage, when everything about the task is new, is characterized by a feeling of being consumed by the task, and by reactive and tactical behaviour; there is a tendency to perceive problems in isolation. People at this stage have challenges recognizing what success looks like, let alone knowing how to make it happen. As one progresses up the ladder, one learns how to apply knowledge and skills, first in straightforward tasks, and then with experience, in more complex and varied situations. People at higher stages experience being "on top of" the task and can generate consistent results. At the "outstanding performer" stage, people are continually monitoring and assessing themselves and the results they are achieving. They perceive issues as part of the larger picture and can manage diverse and complex problems with great flexibility and speed, using their accumulated experience to identify, evaluate and act on emerging trends.

Common sense shows that even at the learner stage superior performers do things that accelerate them along the development path, while others seem to stagnate, plateau, or move along only with great difficulty. Superior performers learn differently, even at the learner stage. By reducing the complexity of the information they have to manage through recognizing common patterns and automating tasks, these individuals create spare thinking capacity that they intentionally reinvest to continually build their expert knowledge base. Reinvestment of spare thinking capacity is the engine that drives superior performance.[2]

The Role of Expert Knowledge

Research in many different fields shows that superior performers simply know a great deal more than average performers and they use that knowledge base in solving their daily tasks. That knowledge base can be roughly categorized into three areas:

- **Academic knowledge or "knowing about"**: Typically learned in training or educational settings, it consists of formal technical or theoretical information learned through courses or reading books and can be generalized to different organizations and work settings.

- **Practical knowledge or "knowing how"**: Practical or "tacit" knowledge cannot be taught directly. It is developed through repeated

---

[2] Carl Bereiter and Marlen Scardamalia, *Surpassing Ourselves: An Inquiry into the Nature and Implications of Expertise* (Open Court, 1992).

real-life problem-solving and, unlike academic knowledge, is tied to a specific domain or context that people work in. Practical knowledge can include knowing the procedures to get work done or knowing what approaches work in an organization and what tends to get valued. It is also difficult to articulate to others.

- **Self-management knowledge or "knowing yourself"**: This is the knowledge necessary to manage oneself, including knowing one's strengths and areas of weakness, the ability to self-reflect and control emotions and, for example, knowing under what conditions one performs at his or her peak. Self-management knowledge controls or regulates the use of academic and practical knowledge.

Competency-based research across many organizations and industries consistently shows that all three types of knowledge are essential for superior performance. Reinvestment of spare thinking capacity is the engine that drives the development of the expert knowledge base.

Reinvestment Is Key

How we choose to reinvest our spare thinking capacity is what differentiates average from superior performers. Average performers tend to rely on routines to simplify their job tasks in order to reduce the number of problems they have to deal with. Once we learn the skill of driving a car, for example, most of us choose to reinvest our spare thinking capacity in other things such as thinking about an upcoming meeting or talking on the phone while driving to work. Unless we intend to significantly enhance our driving skill, we choose not to reinvest our spare thinking capacity in the task at hand.

Superior performers, however, are motivated to reinvest spare thinking capacity, which they gain as a natural consequence of learning, in continually building their expert knowledge base for activities critical to their personal and professional success. Superior performers tend to reinvest their spare thinking capacity by:

- engaging in new formal learning;

- taking on increasingly difficult tasks that continually push them to the edge of their competence; and

- reflecting on their own thinking, building more complex concepts and connections (e.g., linking a business unit's turnover to an organizational culture issue).

Defined in this way, superior performance emerges as something all of us do, depending on the tasks or situations we find ourselves in. The challenge for HR professionals is to motivate and support employees so that they reinvest their spare thinking capacity in the activities that support the strategy and goals of the organization.

SUPERIOR PERFORMING ENVIRONMENTS

The very nature of many organizations—with traditional hierarchies, an emphasis on managed control of information, an aversion to setting people free to take on progressively more challenging tasks, and limited managerial skill in self-reflection and sharing expert knowledge—can inhibit the growth of a culture that supports reinvestment. Superior performing organizations focus on the development of expert knowledge by supporting and rewarding people for reinvesting their spare capacity to continually build their academic, practical and self-management knowledge. These cultures are characterized by four key dimensions (Figure 7):

- sharing expert knowledge
- working at the edge of one's competence,
- enhancing capacity for self-management, and
- experimentation.

Sharing Expert Knowledge

Research in the fields of general education and professional training (for example, schools of architecture[3]) demonstrates individuals can make huge strides by working with expert coaches while applying their knowledge and skill in shared problem solving environments. These opportunities often happen informally. The key is for organizations to make the sharing of expert knowledge happen by design rather than by chance. Professional practicums are a powerful learning tool where an expert coach/manager leads shared problem solving discussions among a group of professionals. The role of the expert coach/manager is to encourage the reinvestment of spare capacity by:

- modelling the thinking process he or she engages in when approaching key job tasks;

---

[3] Donald Schon, *The Reflective Practitioner* (Basic Books, 1983).

FIGURE 7: Superior Performing Environments

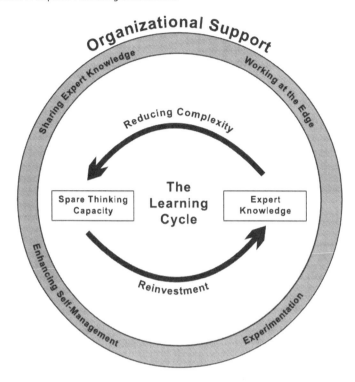

- teaching others to ask the right questions and predict outcomes;
- encouraging others to create learning goals;
- reformulating problems at higher levels; and
- assisting others in identifying alternatives that will lead to success.

Managers can be trained to develop these expert coaching skills and competencies, while employees can be provided with the complementary skills that encourage them to develop their expert knowledge base. In this way, superior performance becomes accepted organizationally as an ongoing process that everyone should engage in.

Working at the Edge of One's Competence

Expert knowledge is also built through real-life problem-solving. People who engage in the process of superior performance are different in that they continually push themselves to take on tasks that are at the edge of their capability. In doing so they gain important experiences in which approaches work and which ones don't; how long it takes to accomplish tasks; the pitfalls one should look out for; and the cues that let one know whether or not he or she is being successful.

Structured on-the-job developmental experiences requiring progressively higher competency levels are key to developing this practical knowledge. These can include individually self-directed activities, partnered activities with a manager or coach, and team-based activities. To achieve maximum benefits, development experiences should also provide an opportunity to build academic and self-management knowledge as well as practical experience.

Development Guides

Development guides are a competency-based tool developed by Hay/McBer for use by both managers and employees in identifying activities targeted at specific competency gaps. Development guides (see accompanying box entitled "Sample Development Guide") contain individual and partnered activities as well as resources including books, training videos and even popular films organized under different competencies (for example, "Impact and Influence").

Sample Development Guide

Client Service Orientation implies a desire to help or serve others. It means focusing one's efforts, anticipating and meeting the client's needs, responding with appropriate solutions and providing prompt service.

For example:
The core of Client Service Orientation is acting in the best interest of someone else. People with this competency think about a situation in terms of the other person's needs, not their own. They fully focus on uderstanding the other person's point of view and make a sincere commitment to helping.

Shown by:
- deciding on the best way to serve the client based on the options available
- taking responsibility to resolve a client's problem even if it goes beyond the normal demands of the job

---

Not shown by:
- offering the same service to every client
- giving someone else the responsibility for difficult client problem

Self-Directed Activities

1. Look for examples of good customer service demonstrated by others.
- This is something you can do in your everyday dealing with the phone company, retail shops, banks. Who does it well?
- What did you like about the service you received? What specific behaviours lead to good services?
- Write down the behaviours you observed. Identify any patterns.
- Identify those behaviours you could incorporate into your own service delivery.

2. Keep a list of any compliments you receive from clients on your desk.
- Keep track of how many work-related compliments you get each month.
- Strive to provide such good service that you receive an increasing number of compliments.
- This list will remind you of rewards of providing good client service and it will also keep track of how well you are doing.

Once an assessment of the employee's competency strengths and areas for development has been completed, the development guide is used to identify appropriate activities. At most, only two or three competencies are developed at a time. The development guides also contain specific examples of what the competency looks like and does not look like on the job to help the employee clearly understand the behaviours he or she is attempting to acquire. The development guides are based on the six principles of competency acquisition:

- recognizing the competency when it is demonstrated by others,
- being able to explain the competency,
- assessing the competency,
- practising the competency by trying out different behaviours,
- applying the competency and integrating it into daily on-the-job performance, and
- receiving feedback from others.

Development Guides have been used successfully for all levels in an organization, ranging from front-line service positions to senior-level executive roles.

Enhancing Capacity for Self-Management

The ability to manage thinking and emotions can be just as important as academic and practical knowledge in predicting success in one's career and personal life. This ability is often called "emotional intelligence," a term popularized in a book of the same name[4]. Superior performers regularly "think about their own thinking," identifying gaps in their own knowledge or capability. They also have a well-developed understanding of themselves. They have insight into their emotions, why they experience particular feelings at particular times, the impact of their behaviour on others, and, most important, how to manage those feelings and behaviours in order to develop more effective interpersonal relationships. This self-knowledge also includes understanding of their motivations and drives, and knowing when they work most effectively. All these aspects of self-awareness—reflection, emotional and motivational management—are also part of the process of superior performance.

There are a variety of approaches that Hay/McBer has used to assist individuals in building self-awareness. These applications fall into several categories:

- **Competency-based assessments**: By far the most widely used, self-assessments and/or full multi-rater assessments provide an individual with feedback on his or her current level of competency performance against the "Just Noticeable Difference" scale within a competency.

- **Managerial style inventories**: These assessment tools focus on an individual's managerial behaviours and how they impact on others, including direct reports, peers and supervisors.

- **Motivation profiling**: Using a series of competency-based and psychological instruments, individuals develop insight into their motivation profile. The resulting profile provides insight into three key areas of the individual's motivation, originally identified by McClelland:

  - **achievement**: the extent to which the individual is driven to set and achieve challenging goals,

  - **affiliation**: the extent to which the individual is driven to form relationships with others, and

---

[4] Daniel Goleman, *Emotional Intelligence* (Bantam Books, 1995).

- **power**: the extent to which the individual is driven to have an impact on others.

The resulting motivation profile can then be used to help the individual achieve a better match between his or her drives and the demands of the job.

- **Emotional Intelligence or "EQ"**: Several assessment questionnaires have recently been developed that assess an individual's capacity to manage his or her emotions. Training programs based on strategies for managing one's feelings and improving interpersonal effectiveness have also become available.

With all of these applications, structured feedback and coaching by an experienced facilitator is key to helping the individual understand the meaning of the developmental information and how it can be used to manage his or her own performance.

Experimentation

Through experimentation all of us develop our own theories about how the world really works. Experimentation is one of the most powerful techniques we have to build practical knowledge. For children, play is a form of experimentation. Through play, children rehearse in a safe and vastly simplified environment representing the adult roles they may take on in future years. As adults, experimentation in daily life helps us to adjust our approach, confirm our understanding, or change our assumptions, especially in situations that are unique or unforeseen.

A culture that supports experimentation is one that encourages people to test out new ways of performing and accepts multiple approaches to similar problems. Experimentation can take place in daily practice, or through structured activities such as business simulations. Like a laboratory, simulations reduce the complexity of a real-world system to its key elements and compresses time so that what would take weeks or months to observe can be experienced over a few hours or days. Simulations allow participants to try out new behaviours and observe the impact of their actions in a low-risk environment. They can be effective tools that support reinvestment by reducing complexity and encouraging reflective thinking.

USING COMPETENCIES FOR INTEGRATED ORGANIZATIONAL CHANGE

Between an organization's strategic value and the results or measures that get paid attention to are the "people levers" an organization has at its disposal to make change happen (Figure 2). Successful change requires the coordinated and simultaneous management of all these elements.

It often becomes apparent that a change in one component, for example, a new competency-based performance management system, may require a change in reward and recognition and in team and job design.

Take a financial services industry example. When developing a competency model for a financial advisor position for a major brokerage firm, "Teamwork and Cooperation" emerged as a key competency that differentiated average from superior performers. This competency was to form part of the new performance management process, yet financial advisors worked in what was termed an "eat what you kill" culture, where people were rewarded for individual transactions (i.e., personal commissions). It was often to financial advisors' disadvantage to work in partnership with their peers. The organization's strategy was to move to a reward structure that emphasized total assets under management versus personal commissions. As a result, "simultaneous re-engineering" was required of the organization's values and culture, team design, and reward and recognition if the new behaviours were to be implemented and sustained.

Determining Readiness for Change

We present below a checklist, organized by topic, which organizations should review before embarking on a re-engineering project. The extent to which you can answer "yes" to each question below is an indication of how well your organization is positioned for implementation of competencies that can act as a catalyst for integrated strategic change.

Leadership:

- Is there a compelling vision that inspires the organization?

- Are leaders as a team viewed as solidly behind the new direction?

- Do individual leaders "walk the talk"? Do their actions support the strategies?

Values and Culture:

- Do people know the values and behaviours needed to achieve desired results?
- Are values communicated and understood?
- Are people behaving in ways that demonstrate the values and culture?

Work Processes and Systems:

- Have key work processes required to support the strategy been identified?
- Are key work processes efficient and effective?
- Does information flow where it is needed when it is needed?

Organization, Team and Job Design:

- Does the way work is designed support the strategy?
- Do team and individual roles support the required work processes?
- Do teams and individuals understand their roles and account-abilities?

Individual and Team Competence:

- Have individual and team competencies (skills, behaviour, knowledge) been identified?
- Is there an adequate talent pool?
- Are the right people in the right jobs?

Management Processes and Systems:

- Do the selection, development, career and succession planning systems support the strategy?
- Has the strategy been translated into specific performance measures?
- Is the performance management process effective?

Reward and Recognition:

- Does reward and recognition support the strategy?

- Is there a clear link between measurement and reward?

- Does reward encourage the demonstration and development of competencies and key performance indicators?

SUMMARY

This chapter began by positioning competencies as a response to the revolutionary changes occurring in business. They are a powerful concept which can assist organizations in providing people with the tools to adapt successfully to an increasingly dynamic and unpredictable environment.

Our purpose has been to demonstrate that competencies have broad applications. To truly raise the bar of people performance through competencies, organizations need to be prepared for significant investment of resources and allow for sufficient time for design and implementation. For those organizations that have taken this challenging route, the investment can provide individuals with the tools to significantly improve productivity and personal ownership of development and growth, leading to sustained competitive advantage over the long term.

CHAPTER THIRTEEN

Developing a Compensation Strategy

John Lewis

INTRODUCTION

THIS BOOK DEALS with the business changes that will be required to respond to the challenges of the future, and the resulting implications of these changes on the Human Resources function. Two areas of change have a particular impact on compensation:

- **the changing nature of the competitive environment**, with new requirements for speed, quality, cost control and technological mastery, and their impact on the skills or competencies required by those doing the work; and

- **the pressure for cost reduction**, with its impact on the relationship between owners and workers and the nature of the bargain struck between these two groups.

Delivering effective and appropriate compensation for today's and tomorrow's organization requires careful attention to be paid to these changes and the resulting changes in an organization's goals. In this chapter, we will explore compensation strategy in three steps. First, we will consider compensation in the context of other HR functions and of an organzation's overall strategy. Second, we will define the underlying principles of compensation design, which despite many other changes in the business environment remain constant. Third, we will explore the delivery of actual compensation programs incorporating both underlying principles and attention to an organization's goals

THE PRINCIPLES OF COMPENSATION DESIGN

The underlying principles of compensation design have not changed; we may usefully review them by examining the following series of straightforward questions:

- What do we mean by "a job"?
- How much is a job worth?
- How much should we pay someone in the job?

What Do We Mean by "a Job"?

Traditionally, a job is a series of tasks or activities within an organization, normally carried out by one person. Many different people can have the same job ("sales representative," "administrative assistant"). Often, the tasks have been closely described in a written job description.

Because jobs as defined by tightly written job descriptions have been seen as restrictive or even irrelevant in a period of rapid change in the work force, it has become popular to think of a job as a series of skills or competencies, and work as being the often fluid application of these skills. In the ideal organization, there is a perfect match between the skills possessed by the employees and the skill requirements of the work to be done; in fact, the skills of the employees determine the work that will be done. In the real world, there will be mismatches; most organizations still require considerable structure in order to operate, and it may not be possible to structure the work to take advantage of the skills possessed by the workers. If employees have more skills than the work requires, there is a choice between thinking of the job as the work to be done or as the set of skills possessed by the employee doing the work.

Organizations that are less structured, that view their future success as being closely linked to the skills of their workforce, and believe that these skills will be in short supply, are likely to want to consider jobs in terms of skills. Organizations that are more structured and more oriented to results in the shorter term are more likely to want to consider jobs in terms of work and results, even where they are keenly interested in improving the skill base of the workforce.

How Much Is a Job Worth?

Most people would agree that different jobs do have different relative worth; for example, the job of Vice-President, Sales, is more valuable than that of sales representative, and the job of plant manager is more valuable than that of plant security guard. It would also appear that, in a general way, there is consensus about the sorts of factors that give value to jobs: the level of expertise required, the difficulty or complexity of the decisions that need to be taken, the accountability for results, and the conditions under which the work is performed. These general sorts of factors have relevance to jobs regarded as sets of skills just as much as they do to jobs regarded in terms of work and results.

There is a broad spectrum of possible ways to translate these general ideas about factors into an actual relative ranking of jobs in an organization. At one extreme, it would be possible to arrive at an overall ranking by doing a comparison of each pair of jobs, subjectively reviewing the entirety of each job. At the other, considerable effort has been put into so-called "hard factor" evaluation systems, where objective data has been used as a proxy for more subjective factors. While these systems do go a long way towards matching the subjective consensus about relative value, they do not appear to completely match it, and they are not in common use. It is still most common to rank jobs relatively, using a system of subjective factors.

Job Evaluation Systems

Over several decades, a large number of these systems have been designed, each of which claims to identify exactly those factors that give value to a job and the extent to which each factor applies to a given job. Known as job evaluation systems, they most commonly are "point factor" systems, in which each factor is divided into a series of levels, and each level is defined and assigned a value in points. Figure 1 shows an example of one factor in a job evaluation system. To determine the relative value of a job, each factor is examined for the level that most closely matches the way that factor applies to the job. The points for each factor are added together, and the total number of points is the relative value of the job.

FIGURE 1: Description of Decision-Making Factor

SKILL: DECISION MAKING / INITIATIVE

Decision making / initiative describes the requirement in the job to choose between alternative courses of action when faced with a problem that has more than one solution. The exercise of this choice requires some degree of judgement and initiative.

Level 1	Solutions involve choice between a small number of well-defined alternatives. The information available conforms to a standard pattern and is sufficient for making the best choice without analysis. There is essentially no opportunity to exercise initiative.
Level 2	Solutions involve simple analysis; the choice can be made by trial and error. The opportunity to exercise judgement or initiative is limited and not significant.
Level 3	Problem analysis involves choosing a subset of the available information and estimating from incomplete information. A number of solutions may be available as a result of the analysis, and a choice must be made between them. This choice requires some level of judgement.
Level 4	Problem analysis involves considering different variables, each of which has an effect on the others. Understanding the action of the variables involves the ability to perform analysis based on technical, commercial or behavioural principles. Arriving at a solution requires the exercise of judgement and initiative.

Different systems give similar, but not identical, relative values to particular jobs. Many organizations choose to design their own systems, while others prefer to purchase one of the systems available on the market. Designing their own system may be most appropriate for organizations that are used to a high degree of employee involvement, and that will involve employee task teams in the selection of factors, the description of levels for each factor and the evaluation of the actual jobs. Organizations that are comfortable with lower levels of employee involvement my choose to purchase a system and to have minimal employee involvement in the evaluation of actual jobs. In either case, successful application requires communication of the system and perceived equity and objectivity in actual evaluation; this in turn depends on good information about jobs being made available.

Job Descriptions

Historically, the main source of information has been a written job description. However, interviews with the job incumbent and the incumbent's supervisor are likely to produce better information. A major concern with written job descriptions is that they tend to degenerate to a list of tasks, and support the idea of restriction and specificity in jobs, rather than the more fluid approach to work that is required in many organizations. Much time can be wasted in discussion and argument around minor changes to written job content.

One solution to this problem is to focus on much more general descriptions that are generic enough to encompass many different specific positions in an organization, so that, for example, all the positions in one sector, or family, of jobs in an organization, such as administrative jobs, may be described in two or three job descriptions. This approach is interesting to organizations that are skill-driven because it highlights the skills and skill levels required for all jobs. Figure 2 shows an example of such a family of jobs; here the general descriptions are linked directly to factors in a job-evaluation system and to the core competencies of the organization.

Pay Equity

In several jurisdictions, legislation has been put in place to support the concept of equal pay for women for work of equal value. Such legislation requires the use of a job evaluation system that is gender-neutral, that is, one whose factors do not relatively undervalue jobs traditionally held by women. Obviously, organizations that operate within these jurisdictions will have to have some form of equitable job evaluation process in place.

How Much Should We Pay Someone in a Job?

Many organizations find it difficult to see how the whole exercise of relatively valuing jobs adds value. To them, the important question is how much a job is worth in the marketplace.

FIGURE 2: Role Description—Secretarial and Administrative Roles

Competency Area: Technical

LEVEL 1

Functional
Basic skills are required, such as ability to carry out basic arithmetical operations (multiplication, division), and ability to operate standard business equipment, including a PC, with a solid working knowledge of Word.

Quality
There is a solid basic understanding of the relevant operational standards, such as Visual Identity Standards.

LEVEL 2

Functional
Basic knowledge of technical or vocational topics is required, such as bookkeeping, or more advanced knowledge of basic skills (calculation of averages, use of tables) and ability to carry out more advanced functions on a PC (advanced level knowledge of Word, straightforward presentations in PowerPoint, basic knowledge of Excel).

Quality
There is a solid and extensive understanding of the relevant operational standards.

LEVEL 3

Functional
Knowledge of basic principles and applications of technical or commercial topics is required, such as accounting or business administration (ability to read and understand a balance sheet, or to complete simple tax returns), or advanced PC skills (use of graphs and tables in PowerPoint, advanced Excel knowledge, ability to use Access).

Quality
There is in-depth and comprehensive understanding of the relevant operational standards.

Competency Area: Client Service

LEVEL 1

Understanding and Relating to the Client
Verbal and written communications skills are effective for normal interchange of information.
Contacts may be inside or outside the firm and are to exchange routine information.
Normal tact and courtesy are required.

LEVEL 2

Understanding and Relating to the Client
Verbal and written communications skills are effective for developing and explaining ideas. Contacts may be inside or outside the firm and are for the purpose of giving or obtaining information where the true information needs are not clearly or completely defined before hand. High levels of patience, tact and persuasiveness are required.

LEVEL 3

Understanding and Relating to the Client
Verbal and written communications skills are effective for presenting and defending proposals.
Contacts may be inside or outside the firm and are for the purpose of resolving problems or negotiating. Solid negotiation skills are required.

Competency Area: Management

LEVEL 1

Evaluation of Problems and Issues
Problems that are identified can be resolved by choosing between a small number of previously-defined alternatives, with little analysis required to make the correct choice.

Decision Making
Work consists of well-defined tasks, presented in a straightforward sequence with reasonable time for completion. There is little need to prioritize between conflicting tasks.

Implementation
The incumbent carries out tasks in accordance with standard written procedures or well-defined standard practice, and has regular access to supervision while the work is in progress and on completion. The incumbent must handle variation of work within the defined standards; deviation outside standards is referred to a supervisor for resolution, but it is expected that the incumbent will contribute to the discussion around resolution.

LEVEL 2

Evaluation of Problems and Issues
Problems that are identified can be resolved by straightforward analysis and trial and error.

Decision Making
Work consists primarily of tasks, with occasional small projects, often presented with a very short time frame for completion, requiring careful organization and planning to ensure timely completion.

Implementation
The incumbent carries out tasks and projects in accordance with standard practice, and has access to supervision when needed, primarily to confirm that completed work adheres to standard practice. The incumbent must solve problems within standard practice; unusual problems are referred to a supervisor with a recommendation for resolution.

LEVEL 3

Evaluation of Problems and Issues
Problems that are identified can be resolved by collecting data, summarizing and extrapolating from it, and choosing between different alternatives defined by the incumbent.

Decision Making
Work consists of both tasks and non-complex projects of relatively short duration, presented from different sources with conflicting time frames for completion, requiring good judgment and knowledge of the organization, and well-developed planning skills, to ensure the most effective completion.

Implementation
The incumbent carries out tasks and projects in accordance with generally accepted standards and agreed objectives, and has access to supervision when needed, primarily to confirm that completed work adheres to objectives and is technically sound. The incumbent must solve problems within general standards; unusual problems are discussed with colleagues or a supervisor so that the incumbent can propose a resolution.

Competency Area: Leadership

LEVEL 1

Motivating and Inspiring Others
Consistently demonstrates willingness to help others and models commitment to vision and values.

Team Building
An effective and willing participant as a junior member of teams.

LEVEL 2

Motivating and Inspiring Others
Initiates relationships that build mutual support.

Team Building
An effective and enthusiastic participant as a working team member.

LEVEL 3

Motivating and Inspiring Others
Is widely viewed as an outstanding role model and natural leader to whom others turn for advice and assistance.

Team Building
An effective participant as an active and enthusiastic team member and team leader. Training and coaching skills are required from time to time.

It is certainly important to know what the marketplace is paying for jobs, because at the end of the day an organization is going to pay the market rate. If I offer my employee substantially less than the market rate, he or she is unlikely to join my organization or stay with it; on the other hand, if I offer substantially more than the market rate, I am wasting money that could be put to better use elsewhere in the organization. Of course, this is a considerable simplification; it implies that we know what we mean by "marketplace," "market rate" and "substantially," and it implies that there is an open marketplace for both jobs and employees.

Marketplace

Let us first discuss the idea of marketplace. A useful definition of marketplace in a particular organizational context is that group of organizations from which we intend to recruit our employees, or to which we risk losing our existing employees. Obviously, that definition will produce different results for different groups of employees. For example, if we have a group of administrative assistants in Halifax, pay rates for these jobs in Winnipeg are unlikely to be relevant; the relevant marketplace is likely to be all organizations in Halifax. If we have senior research scientists in polymer chemistry, the relevant marketplace is likely to be other organizations across Canada, or possibly even further afield, that employ such scientists.

We can see that one organization may have many different definitions of marketplace for different groups of employees.

Market Rate

The market rate for a particular job in any given marketplace can be defined as the average rate paid for mature, competent performance of that job in that marketplace.

There are several difficulties in attempting to directly measure the market for all the jobs in an organization:

- **Difficulty in getting accurate data:** For example, to obtain a market rate for the research scientist in polymer chemistry, we would have to identify the other organizations and obtain the pay rates they were using for their research scientists, and we would have to be confident that those jobs were in fact the same jobs as ours. If we were able to do all these things, we would still have a problem if the sample size of similar jobs was very small, because we would have the concern that our sample result might have been a statistical anomaly; for example, if the real market for these scientists consisted of one hundred jobs, and we had obtained information on ten, there is a good chance that the results for the ten do not accurately reflect the one hundred. Experienced compensation analysts will generally agree that it is an almost impossible task to get good data for specialist jobs using pure market data alone.

• **A common approach to jobs**: Organizations that have an overall approach to Human Resources and that try to link their various HR initiatives together will commonly have adopted a skill-based approach to employees and jobs. This tends to de-emphasize specific technical skills as the driver of job worth in favour of more generic skills. It would be very difficult for these organizations to justify pay scales based on specific functional family membership, unless it can clearly be shown that there is a shortage of these functional skills in the marketplace. Such shortages do occur from time to time—and we will address some ways of dealing with these "hot market" shortage issues later—but not nearly as often as the holders of the functional skills allege! In general, there is an open market in jobs and no reason to believe that one family of skills commands a premium on the market.

Most organizations find it very useful to rank jobs using a job evaluation system, because they can combine the relative ranking of all jobs produced by that system with the good reliable market data available for some jobs to produce a calculated market rate for all jobs. If we believe that, in general, there is an open market in jobs, then this calculated rate will be an accurate substitute for direct market measurement in cases where a reliable direct measurement is not possible.

We are still left with the concept of different marketplaces for different jobs, but on a regional rather than functional basis. For example, it is quite common to have one marketplace for all administrative jobs in Halifax and another for all administrative jobs in Vancouver. The higher the value of the job in the organization, the less regional the marketplace; for example, many organizations treat Canada as one marketplace for managerial jobs and it is becoming common to treat all North America as one marketplace for senior executive jobs.

Hot Markets

We mentioned above the concept of "hot markets." These are job families in which a significant shortage of individuals with the required specialized skills leads to an increase in competitive pay levels for the relatively few qualified individuals over and above the level that would normally derive from the job value, as measured by a system of internal relativity. These job families are found, for example, in the information systems application implementation field, where new specialized applications are being sold into the market at a rate beyond the job market's ability to find individuals qualified in these applications. Over the course of time, the marketplace should rectify the shortage, but in the short term the skills shortage is severe and leads to large upward pressure on pay rates.

Since it is not possible to pay below market rates for any length of time and retain an employee with "hot market" skills, in the medium term the organization has to identify and pay at the "hot market" rate. Paying the extra earnings in the form of a special regular "hot market" allowance, rather than folding them into regular pay, reduces the concern of other employees, and also allows the extra payment to cease if the skill shortages causing the "hot market" conditions cease at any point. In the short term, it is possible to defer the extra payment through stay bonuses for fixed-term employees or through learning bonuses for indefinite-hire employees; this has the further advantage of controlling turnover in the short term.

DELIVERY OF COMPENSATION

We have seen that the following basic concepts underlie any compensation program:

- an agreement about the content of what is to be done, either in terms of a description of the types of task that are to be accomplished, or in terms of the set of skills that are to be brought to bear on tasks, or ideally a combination of the two;

- a methodology for valuing this content, both relative to others and to the marketplace; and

- a description of the competitive marketplace.

Cash compensation can be delivered in different ways. Conventionally, these are divided for discussion purposes into three general types of delivery:

- **salary**, which is paid regularly (weekly, monthly or some other regular frequency); traditionally, the rate of salary is reviewed and adjusted once a year and the metrics that determine how much salary is delivered for the following year are normally measured over the prior one-year period, or possibly over a series of these prior one-year periods;

- **short-term incentive**, which is paid periodically (normally once a year, but perhaps more frequently); again, the metrics that determine how much is delivered are normally measured over a one-year period prior to the date of delivery; and

- **long-term incentive**, which is paid periodically, but for a period longer than one year (perhaps three or five years); here the metrics are measured over a period of perhaps three or five years.

Each organization will determine its own mix of these methods of delivering cash value, and we will discuss how an organization might go about making this determination in a later section.

Once the marketplace has been measured, an organization will wish to compare its own pay for each job with the marketplace rate of pay for that job. Generally, the organization will have developed a policy for its pay rates compared to the marketplace it has selected. This is unlikely to call for rates of pay below the market rate, and commonly may call for rates of pay close to the market rate. Some organizations may choose to pay above the market, for various reasons (they wish to reduce turnover rates, they have high expectations of their people, they have an organization self-image that relates to high pay rates).

Many organizations only measure the salary marketplace when attempting to determine a market rate for a job. For less senior jobs, this may be quite acceptable, since relatively little value is delivered in the marketplace for these jobs by other means than salary. However, for jobs at managerial level, it is more common than not in the general marketplace to deliver a significant minority of total cash value through short-term incentive and (less commonly) long-term incentive; measuring job value by salary only for these jobs results in underestimating job value.

An organization may choose to deliver its cash compensation in the form of salary only at these more senior job levels, but, if it wishes to be competitive in cash delivery, its salary will need to be higher than the market salary, since the extra salary will take the place of incentives paid in its competitor organizations. Conversely, if an organization chooses to pay incentives that are substantially higher than those paid in its competitive marketplace, and wishes to be competitive in total cash value, then it must set its salaries below competitive levels. It is unlikely that an organization will be competitive at both the salary and total cash level; this would require setting its incentive payout levels to exactly match what the market pays in incentives, and this is only coincidentally going to be a sensible basis for setting incentive payout levels.

How Individual Pay is Decided

With the exception of unionized workers, whose pay levels are governed by the collective bargaining process, it is unusual to find each one of a group of workers, whose jobs have the same value to their organization, and who are in the same marketplace as each other, being paid the same as all the others in the group, or the same as the job value. In other words, organizations reward differentially for the value generated by individuals in a job in addition to rewarding differentially for the value inherent in each job.

With the exception of a few organizations who pay on an arbitrary or completely subjective basis, there are more or less well-defined mechanisms in organizations for deciding how individuals will be paid.

The metrics used vary considerably:

- At one end of the spectrum, individuals may receive a payment based on some measurement of the **performance of the entire organization**.

- At the other end of the spectrum, individuals may receive a payment based on some measurement of **personal performance**.

- In between these two, measurements based on **team performance, unit performance, divisional performance** and so on are possible.

When it comes to deciding on payment from an incentive plan, several different metrics may be used in combination; personal performance is most commonly used when it comes to deciding on how much salary to pay an individual.

Whatever its decision on how to deliver cash compensation, an organization must be able to address certain fundamental compensation questions:

- Do we wish to reward **high performers** more than average performers? If so, how much more? Over what time period do we measure
  performance?

- Do we want employees to share in the **financial achievements of
  the organization**? If so, how big a share of the gain do we want to
  give them? Does this apply on the downside (they share the loss) as
  well as the upside?

The answers to these questions will depend on the organization's
views on the critical issues we identified at the beginning of the chapter.
For example, if the organization believes strongly in the development of
core competencies, it is likely to want to significantly differentiate compensation paid to high performers, whom it will identify as those
employees who demonstrate high competency levels, and it may want
to do so over a short time frame (in other words, the concept of maturi-
ty and moving steadily up in salary may not have much meaning for
such an organization). An organization that wishes to encourage a community of interest with its workforce and eliminate entitlement may
want to strongly weight its compensation delivery towards incentives,
and determine pay-outs based on firm or unit metrics.

From a different perspective, the issue of variability of pay is linked
to the issue of results versus skills that we discussed at the beginning of
the chapter. Those organizations whose business is focused on results
in the relatively short term, and whose employees can have an impact
on short-term results, may be prepared to put more of their employees'
total cash compensation at risk in the short term and allow incentive
payouts to vary considerably by organizational performance. Organizations whose view is somewhat longer-term may focus on continuous
skill development, which would argue for less focus on short-term
incentive payment, but more focus on considerable differentiation in
salary, based on personal performance measured by skill acquisition.

Of course, most organizations would argue correctly that both the
short and long term are important, and this logically leads them to look
at a mixed approach, with significant variability in both salary and
short-term incentive payout. This is the most prevalent combination;
for example, between 60% and 80% of organizations make short-term
incentives available to managerial-level employees, and pay-outs from
these programs vary roughly between 5% and 20% of total cash at this
level in the organization. This in turn restricts the scope of the decision

for most organizations; if the marketplace pays, say, 85% of the total cash dollar in salary, it is difficult to convince employees that your organization is so different that you will pay only 50% of the same total dollar in salary.

Salaries

Many organizations deliver salaried compensation using a traditional type of performance salary system, which allows for a range of salaries for each job. The range traditionally has a value in it defined as the midpoint, or a region of values known as the midrange, and the midpoint or midrange represents the market comparison point; for example, an organization that intends to pay, for a particular set of jobs of equal value, salaries that are median in its marketplace would set its midpoint for that set of jobs equal to the market salary rate. The midpoint or midrange also represents the salary that the organization will pay an employee in a job who has exhibited mature, competent performance in that job. As we noted previously, performance may be measured as a function of skill development, of results achieved, or both. Each section of the range is associated with a different level of performance; for example, a typical mapping for an organization with a five-level performance rating system is shown in Table 1.

TABLE 1: Sample Five-Level Performance Rating System

Performance Rating	Section of the Range (expressed as a % of the range midpoint)
Outstanding	112% - 120%
Exceeds Expectations	104% - 112%
Competent / Meets Expectations	96% - 104%
Meets Some Expectations	88% - 96%
Fails to Meet Expectations	80% - 88%

One option for an organization would be to pay an individual in the portion of the range corresponding to the most recent performance rating. However, many organizations have been unable to cope with two consequences of this approach:

- large increases awarded to employees whose performance has improved, and
- decreases required for employees whose performance has declined.

Traditionally, these organizations (either deliberately or unknowingly) have effectively taken a longer view of performance, whereby the employee's position in the range is a function of performance over several measurement periods and the employee moves towards (rather than to) the position in range that corresponds to the most recent performance measurement. Even this approach has run into difficulties, because it still requires that small or no increases be awarded to individuals whose performance is in decline (often employees who have been in the job for some while), and managers have proven to be unwilling to follow this rule. Over time, these systems can deteriorate so that it appears that seniority is the most important determinant of salary.

In an attempt to address this issue, some organizations have effectively reduced the width of the range by cutting out the portion above 100% and transferring value to a type of short-term incentive plan (so-called "re-earnable merit"). However, since making awards from such a plan requires making the same measurement of individual performance and addressing the same types of unwillingness to deliver "bad news" to employees with declining performance, it does not really address the issue for organizations that intend to make personal performance an important metric. Put another way, modifying the salary delivery system is not a solution for organizations that have problems with their performance management systems. Organizations that are serious about making a direct link between salary and performance or skill development must face up to the requirement to give bad news as well as good news.

Short-Term Incentives

As we noted above, short-term incentives are appropriate in organizations:

- where results that are most significantly related to organizational success can be measured over the short term (one year or less), and
- where these results are significantly in the control of plan participants (rather than due to external influences) either personally or as a member of a team or unit (the so-called "line of sight" criterion).

It should be noted that organizations can achieve surprisingly successful outcomes in encouraging employees who would appear to have very little control on results (such as administrative staff) by using an incentive plan based on a simple, visible and well-communicated measure of organizational performance (such as total revenue, or total profit). This would suggest that a "line of sight" test for deciding whether or not an incentive plan is appropriate does not tell the whole story.

Even where the above conditions are met, the design of a short-term incentive plan may cause failure of the plan to assist in improving organizational results, for several reasons:

- The plan may have an **incorrect or incomplete set of metrics**; the resulting focus of the plan participants on metrics in the set, rather than on all the metrics that influence organizational performance, may cause important areas to be neglected (for example, a plan that focuses on sales generation rather than profitability may encourage sales that are not to the organization's benefit).

- The organization may be **unwilling to allow significant variation in payment between good and poor performance** (ideally, the plan should encompass the possibility of zero payment); as a result, there is no incentive to achieve the results required (if the top performers see no significant link between their efforts and the reward obtained, they have no incentive to put their abilities to use for the organization's benefit).

- There may be **no confidence in the way the required results are set**, and so the required behaviours will not be generated (for example, "top-down" revenue targets that have not been bought into by plan participants will generate either apathy or, worse, a variety of counter-productive behaviours such as artificial sales, inventory generation, and so on).

- The organization may either **not be willing to allow participants to share in the gains** to the extent required to allow for significant payment for achievement (similar to the second bullet point, participants see no link between effort and reward, and have no incentive to make the effort) or, conversely, may have designed the plan so badly that the entire gain is put into the participants' hands (the plan is wildly successful from their perspective but a complete failure from that of the organization).

Long-Term Incentives

While short-term incentives are appropriate where results that are most significantly related to organizational success can be measured over the short term, there is another category of organization where success is more appropriately defined over the longer term. For example, a start-up bio-research organization may take years to develop and market its first successful product; there are certainly measurable short-term factors that will have an impact on the organization's ultimate success, but they are secondary to long-term factors that cannot be measured over this time period.

At its simplest, a long-term incentive plan is simply a short-term incentive plan with a longer period of measurement and the same concerns that applied above in determining a plan's success apply here also. However, there are two additional issues to consider:

- Equity-based plans are of considerable interest, both because share value may well be a good measure of performance in the longer term and because equity-based plans can provide tax-effective delivery of value.

- Measurement of the actual value of long-term incentives is more complex and more subject to dispute. If a significant portion of total value is being delivered in this form, it may be more difficult to establish whether the overall value of compensation delivery is competitive in the marketplace. Thus value delivery in this form may present problems for organizations that believe accurate measurement of competitiveness, and communication of this, is important.

Employee Benefits

Traditionally, the value delivered to employees by an organization in the form of various benefit plan coverages (such as supplementary health coverage, life insurance and disability coverage) has been considered separately from cash value; competitiveness has been determined for cash and benefits separately. In addition, the competitiveness of an organization's benefit program has been measured on average over the entire employee population, without taking into account the considerable variation in delivered value that occurs between different members of that population. Typically, with traditional benefits plan designs, this variation has been a function of age, service and marital status, and only secondarily a function of performance.

This type of value delivery (often described as "entitlement-based" because value typically increases with age and service) is at odds with the messages of skill-based value delivery and individual responsibility that many organizations are now attempting to deliver to their employees. As a result, many organizations are now attempting to remodel their benefit plans in the direction of individual responsibility; a fixed sum of money or its equivalent is made available to an employee—salary-based, a fixed amount, or a combination—and the individual chooses how to make use of that fixed value, either to obtain benefit plan coverage or to take cash. Examples of this type of change are replacement of defined benefit pension plans with defined contribution plans or group RRSPs, and replacement of traditional health and dental plans by private health services plans.

HOW DOES COMPENSATION FIT INTO OVERALL BUSINESS STRATEGY?

An organization cannot effectively review and remodel its compensation systems either in isolation or based on what is seen to be effective elsewhere. A compensation strategy is effective to the extent that:

- it is integrated with other HR initiatives, and
- it reflects the goals of the organization.

To survive and prosper, organizations must have a clear vision of who they are, what they do and why they do it better then their competitors. Fundamental HR work, described in other chapters of this book, includes identifying the skills required to put these goals into operation and ensuring that these skills are available and continuously sharpened, and lead to better results. Compensation is not a direct contributor at this fundamental level, but it must be used in support of these other initiatives. For example, compensation delivery must support achievement and maintenance of critical differentiating competencies. Put more simply, a manufacturer of aluminum can stock will want to significantly reward, and continue to reward, the team that can discover how to keep improving the consistency of the thickness of rolled aluminum sheet, since that is a key differentiating competency in that business. It also must reward key results; for example, the marketing team in a pharmaceutical company working to have its product displace another company's product on a provincial formulary needs to know that success in this area will be a key factor in their incentive

FIGURE 3: Relating Organizational Factors to Compensation

If Highly Important Differentiating Factors are:	Technology/ Expertise	Price	Delivery Speed and Responsiveness to Customers
Factors in Compensation Delivery			
Job Evaluation	Skill-based	Job-based	Role-based
Marketplace	Similar skills	General	General
Salary	Average to above	Above average	Average to below
Short-Term Incentive	Below average, based on individual performance	None on an individual base; moderate firm-wide profit sharing	Average to above, team-based
Long-term Incentive	Significant, based on individual and firm performance	None	Moderate, based on firm performance

plan. Obviously, in order to ensure that compensation does support the organization in this way, we have to identify what these competencies and desired results are.

Linking Organization Factors to Compensation

We have described in earlier sections how different organizations may view compensation elements such as job evaluation and incentive compensation in different ways.

Figure 3 shows directionally how we may attempt to link differentiating factors of organizations with different approaches to compensation delivery at the macro level. The specific design of each component will, of course, vary with the characteristics of each organization, driven by the elements we have discussed throughout the chapter, and also by such things as the degree of employee involvement sought (high employee involvement is possible, particularly in areas such as competency modelling, job design and job evaluation, but possibly extending to salary planning) and the degree of structure and centralization in the organization (for example, large organizations may not be able to ensure consistency without tight guidelines for salary planning).

FIGURE 4: Impact of Organization's Outlook on Performance

If the Organization is:	Renewing	Stagnating
Factors in Compensation Delivery		
Job Evaluation	Role-based or skills-based; general descriptions of roles	Job-based; tight description of tasks
Marketplace	Specific; based on identified competitors	General; based on high payers
Salary	Low; varies significantly by individual performance	High; varies by length of service
Short-Term Incentive	Average to high, based on team and individual performance; significant variation in payout	Low; little variation in payout
Long-Term Incentive	High, based on organization performance	None
Benefits	Low to none; little variation in value by age, service or marital status	High; entitlement-based; large variation by age, service and marital status
Expected total compensation	Average	Above average
Variability in total compensation	Very high; varies with both individual and organization performance	Very low; varies most significantly with length of service

Different macro approaches to compensation are appropriate for different organizations; not everyone can be on the leading edge of technology. However, looked at from another perspective, Figure 4 shows how failure to continually renew and refresh the organization's approach to key Human Resources issues leads to stagnation in compensation policy.

The organization that does not continually renew its approach risks allowing its compensation programs to deteriorate so that they are not linked to the goals of the organization and are no longer appropriate.

SUMMARY

The basic concepts of compensation design, as we listed them at the beginning of the chapter, are straightforward to understand and apply. With the exception of some of the detail work in long-term incentives and benefits, compensation is not a high-technology function, but it does require logical thinking and an uncluttered approach. You are not likely to go far wrong if you follow these guidelines:

- Be guided by the organization's mission, the key skills required to fulfill the mission, the most important time frames, and how the organization will differentiate itself.

- Translate these statements into how the organization will approach valuing work, how it will identify its marketplace, and how it will compete in that marketplace.

- Refuse to consider the detail of compensation plans before the strategy has been identified, both at the overall level ("How much should we deliver altogether?") and at the macro level within each component ("How much salary, incentive, benefit value, should we deliver?" and " How will we vary the delivery?").

- Apply Occam's Razor (We can translate this for our purposes as "If there are different ways of resolving an issue, the simplest is likely to be the best").

- Mistrust solutions that are looking for problems; something that worked brilliantly for another organization will only work brilliantly for you by the merest coincidence.

- Communicate what you are doing to your employees honestly, fully and openly.

CHAPTER FOURTEEN

Paying for Competencies that Drive Organizational Success

THE HB GROUP INSURANCE STORY

Ellie Maggio, Principal,
William M. Mercer Limited

COMPETENCY-BASED PAY has come a long way lately. Some business people would say it's about time. Put simply, competency-based pay ties an organization's compensation policies directly into its strategic positioning. In the process, senior management begins to see the Human Resources department as something other than a "necessary evil," a cost centre divorced from the operations, a producer of buzz words and "feel good" workshops.

In this chapter, we discuss how HR professionals can contribute to corporate success by taking a new approach to compensation, introduce the concept of competency-based pay, and review a case study.

HB Group Insurance, and its Direct Protect group, illustrates the power of an innovative pay policy to drive a corporate success story. HB has used competency-based pay to make direct sales—a routine, repetitive and often thankless job—into a powerful engine of corporate growth.

THE NEW ROLE OF COMPENSATION AND HR MANAGEMENT

We begin with the changing role of compensation, and the potential for competency-based pay and performance management to link a CEO's vision with the everyday worklife of line employees. Traditional goals for compensation included:

- attracting, retaining, and motivating employees;
- using compensation dollars effectively; and
- minimizing employee dissatisfaction. Traditional Human Resources and compensation management had a strong focus on jobs and on individual performance in achieving job objectives.

Traditional Human Resources and Compensation	Emerging Issues and Focus
• jobs and job entitlement	• individuals and individual contributions
• cost containment	• cost containment and investment in human capital
• cost containment within job grades	• linking pay to economic fluctuation
• incentive programs for senior and sales employees	• broad-based incentives for more employee groups
• avoiding or eliminating risk-associated programs	• a greater proportion of pay-at-risk and performance-based programs
• equating equity with demonstrable uniformity	• defining equity as individual differentiation based on contribution
• focusing on internal job comparisons	• focusing on external benchmarking

Although the traditional job focus and pay goals are still valid, the compensation rationale has become more complex. Now, additional pay goals include:

- linking reward systems to organizational needs.
- focusing employees on team and organization performance;
- integrating quality and service as prime measures;
- eliminating internal competition and department and employee levels; and
- including employee and customer feedback in plan design.

FIGURE 1: Emerging Compensation Goals

New compensation systems reward for value, not just time on the job. But a compensation philosophy—a broad statement of company values—and a compensation strategy—a detailed plan of action—are musts:

COMPENSATION PHILOSOPHY

- Reflects an organization's values, culture and objectives.
- A "big picture" statement communicating what the company believes in and what ideas it supports in its compensation systems.

COMPENSATION STRATEGY

- A well-reasoned plan to achieve a set of objectives.
- Composed of specific, actionable steps that logically and clearly result in high probability of achieving the objectives.
- Has a measurable impact, is predictable and consistent with organizational needs.
- Sets economically anchored end goals for a business organization.

New Employment Contract

It is no secret that we are witnessing a fundamental change in the employment contract between workers and management. Today, organizations cannot guarantee lifetime employment even if employees want to commit themselves to the company. In the process, employee loyalty has become loyalty to the individual and to personal accomplishments, rather than loyalty to the firm.

Organizations are moving toward a contract that emphasizes employees' responsibility for sustaining their own commitment, motivation and performance in return for the opportunity to enhance their skills, talents and marketability. One challenge for HR practitioners is to design a compensation system that encourages a partnership approach between employer and employee. The employee must understand how to enhance those competencies which will contribute directly to the success of the overall enterprise.

To make this happen, employees need very explicit information about what is expected of them and how they will be rewarded if they meet those expectations.

FIGURE 2: A Partnership Approach to Career Management

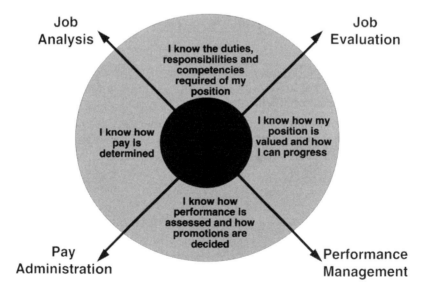

FIGURE 3: The "What" and "How" of the Partnership Approach

MOVING TOWARDS COMPETENCY-BASED HUMAN RESOURCES

In 1996, William M. Mercer Limited conducted a survey of performance evaluation techniques used for non-union employees at 471 organizations operating nationwide in Canada. While 90% of the organizations surveyed still assessed performance using results-against-objectives, 54% were planning to use behaviours as performance criteria, and 43% were planning to use competencies. The results indicate that expectations were leading practice—but clearly Human Resources management, including total compensation policies, is about to move on. Competency-based pay is becoming an attractive strategy to deal with the new marketplace and the new workplace.

Some Background Research on Competencies

Competencies have been researched for decades to better predict and understand human behaviour. Used for years by HR practioners as assessment and development tools, competencies in recent years have become the foundation of broad-based human resource strategies and programs, including pay programs.

There is still no universal accepted definition of competencies, but most descriptions have the following common features:

- Competencies are characteristics that predict superior performance.

- Competencies differentiate top performers from all others.

- Competencies describe how individuals should perform and what results should be achieved; they are defined for each particular organization to focus employees on the desired goals.

- Competencies can be attached to pay.

CORE COMPETENCIES ARE...

Groups of interrelated competencies (skills, knowledge, behaviours, motives) required by employees which are:

- focal points for achieving superior performance,

- essential to the organization's ongoing success,

- able to predict outstanding performance,

- generic enough to apply to all employees in the organization,

- aligned with organizational business strategies.

NON-CORE COMPETENCIES ARE...

Competencies (skills, knowledge, behaviours, motives) required by employees which are:

- derived from core competencies,

- aligned with and distinguish superior performance at the division, employee group, job family and/or job level, and

- different for different divisions, employee groups, job families and/or job levels.

When defining competencies, it is important to state what they are not. Competencies are not a psychological construct. They are a collection of observable skills, knowledge and behaviours. Most competencies are presented in the form of a model, or grouping of competencies, to represent excellence in a particular type of work. For example, "Customer

Service" is a grouping that describes how an employee demonstrates customer responsiveness through behaviour on the job (see accompanying box entitled "Competency Example).

COMPETENCY EXAMPLE: CUSTOMER SERVICE

Competency

- Recognizes that the purpose of the organization is to serve its customers; maintains awareness of conditions or factors that affect the client's ability to use services or satisfaction with the services; maintains awareness of clients need and ability to use one's work output.

Behavioural Indicators

- Looks for creative approaches to providing or improving services.

- Works to remove barriers that get in the way of giving clients top-notch service.

- Takes a variety of actions to meet a customer's needs, as required until the need is met.

- Responds to customers with an appropriate level of urgency.

Core vs. Non-Core Competencies in Compensation Plans

Competencies are often grouped into the categories "core" and "non-core" (see accompanying boxes). In most organizations, core competencies are defined as those essential for all job classes. Starting at the top of Figure 4, we see the competencies which are core to the whole organization.

Identifying and aligning competencies by level is a challenging endeavour. Moving deeper into the structure, we can identify business-unit or function-specific competencies which supplement the core competencies. These can be related to a department, a job family, or even specific jobs. Just how far competencies have to be developed depends on the variety of tasks within an organization. Using core competencies to develop a pay structure is a macro approach and has a higher success rate than using non-core competencies. We attribute this success to the correlation between core competencies and a business's organizational strategies.

FIGURE 4: Aligning Competencies with the Organization

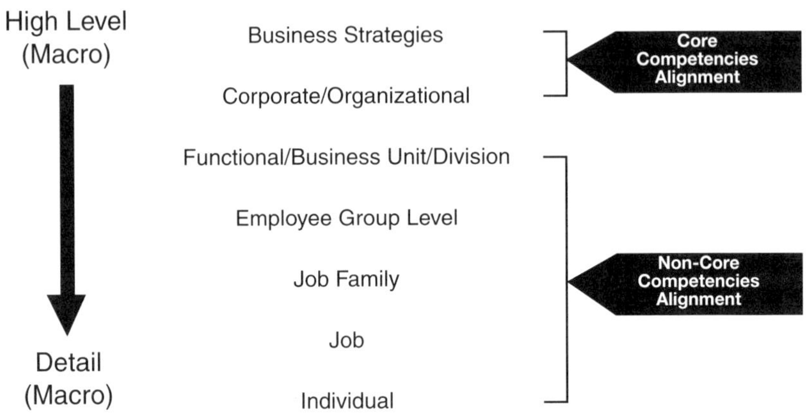

High Level
(Macro)

Business Strategies

Core
Competencies
Alignment

Corporate/Organizational

Functional/Business Unit/Division

Employee Group Level

Job Family

Non-Core
Competencies
Alignment

Job

Detail
(Macro)

Individual

IMPLEMENTING CONTRIBUTION-BASED PAY AT HB GROUP INSURANCE

HB Group Insurance, a company of approximately 400 employees with ten offices across Canada, provides a dramatic case study of the potential benefits in competency-based compensation. In the discussion that follows, we will examine the planning and launch of HB's Direct Protect program, whose success has been attributed to the company's decision to reinvent the way direct sales emplyees are paid.

HB Before Direct Protect

Founded in 1980, HB Group Insurance marketed property and casualty insurance programs to employee groups. By the early nineties, HB was experiencing considerable difficulties. The market for group property and casualty business was increasingly competitive, and the company faced a $60-million loss.

In December, 1992, Jeff Contant was promoted from Senior Vice-President, Sales, to President. Under his direction, HB, like many companies at that time, worked to reduce costs and improve service. The workforce was reduced by about 25%, and virtually all middle managers were eliminated. Contant's mandate was not only to improve the bottom line but also to increase group business and to develop new markets in which to launch HB's insurance products.

Contant began exploring possibilities for growth; there appeared to be an opportunity in direct sales to consumers. HB addded to its traditional distribution channels—through employers, associations, and affinity groups—by launching Direct Protect, a home and auto insurance program sold directly to consumers over the telephone.

Direct Protect was launched in early 1996, but not before HB invested heavily in the technology to support a leading-edge call centre in its Mississauga head office. The call centre makes extensive use of computer telephone integration and interactive voice response systems, resulting in one of the most sophisticated applications of technology in the industry.

Senior management recognized that sustained growth and success would not be supported simply through technology. Equally important was a focus on people. Now, many companies talk about their staff being their most important resource, but few appear willing to actually design policies that recognize this. HB saw a different approach.

Transforming the Call Centre

Typically, call centres are staffed by part-time, low-skill employees. The job can be fairly simple: ask callers questions and feed responses into a computer which then tells them whether or not to offer insurance at a competitive rate. To "open the funnel" to a wider range of customers, HB wanted its call centre manned by staff who would think, and use technical tools to support their work efficiently. Rather than turn down business based on a computer-driven decision, they wanted licensed insurance representatives who could assess situations and offer advice, for example, suggesting a higher deductible on car insurance, which would result in lower premiums.

Meeting the expectations of consumers while keeping down costs requires staff with particular skills and competencies. However, insurance companies typically pay the most to people who do not deal directly with customers: underwriters, experts, marketers and supervisors. They were telling the front-line people, if you're any good, go elsewhere, forcing them into a different career path if they wanted more money and prestige.

HB needed a way to attract and retain front line "insurance professionals" who would be happy and rewarded for their effort. In addition, the entrance of several other companies into the market was increasing the demand for trained insurance representatives, making "good" reps a highly marketable commodity. HB needed a new system to reward front-line professionals for doing what they do well, for their contribution to the success of the company.

A New Reward System

A lot of thinking went into what HB wanted out of a new reward system. Having successfully turned itself around HB needed to ensure its new employees would support the cultural change the company had been through. The system had to:

• tie individual pay to organizational goals,

• be suitable for integration with other Human Resources systems such as training, performance management, and recruiting,

• be deemed "fair" by all of their employees, and

• be easy to administer.

After a lot of investigation into different types of compensation plans, HB decided to implement a system of competency-based, or contribution-based, pay. The solution was so simple it was novel, so self-evident it was elegant: HB invested significantly in changing its people from reactive phone answerers to pro-active relationship builders.

HB took a new approach to call centres, necessary to achieve its plan of high growth and high responsiveness. Then, as Contant said, "How can you train and retain that type of front-line staff when your own pay structure is telling them that they are not valued for what they are doing?" HB had been using a traditional pay model. Employees highest on the scale were specialists: underwriters, insurance specialists, marketers and management. Turning this on its head, and working with compensation consultants at William M. Mercer Limited, HB's senior management developed and put in place a competency-based, pay-for-performance system.

Contribution-Based Pay

Making a cultural and business change meant developing and implementing a new pay and performance management system. At HB, it is called "contribution-based pay" because "contribution" was seen to be

FIGURE 5: Methodology

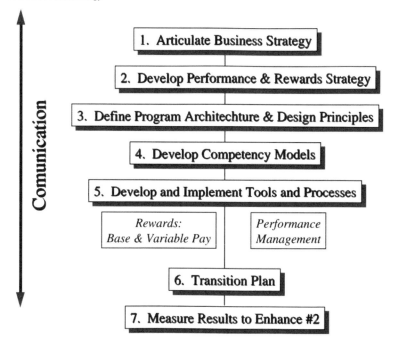

more relevant and meaningful to the employee audience than "competencies," an intimidating word that smacks of warm, fuzzy HR jargon.

The process began and ended with a strong communication program, including:

- working group/design team impact on plan design and implementation;

- focus groups to test and validate tools and results;

- employee group meetings; and

- formal communication by way of presentations, memos, documents, e-mail and tool kits.

Step 1: Organization Audit

The first step in building the strategy was an organization audit that examined the readiness of the organization for a competency-based pay program. HB and Mercer examined:

- existing compensation and Human Resources programs; and

- employee attitudes towards pay and performance management policies and practices.

The audit identifed the organization's core competencies.

Using the organizational audit findings, senior management—including business unit leaders and HR representatives—began developing a career management philosophy with emphasis on pay and performance management. The strategy clearly outlined the need to develop an integral Human Resources system that would use business strategies and core competencies as the foundation and link between each element.

The strategy required:

- a clear correlation between performance and rewards;

- guiding principles for overall program architecture (e.g., market pay positioning, communicating the new plan design, implementing the new program, training requirements); and

- criteria for measuring success.

FIGURE 6: New Concept Integrated Systems

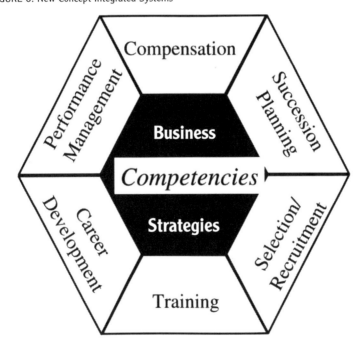

Clearly, it was not a simple task or process. Key challenges included reaching consensus on business goals, accommodating different sub-cultures, identifying core organizational capabilities distinct from those that make the organization competitive, and keeping focused on performance strategy rather than on Human Resource programs.

Step 2: Designing the Program

The next step was to define the program architecture and design principles. A base and variable pay plan model was constructed incorporating core contributions also used in the performance management model. The model was developed with senior management and tested in employee focus groups.

In assessing alternative designs, a review was made of how competency-based pay and performance management is used in other organizations. Published information was reviewed and meetings held with other companies.

HB was ready at last to define performance excellence, set up success measures, create a design blueprint along with a detailed development plans and timetable for implementation, and build a communication plan.

The biggest challenge was for HB to get its people to think outside the box and beyond current plans, priorities and agendas. It also had to balance its appetite for change against the company's ability to digest change. It had to weigh the views of experts against the opinions of business unit leaders and employee groups, and the relative merits of sub-unit autonomy and integration. Finally, it needed to show progress as the project unfolded.

Step 3: Developing a Competency Model

The next step was to develop a competency model. A working group/design team was appointed and trained with representatives from each business unit. The working group identified competencies by employee group and business unit. Teams also worked on validating the behavioural indicators for each core competency. The design team studied the workforce profiles—various functions, business units and job families—and determined the most appropriate business unit for a prototype or pilot test. This was done by using four critical steps, and each step had different participants, key challenges and outcomes.

FIGURE 7: Develop Competency Model(s)

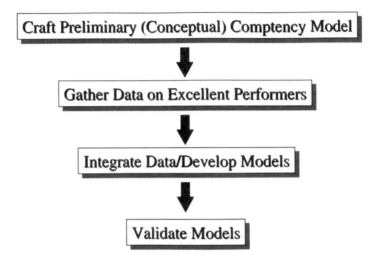

Developing a Competency Model

1. Draft Conceptual Competency Model

Participants

- Executives

- Business Unit Leaders

- Human Resources

Key Challenges

- Avoid emotional commitment to Models without "Hard Data"

Outcome

- "Ideal Model" Aligned with Business Strategy

2. Gather Data On Excellent Performers

Participants

- Excellent Performers

- Stakeholders to Provide "Customers' Perspective"

Developing a Competency Model (cont.)

Key Challenges

- Balance Buy-in vs. Efficiency vs. Validity
- What is "Excellence" Here?
- Adhere to Business vs. Personal Definition of Excellence

Outcome

- Skill and Knowledge Requirements
- Behavioural Definition of Excellence

3. Integrate Data/Develop Models

Participants

- Human Resources
- Select Competency Architecture that Meets Needs of All Applications
- Keep Models Simple/ Focused

Key Challenges

- A constellation of 5-9 Competencies for Each Model
- Specific Behavioural Indicators for Each Competency
- Documented Skill and Knowledge Requirements

Outcome

- A constellation of 5-9 Competencies for Each Model
- Specific Behavioural Indicators for Each Competency
- Documented Skill and Knowledge Requirements

4. Validate Models

Participants

- Sample of Workforce and Their Supervisors

Key Challenges

- How to Validate "Future" Competencies
- Persuade Organization to Take the Time

Outcome

- Models Demonstrably Linked to High Performance
- Awareness, Understanding and Greater Commitment to the Program

Comparison of Traditional Job Evaluation vs. Contribution-Based Pay Evaluation

	Traditional Scored Questionnaire Approach	Competency/Contribution-Based Approach
Philosophy	Pay for the job performed	Pay for individual competency
Tool	22 factors with 5 to 9 levels; questionnaire to collect information.	2 major factors on a matrix with scaled language to describe levels; questionnaire optional
Design Process	Participative: employees, committee with line managers	Participative: focus groups with employees and guidance from design team with line managers
Evaluation	Jobs	Positions and individuals
Ranges	Traditional grade structure	Flexible structure/ broadbanding is an option
Link to Market	Ranges built from pay line through market rates	Positions linked directly to market
Base Pay Administration	Driven by established policy; adjustments once per year	Driven by business needs and individual contribution; adjustments as required/earned
Ownership	Human Resources	Individual line managers
Link to Business Strategies	Indirect	Direct
Performance Management	Separate	Linked
Career Planning	Separate	Linked

Step 4: Planning Implementation

The next step was to develop and implement tools and processes. Pay and performance management tools and processes were developed simultaneously to ensure linkage between programs and continually tested with employees using focus groups.

Since the pay model was based on varying competency requirements, HB positions were assessed and assigned using the model as the focal point for job evaluations. We tested each position assessment with the pay model to ensure internal equity and market competitiveness.

The seven steps of implementation at HB were:

1. Career paths/progression descriptions for each job family were developed to show the differentiating competencies, activities, education and experience required for each level.

2. Management workshops were conducted to assess each employee using the competency-based tools but without referencing pay.

3. Costs associated with the new workforce distribution were analyzed and a feasible transition/implementation plan was developed.

4. The final assessment of positions and incumbents was validated, and two comprehensive performance and reward guideline documents were written, one for senior managers and the second for all other employees.

5. A career management tool kit was built to equip employees with sufficient information for them to take greater control over their careers. The kit included information and instructions on the pay and performance management programs, as well as career pathing information.

FIGURE 8: Competency-Based Pay Development Process

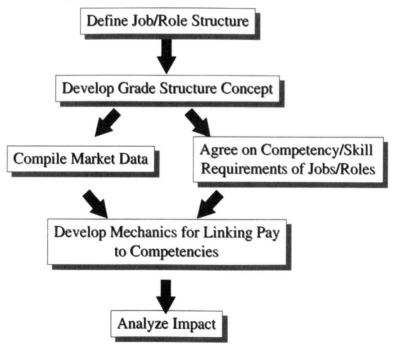

6. Training materials and workshops for users (managers and employees) were also developed to ensure a smooth transition.

7. Finally, there was a step for monitoring success, including a process for testing/auditing the new program practices and the change in workforce.

The Tools for Success

The two key factors for successful implementation are:

• keeping it simple, and

• communicating as much as possible to all stakeholders.

Successfully implementing the program meant developing both a competency-based pay program and a performance management program. They were linked together by competencies and by the six tools in the career management tool kit provided for all employees.

All six of the design, implementation and communications tools refer to THE BIG 10, HB's core competencies which drive organizational success and link integrated compensation and performance management.

FIGURE 9: The Tool Kit

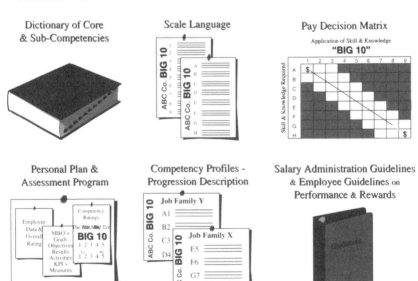

The Dictionary

The first tool, the Dictionary, gets employees focused on competencies driving organizational success. It defines and gives behavioural indicators both for the ten core competencies and many other sub-competencies.

The HB Big 10 are:

1. **Accountability**: Demonstrates responsibility or answers for required decisions, actions, advice or counsel and their resulting consequences on customers and/or the Company. This competency covers both operational and ethical decision-making.

2. **Communication Skills**: Effectively transfers thoughts and expresses ideas using written/oral communication in individual or group situations; demonstrates active listening skills through attending to and fully comprehending what others are saying. This covers the ability to understand and differentiate audiences, to organize work and communication and to listen and ask questions.

3. **Customer Service and Customer Relations**: Focuses efforts on discovering and meeting internal and external customers' needs in a manner that satisfies the customer and the Company within the resources that can be made available. Covered are the ability to ask questions and probe customer needs, and also the tendency to look for creative approaches to providing or improving services. One point notes the attitude necessary: "Keeps own emotions from interfering with responding effectively to customer's needs."

4. **Interpersonal Skills**: Builds rapport with individuals by demonstrating an understanding of others' concerns, motives, feelings; gains agreement for or acceptance of ideas, plans, activities, or solutions through effective communication and interpersonal styles. This competency grouping includes a number of sub-groups: relationship building, interpersonal sensitivity, persuasiveness, and conflict resolution.

5. **Leadership, Mentoring and Coaching**: Develops and uses effective strategies and interpersonal styles to influence and guide others toward the accomplishment of identified objectives/goals, performance of individuals or development of skills, knowledge and career.

6. **Learning Orientation**: Responds to change with a positive attitude, an eagerness to learn new skills, to accomplish work activities and objectives; demonstrates a commitment to continuous improvement. The learning orientation competencies are defined to make it clear that learning on the job is a key objective. Employees are asked to improve internal procedures, to challenge conventional practices when new services will work better, to constantly seek to improve results, and to adapt to change quickly.

7. **Practical Problem-solving and Judgement**: Builds a logical approach to address problems or opportunities, or to manage the situation at hand by drawing on own knowledge and experience base and calling on other references and resources as necessary.

8. **Results Orientation**: Sets and meets challenging objectives; finds better or more efficient ways to accomplish defined goals.

9. **Skills and Knowledge for the Position**: Applies, maintains and improves specialized knowledge and skills to accomplish a result or serve internal and external "customers" effectively. ("Customers" can be co-workers, peers or management as well as external consumers of a service). For HB Group, the specialized positions included sales, underwriting, operations, marketing, claims, accounting, administrative services and systems.

10. **Time and Deadline Management**: Determines priorities and allocates time and resources effectively; able to meet normal commitments; handles situations or deadlines as required or special work assignments.

Scaled Language

The Scaled Language tool has two parts, "skill and knowledge required" and "application of skill and knowledge."

Scaled language provides definitions and descriptions of both the skills and knowledge requirements for a job and for their application. The skill and knowledge descriptions begin at a basic level, and move through enhanced knowledge and more important applications, through to expert status at a level which may represent a leading role in the organization as a whole. In the area of application, the basic level can be represented as an entry level position needing continuous supervision and exercising little discretion. As the application develops, the employee will move through more learning stages, more supervision of others and more internal responsibility. The highest levels of application of a particular skill include mentoring and coaching other employees, planning the relevant activity and problem-solving in difficult or ambiguous situations.

FIGURE 10: Sample from Scaled Language

Sample from Scaled Language

Scaled Language for Contribution Pay Decision Matrix

All ABC Co. Big 10 competencies are expected of every employee. The brief descriptions below indicate the core competencies that distinguish a more advanced position from all those listed before it. You should assume that any position requires all previously listed position competencies. When more regular or recurring use of that competency is required or the scope of the effort is greater, that competency will be highlighted again.

Skill & Knowledge Requirements

A. Basic knowledge of administrative policies, systems and procedures; Learning on the job; Interpersonal skills in workgroup; Tactful internal and external communication

B. Greater knowledge of administrative programs, procedures and methods; understanding of certain aspects of a specific function. Some specific knowledge of ABC Co. operating procedures and policies; Limited deadline management to complete structured assignments under supervision; Discretion in required communication with internal and external contacts

C.

D.

E.

F. Expert knowledge of a broad and complex functional area; Advanced analytical and evaluative skills, with knowledge of financial and budget considerations; Customer service initiative to determine their needs based on in-depth knowledge of specialized requirements; Considerable accountability for solutions and recommendations, subject to approval at more senior levels

G.

H.

I.

Application of Skills & Knowledge

1. Frequent, but highly structured internal contact, with continuous supervision; Results orientation demonstrated in dependability and accuracy; Interpersonal skills shown in enthusiasm and co-operation with work team; Positive attitude toward learning

2. Frequent contact and communication internally and externally; Responsiveness to non-continuous supervision; Learning orientation toward alternative work procedures; Occasional coaching in direction/instruction of more junior employees

3.

4.

5.

6. Mentoring and coaching of other employees -OR- Planning activities of a small department; Problem-solving to deal with ambiguous or conflicting data. Accountability for planning activities of and the results achieved by a work team; Learning orientation and innovation to modify procedures or administrative methods

7.

8.

9.

The two scales outline varying levels of core competencies (not unlike the Just Noticeable Difference scales) in the organization and relate to the pay plan model or pay decision matrix. They are based on core competencies that are sufficiently generic to apply to the organization from top to bottom.

The third tool is the competency/contribution-based pay decision matrix:

- This is a two-dimensional pay decision matrix used for base and variable pay, job evaluation, individual assessment and organizational staffing decisions ; this information can be found in each cell on the matrix.

- Figure 11 is a simplified version of the decision matrix.

- Lower-valued positions with lower competency levels and would be assessed in the top left corner.

- Conversely higher-valued positions requiring higher competency levels would be assessed in the bottom right corner.

FIGURE 11: Sample from Pay Decision Matrix

	1	**2**	**3**
A	$19,800 *(Entry)* $22,000 *(Full)* $24,200 *(High)*	$20,600 $22,900 $25,200	$21,400 $23,800 $26,200
B	$21,400 $23,800 $26,200	$22,600 $25,100 $27,600	$23,600 $26,200 $28,800
C	$23,100 $25,700 $28,300	$24,800 $27,500 $30,300	$26,200 $29,100 $32,000

Skill & Knowledge

- There must be an organizational need for promotion.
- An individual assessment may differ from the position assessment if the individual demonstrates more or less in the way of competencies.
- Positions can be broad-banded for pay administration.
- A broad-based variable pay program is built into the pay decision matrix indicating different targets for different employee groups/levels.

The skills and applications are hard-wired into the pay system through a pay grid which allows employees to advance in a number of possible directions. Employees can progress laterally, as well as up the traditional hierarchy. The grid demonstrates to HB Group front-line customer service staff that they can progress by increasing their application of the skills and knowledge core to the needs of the HB Group.

Performance Management

Fourth is the performance management system It includes a section on competencies and one on objectives/results, and another on development. The BIG 10 core competencies serve as the link between pay and performance management.

FIGURE 12: Sample Competency in the Performance Management Program

Learning Orientation

Response to change with a positive attitude and an eagerness to learn new skills to accomplish work activities and objectives; demonstrates a commitment to continuous improvement.

	Moderate	Considerable	Significant
Degree required in this position:	❏	❏	❏

	Continues to Develop	Fully Acceptable	Significant Strength
The degree to which the competency has been demonstrated:	❏	❏	❏

This competency is demonstrated by:
• Identifying new ideas, solutions, or directions to build business or improve internal capabilities.
• Actively pursuing learning and self-development.
• Adapting to change quickly.

Comments/Representative Examples:

FIGURE 13: Sample Progression Description

PC Support Analysts   Systems

PC Support-Analyst – Junior (D3)

• Provide basic AS/400 CL support (i.e. check status of lines, controllers and devices, message queue, system status, active jobs)

• Provide basic Novell LAN support (i.e. SYSCON utility, FILER utility, basic LAN commands)

• Provide basic DOS and Windows support (i.e. DOS editor, file manager, setting up icons)

• Provide first-level technical support for user-related problems (i.e. workstation/printer not functioning, basic PC hardware/software problems, LAN & AS/400 login problems)

• Provide basic MS Software support (i.e. create form letters, create basic spreadsheets and databases, maintenance of existing forms/spreadsheets/databases, act as a liaison with MS Technical Support)

• Act as a liaison for departments and remote branches

PC Support Analyst – Intermediate (D4)

• Provide advanced Novell LAN support (i.e. assigning user right and authorities, maintaining LAN profiles, setting up printers and queues, advanced LAN commands)

• Provide advanced DOS and Windows support (i.e. maintaining system and configuration files maintaining LAN profiles)

• Provide second-level technical support for user-related problems (i.e. advanced PC software problems, Rumba/400 and PC Support/400 problems)

• Provide advanced MS Software support according to user-defined requirements (i.e. design and create documents/forms, design and create spreadsheets, design and create databases)

• Provide one-on-one basic user training

• Basic analysis of new software products

• Provide a technical resource for user-defined projects

• Act as a liaison for departments and remote branches

PC Support Analyst - Senior (D5)

• Design and implement technical solutions to meet user-defined requirements

• Provide technical support

• Design, schedule and conduct user training

• Design or adapt training materials

• Evaluate, recommend, and acquire new hardware/software

• Implement and support new hardware/software

• Provide direction for junior/intermediate staff

• Act as a liaison for departments and remote branches

Fifth are the progression descriptions which provide specific job family and position level information pertaining to the competencies required, position-specific activities, education, and experience as well as the position assessment. This tool supplements the scaled language which is generic enough to apply to all positions in the organization. It provides information to employees about career opportunities (position, progressions).

Salary Guidelines

Finally, come employee guidelines on performance and rewards. These are instructional in nature and provide tips for understanding and using the new competency-based pay-for-performance programs.

Linking pay to performance is an option which appeals to many organizations. Keeping it simple and easy to explain is a challenge, but also an absolute necessity. This integrated approach allowed HB Group to identify each individual's ideal competencies and performance, actual levels of both, and the gap between ideal and actual.

Employees progress paths can be very fully delineated using this type of system. Figure 14 is a sample progression description for a systems support analyst.

FIGURE 14: Sample Progression Description

Education

Undergraduate degree or community college diploma

Experience

• Five years programing and analysis experience on life insurance and/or financial business application

• Programing experience with COBOL, IBM mainframe, TSO, VSAM, CICS, DB2

• Experience working on platforms such as IBM mainframe, AS/400 and/or RS/6000.

• Knowledge of insurance and/or financial products

Activities

• Analyzes and designs enhancements to the system based on business requirements

• Writes technical specifications from functional specifications which define business requirements

• Programs and texts system changes from technical specific functions

• Trains clients on the architecture, operation and maintenance of the system

• Installs and tests INGENIUM at user site. Post-implementation support

• Programs and tests conversion programs based on pre-defined specifications

---

Competency Emphasis

Core Competencies		Additional
❏ Customer Service	❏ Organizational Awareness	❏
❏ Specialized/Technical Expertize	❏ Organizing and Planning Cost Control	❏
❏ Judgement/Decision Making	❏ Goal Attainment	❏
❏ Problem Solving	❏ Initiative	❏
❏ Teamwork	❏ Flexibility/Ability to Adapt to Change	❏
❏ Communication	❏ Innovation/Creativity	❏
❏ Work Relations	❏ Professional Image	❏
❏ Leadership/Membership/ Coaching of Others	❏ Integrity/Professional Standards	❏

An important element in this design is the focus on HB Group's competencies, not just competencies in general. Employees are not rewarded just for time on the job, for seniority, or for educational attainment. Rather, employees know, and are assessed against, Key Performance Indicators for the company: loss ratios, average claim costs, retention, number of policies, the sales/quote ratio and service quality. Employees are also assessed on their performance in coaching and mentoring others. It is not just the numbers they produce on their own; their success and advancement depends on the contribution to the success of the company as a whole.

A Work in Progress

The HB project, like any HR initiative, is a work in progress. A career management review committee monitors the program, it evaluates suggestions for tool kit improvement, and reassesses positions within the program as necessary. The committee also monitors the outside environment for customer expectations and changes in the marketplace.

So far, the results are dramatic. The company opened a second, and soon will open a third direct phone centre. Its expense ratio is one-third lower than industry average and savings are passed on to customers. Policy premium growth and retention at renewal are above industry average. Staff productivity has increased at a very high rate and staff retention is high. With a mission to provide outstanding coverage at competitive prices, the company has won a number of quality awards and is a leader in Canada's financial community and North America's call centres.

SIMPLE DO'S AND DON'T'S

There are some basic do's and don't's central to the implementation of an effective competency-based compensation system.

- Do not implement competency-based pay in the absence of a real business strategy. If senior management has not developed and committed to a strategy that is clearly defined—or if senior managers do not agree on the strategy—the Human Resources reorganization will soon become mired in conflicting interests.

- Do not initiate the program in a layered bureaucracy. If the command structure of the enterprise has precedence over the actual jobs to be performed, competencies become relatively irrelevant.

- Do not move to competency-based pay without the commitment, and the budget, to follow through from Day 1 on research, communication and training.

- Do not implement the program unless there are opportunities for competency development. If, for example, the enterprise is fighting a rearguard battle, there are unlikely to be avenues for growth or the financial resources to reward growth. There is a survival strategy called for, but it is not competency-based compensation.

- Do not be impatient. It takes time to gather data on excellent performance. At each step of the process, findings and tools should be validated through pilot projects and focus groups. Next, the training and communication programs will take considerable time. The actual compensation program cannot be launched until the entire organization understands the system.

At the same time, an organization must:

- Have a need for change. The best time to initiate competency-based pay is when the need for change is evident to all. If the market is changing and the jobs within the organization are being radically reorganized, then a new system has a lot to offer—and will be more eagerly embraced.

- Have a clear, unequivocal business rationale. Make this integral to all communication efforts and repeat it constantly.

- Develop the vision, values and competencies particular to the organization. While the steps followed in the HB initiative are applicable to most organizations, the vision must be specific and particular.

- Take a systematic approach. All the steps in the seven-step methodology for implementation need to be addressed, and work-in-process should be documented. Human Resources needs to know what needs to be achieved, and to measure progress every step of the way.

- Devote as much time and effort to implementation as to development. It is tempting to focus on the "interesting" stages of development, the research and focus groups, and then lose steam when it comes time for implementation. Do not pass off responsibility for training and pay decisions.

- Leverage the effort put into competency-based compensation. The competency-based pay grid is just one part of a Human Resources system that can be made integral to organizing and implementing the corporate culture. It is the communication tool for performance assessment and, as such, provides invaluable guidance for both employees and their managers. Many managers are poor at performance management, usually because they have not been given adequate information and training themselves. The training and tools that are used to support competency-based pay also train the trainers. The system is also used for recruiting, career planning, succession planning and future training programs.

Competency-based compensation is, upfront, a resource and an intensive Human Resources strategy—and it is one which is still evolving. Once a system for it is in place, its administration is relatively simple, but the messages must be continually repeated and reinforced.

There are relatively few formal descriptions or learning tools, so it is not for the faint-hearted organization or Human Resources professional. But for those organizations which are progressive-minded, it has proven to be an extremely powerful tool to support cultural change and pursue organizational success.